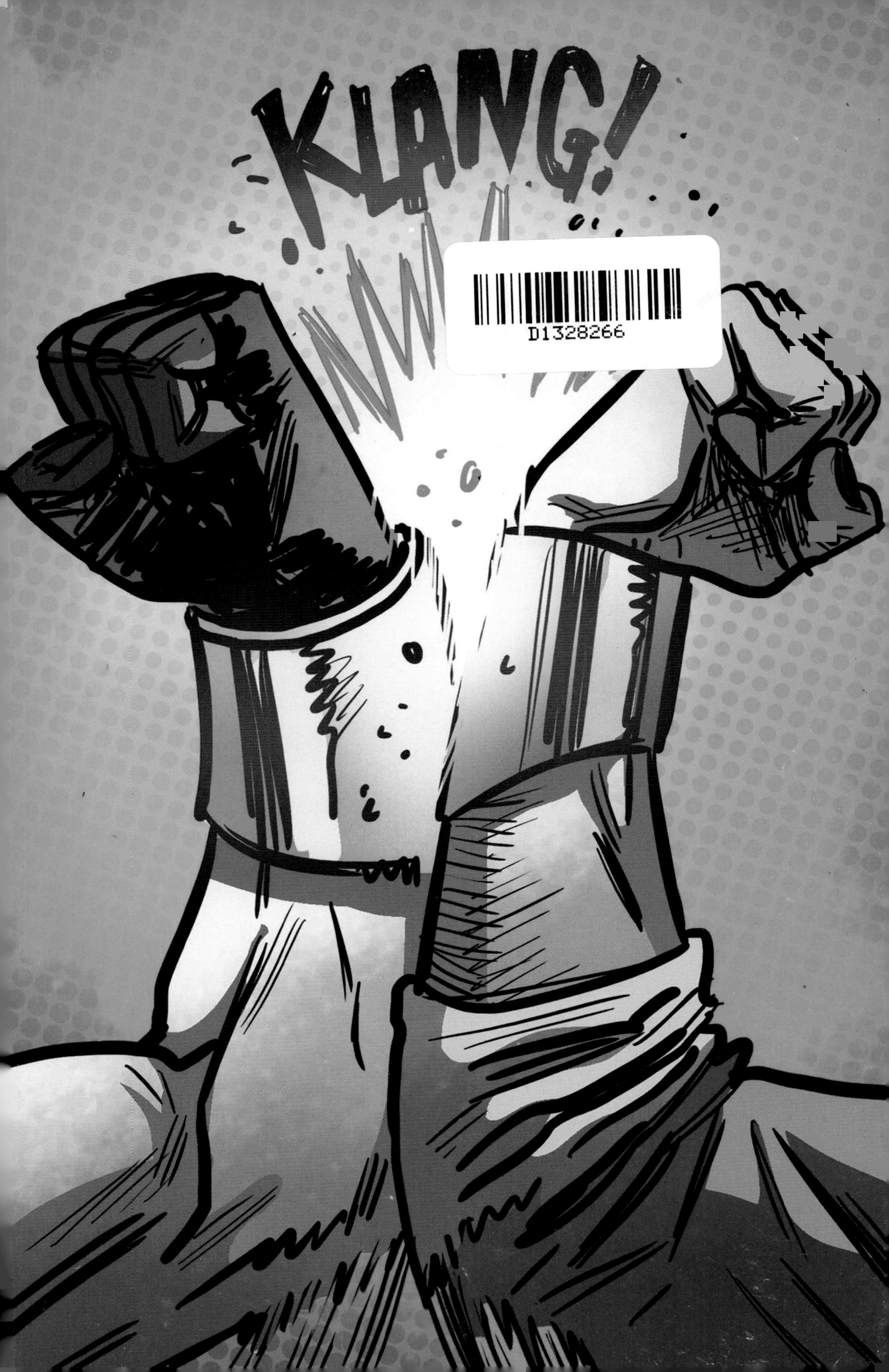
KLANG!

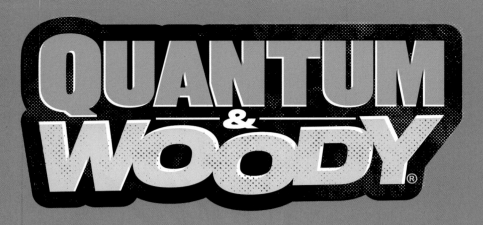

QUANTUM & WOODY®

WRITER
CHRISTOPHER HASTINGS

ARTIST
RYAN BROWNE

COLORS
RUTH REDMOND

LETTERER
HASSAN OTSMANE-ELHAOU

COVERS BY
DAVID NAKAYAMA

ASSISTANT EDITOR
DREW BAUMGARTNER

EDITOR
HEATHER ANTOS

GALLERY
REILLY BROWN with JIM CHARALAMPIDIS
RYAN BROWNE
GURIHIRU
CHRISTOPHER HASTINGS
ERICA HENDERSON
DAVE JOHNSON
STEVE LIEBER with RON CHAN
DAVID LOPEZ
TODD NAUCK with JIM CHARALAMPIDIS
JOE QUINONES
RAMON ROSANAS
CASPAR WIJNGAARD

COLLECTION COVER ART
DAVID NAKAYAMA

COLLECTION FRONT ART
RYAN BROWNE
DAVID NAKAYAMA
REILLY BROWN with JIM CHARALAMPIDIS

COLLECTION BACK COVER ART
RAHZZAH

COLLECTION EDITOR
IVAN COHEN

COLLECTION DESIGNER
STEVE BLACKWELL

VALIANT®

DAN MINTZ Chairman **FRED PIERCE** Publisher **WALTER BLACK** VP Operations **MATTHEW KLEIN** VP Sales & Marketing
TRAVIS ESCARFULLERY Director of Design & Production **PETER STERN** Director of International Publishing & Merchandising
LYSA HAWKINS, HEATHER ANTOS & **DAVID WOHL** Senior Editors **JEFF WALKER** Production & Design Manager
JOHN PETRIE Senior Manager - Sales & Merchandising **DANIELLE WARD** Sales Manager **GREGG KATZMAN** Marketing & Publicity Manager

RUSS BROWN President, Consumer Products, Promotions & Ad Sales

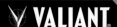

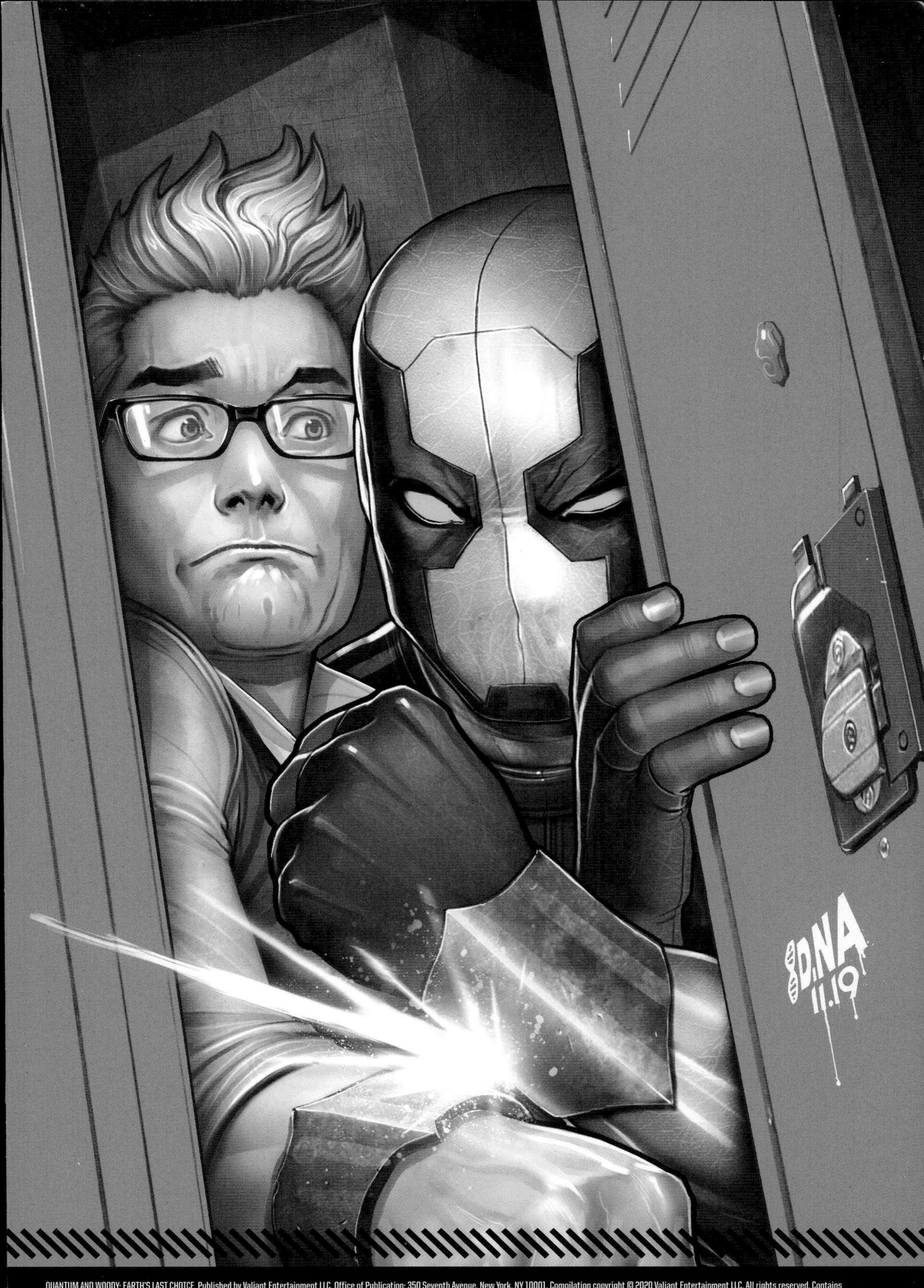
D.NA
11.19

QUANTUM AND WOODY: EARTH'S LAST CHOICE. Published by Valiant Entertainment LLC. Office of Publication: 350 Seventh Avenue, New York, NY 10001.
Printed in Korea. First Printing. ISBN: 9781682153628.

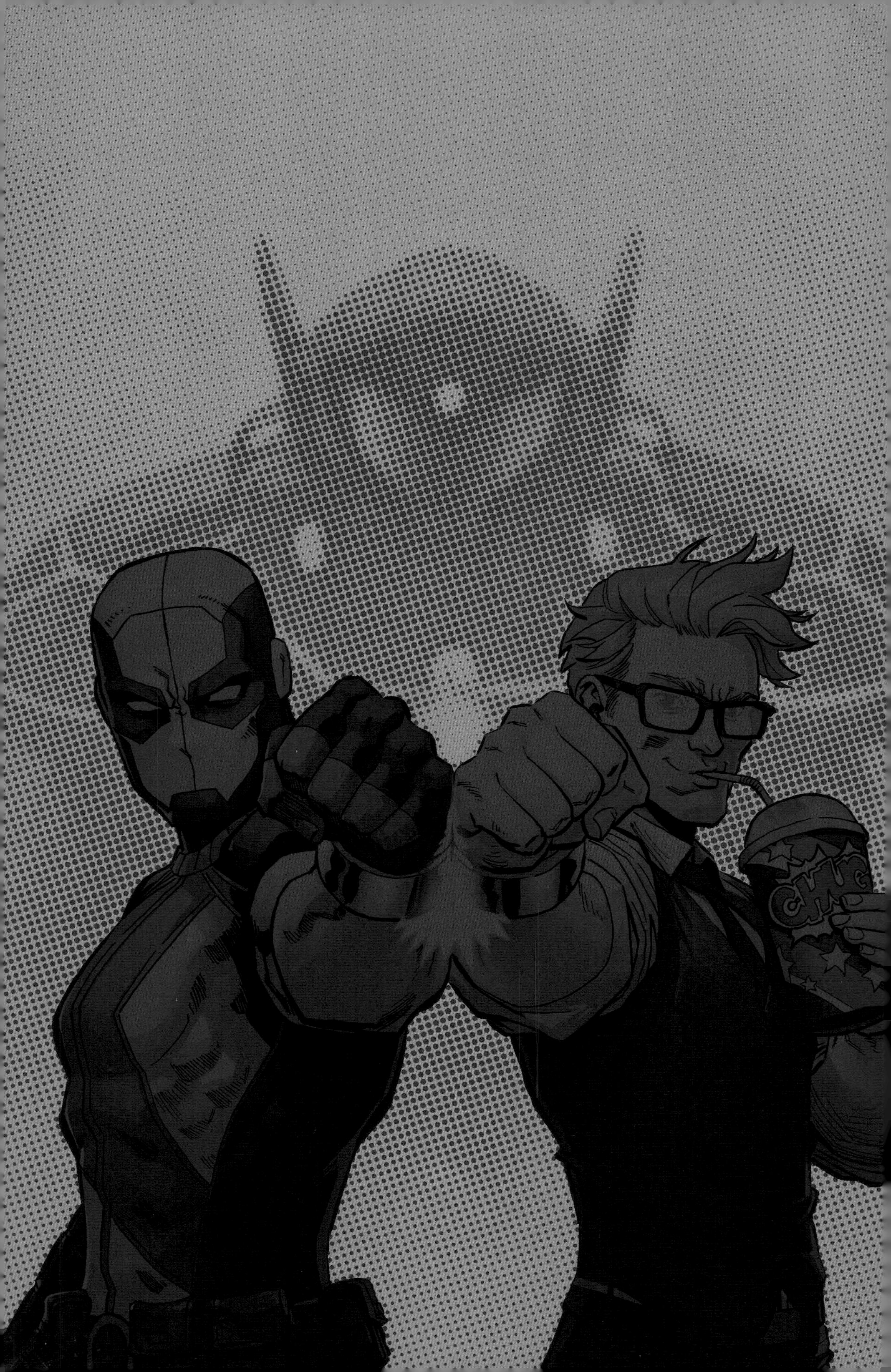
CHUG

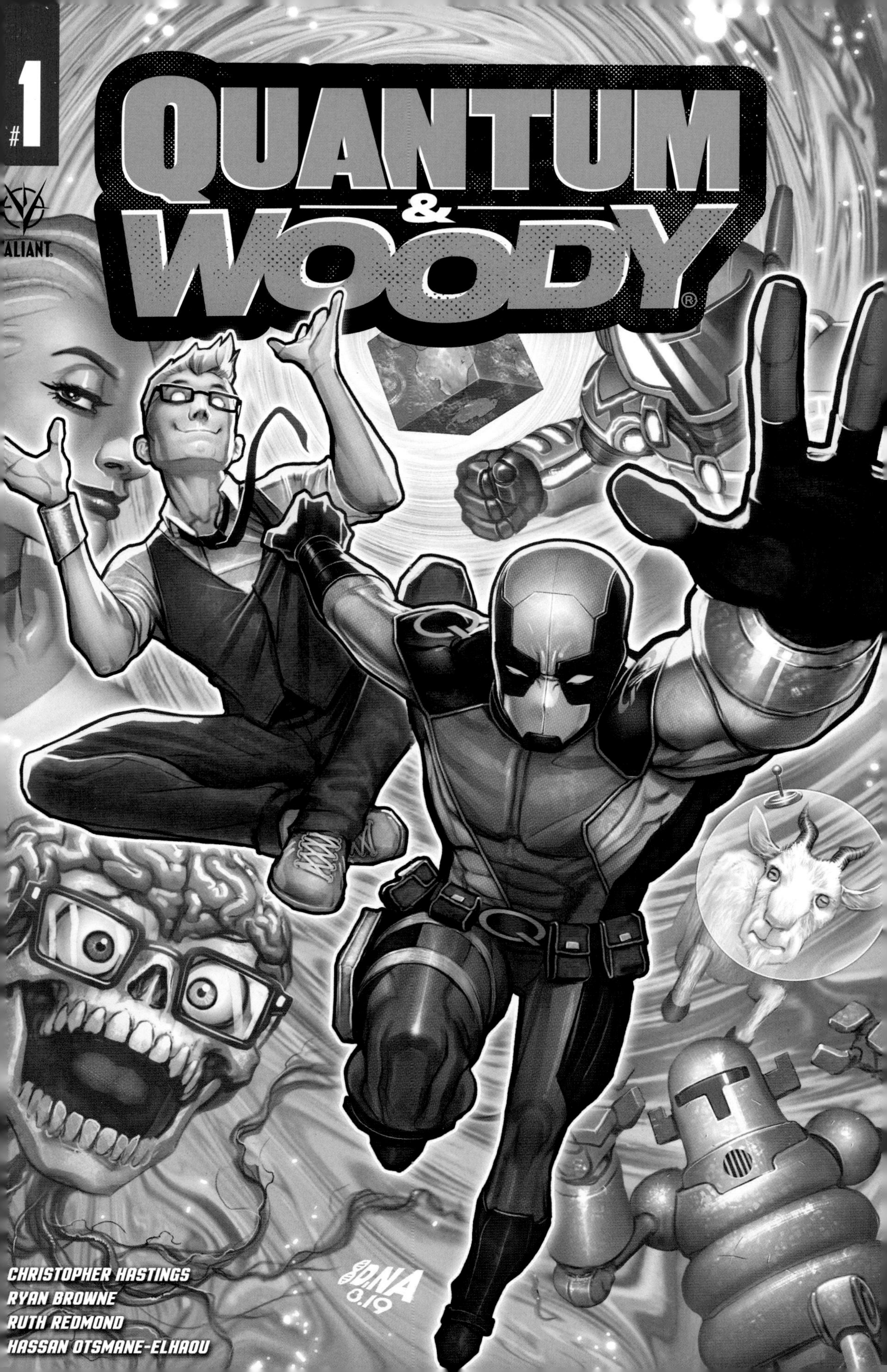

#1
VALIANT
QUANTUM & WOODY®
DNA 8.19
CHRISTOPHER HASTINGS
RYAN BROWNE
RUTH REDMOND
HASSAN OTSMANE-ELHAOU

VOICE IT

Search

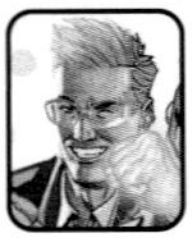

White_Chocolate
69k Cheers

v/DListDisasters Posted by OhThatTyler 16 hours ago

17.5K

SPOTTED: Fake Fugitive Superheroes Quantum & Woody on the Run

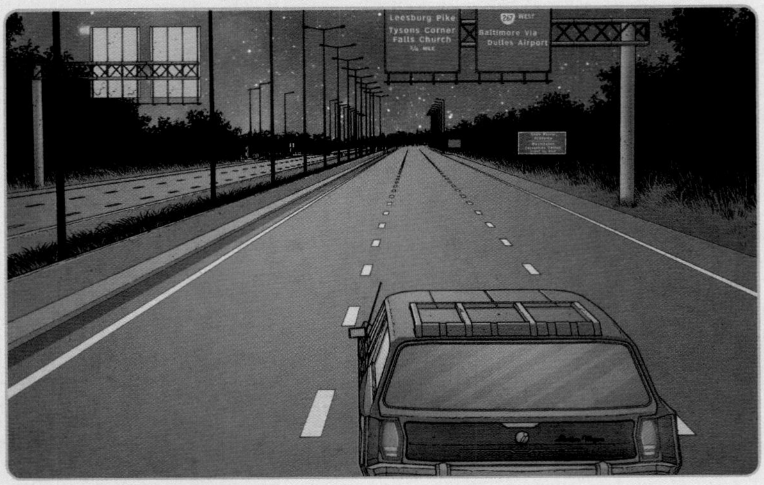

Leesburg Pike
Tysons Corner
Falls Church
Baltimore via
Dulles Airport

237 Comments Share Hide

"Say Something!"

B U I

VOICE IT

White_Chocolate - 5.3k cheers - 14 hours ago
Hellz to the yeah, baby! @BlackMamba we did it! WE HIT THE BIG TIME!!!@#%@!&@!!!!@
Reply Report

justerocknow - 2.4 cheers - 14 hours ago
wait whut
Reply Report

BlackMamba - 7.1k cheers - 12 hours ago
Take this down right now, Woody! I'm serious!
Reply Report

White_Chocolate - 2.1k cheers - 11 hours ago
<iframe src=gifs/-drake-started-from-the-bottom-now-we-here</a></p>
Reply Report

BlackMamba - 1.3k cheers - 8 hours ago
This is it. This is how we die.
Reply Report

OhThatTyler - 3.6k cheers - 8 hours ago
U kno ur IP can be traced, rite???
Reply Report

White_Chocolate - 4.5k cheers - 6 hours ago
the internet cant be tracked u noobz
Reply Report

OhThatTyler - 15.3k cheers - 4 hours ago
theyre in D.C.
Reply Report

justerocknow - 2.1k cheers - 3 hours ago
more like LOSER heroes, amirite?!?
Reply Report

GOATgoat - 961.7k cheers - 4 seconds ago
meh
Reply Report

v/DListDisasters

651 ONLINE | **177K** MEMBERS

The "Who's Who" of internet fame -- A place to follow celebrities even TNZ thinks aren't worth their time! Find your cult following here!

SUBSCRIBE

CREDITS

Writer...**Christopher Hastings**
Artist...**Ryan Browne**
Colorist...**Ruth Redmond**
Letterer...**Hassan Otsmane-Elhaou**
Cover Artist...**David Nakayama**
Variant Cover Artists...**Dave Johnson, David Lopez, Erica Henderson**
Assistant Editor...**Drew Baumgartner**
Editor...**Heather Antos**
Senior Editorial Director...**Robert Meyers**

TRENDING COMMUNITIES

v/ValiantComicFans 167k members JOIN
v/legionofthunder 33k members JOIN
v/MythosOrMadScience 22k members JOIN
v/deadsidedeadbeats 4k members JOIN

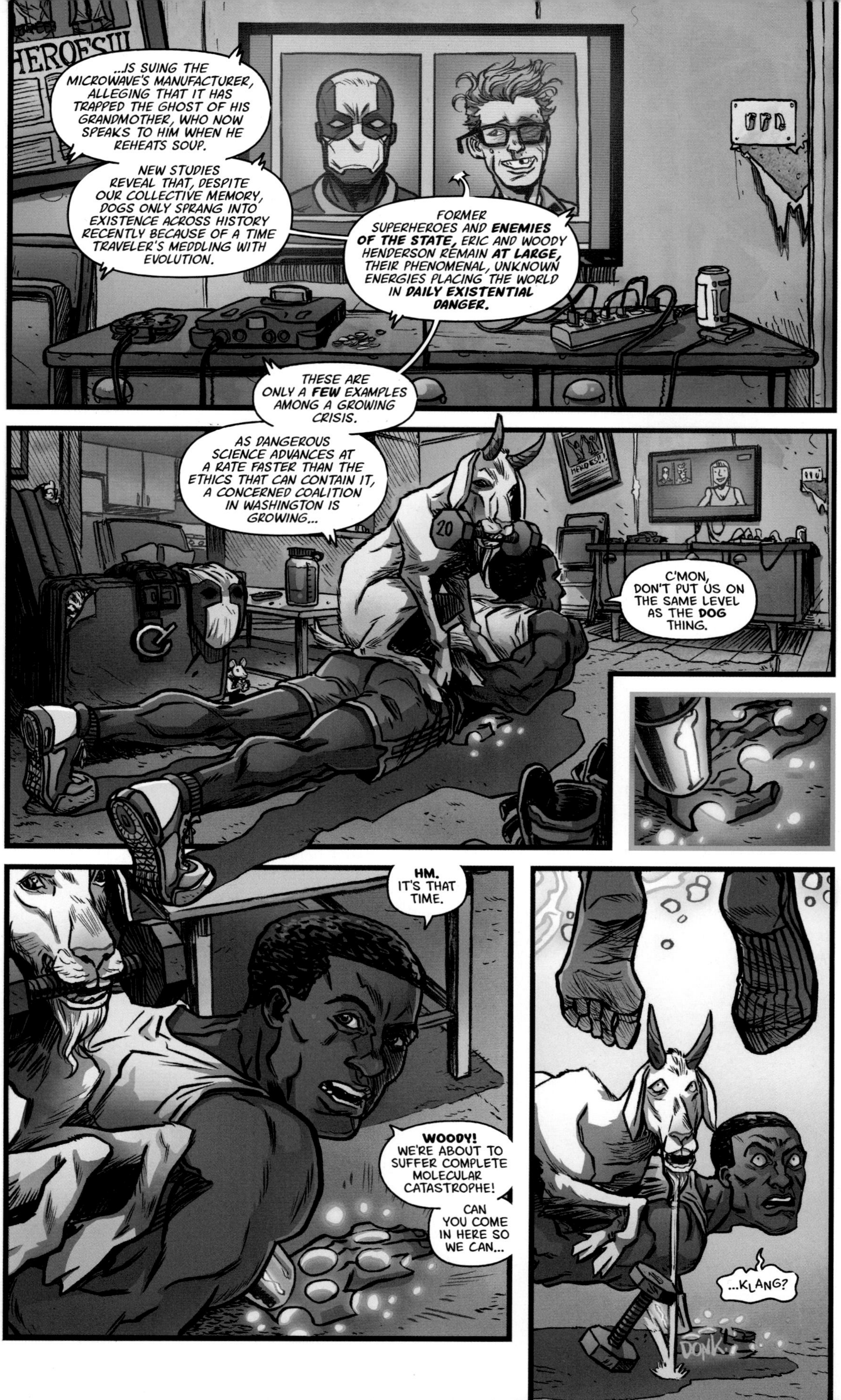
HEROES!!!
...IS SUING THE MICROWAVE'S MANUFACTURER, ALLEGING THAT IT HAS TRAPPED THE GHOST OF HIS GRANDMOTHER, WHO NOW SPEAKS TO HIM WHEN HE REHEATS SOUP.
NEW STUDIES REVEAL THAT, DESPITE OUR COLLECTIVE MEMORY, DOGS ONLY SPRANG INTO EXISTENCE ACROSS HISTORY RECENTLY BECAUSE OF A TIME TRAVELER'S MEDDLING WITH EVOLUTION.
FORMER SUPERHEROES AND **ENEMIES OF THE STATE**, ERIC AND WOODY HENDERSON REMAIN **AT LARGE**, THEIR PHENOMENAL, UNKNOWN ENERGIES PLACING THE WORLD IN **DAILY EXISTENTIAL DANGER.**
THESE ARE ONLY A **FEW** EXAMPLES AMONG A GROWING CRISIS.
AS DANGEROUS SCIENCE ADVANCES AT A RATE FASTER THAN THE ETHICS THAT CAN CONTAIN IT, A CONCERNED COALITION IN WASHINGTON IS GROWING...
20
HEROES!!!
C'MON, DON'T PUT US ON THE SAME LEVEL AS THE **DOG** THING.
HM. IT'S THAT TIME.
WOODY! WE'RE ABOUT TO SUFFER COMPLETE MOLECULAR CATASTROPHE!
CAN YOU COME IN HERE SO WE CAN...
...KLANG?
DONK

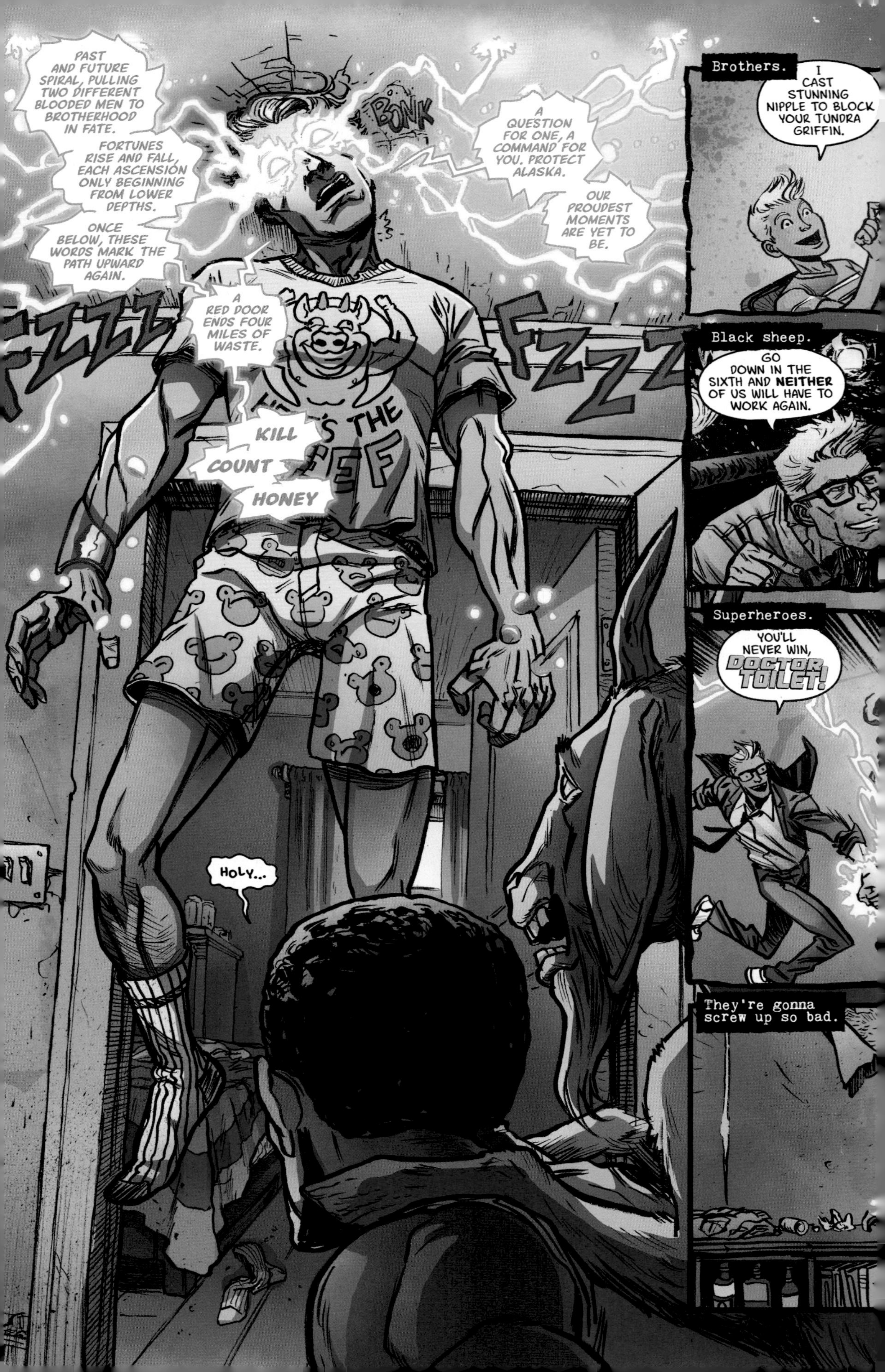

PAST AND FUTURE SPIRAL, PULLING TWO DIFFERENT BLOODED MEN TO BROTHERHOOD IN FATE.
FORTUNES RISE AND FALL, EACH ASCENSION ONLY BEGINNING FROM LOWER DEPTHS.
ONCE BELOW, THESE WORDS MARK THE PATH UPWARD AGAIN.
BONK
A QUESTION FOR ONE, A COMMAND FOR YOU. PROTECT ALASKA.
OUR PROUDEST MOMENTS ARE YET TO BE.
FZZZ
A RED DOOR ENDS FOUR MILES OF WASTE.
FZZZ
KILL
COUNT
HONEY
HOLY...
Brothers.
I CAST STUNNING NIPPLE TO BLOCK YOUR TUNDRA GRIFFIN.
Black sheep.
GO DOWN IN THE SIXTH AND NEITHER OF US WILL HAVE TO WORK AGAIN.
Superheroes.
YOU'LL NEVER WIN, DOCTOR TOILET!
They're gonna screw up so bad.

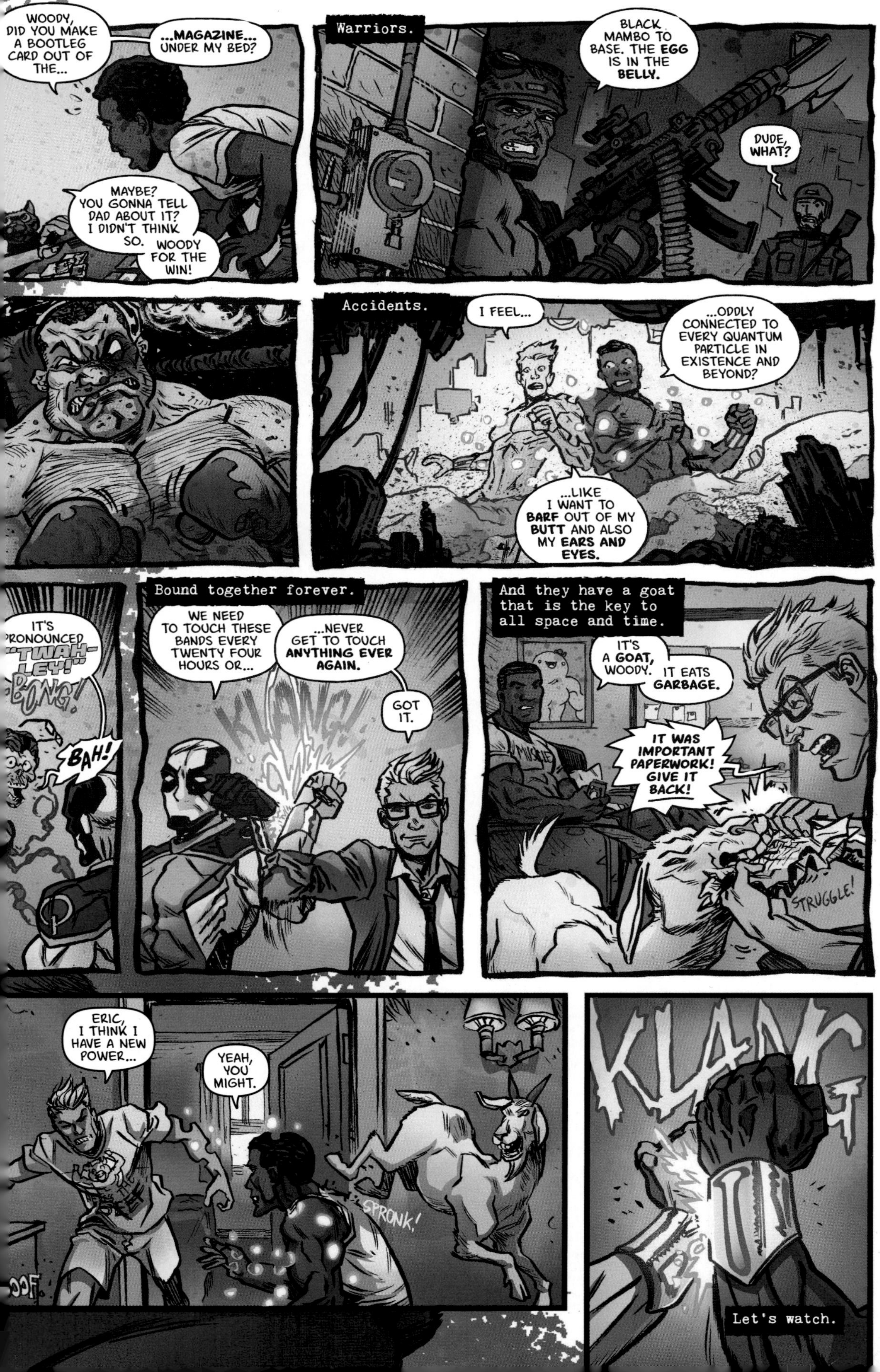
WOODY, DID YOU MAKE A BOOTLEG CARD OUT OF THE...
...MAGAZINE... UNDER MY BED?
MAYBE? YOU GONNA TELL DAD ABOUT IT? I DIDN'T THINK SO.
WOODY FOR THE WIN!
Warriors.
BLACK MAMBO TO BASE. THE EGG IS IN THE BELLY.
DUDE, WHAT?
Accidents.
I FEEL...
...ODDLY CONNECTED TO EVERY QUANTUM PARTICLE IN EXISTENCE AND BEYOND?
...LIKE I WANT TO BARF OUT OF MY BUTT AND ALSO MY EARS AND EYES.
IT'S PRONOUNCED "TWAH-LEY!"
BONG!
BAH!
Bound together forever.
WE NEED TO TOUCH THESE BANDS EVERY TWENTY FOUR HOURS OR...
...NEVER GET TO TOUCH ANYTHING EVER AGAIN.
KLANG!
GOT IT.
And they have a goat that is the key to all space and time.
IT'S A GOAT, WOODY.
IT EATS GARBAGE.
IT WAS IMPORTANT PAPERWORK! GIVE IT BACK!
STRUGGLE!
ERIC, I THINK I HAVE A NEW POWER...
YEAH, YOU MIGHT.
SPRONK!
OOF.
KLANG
Let's watch.

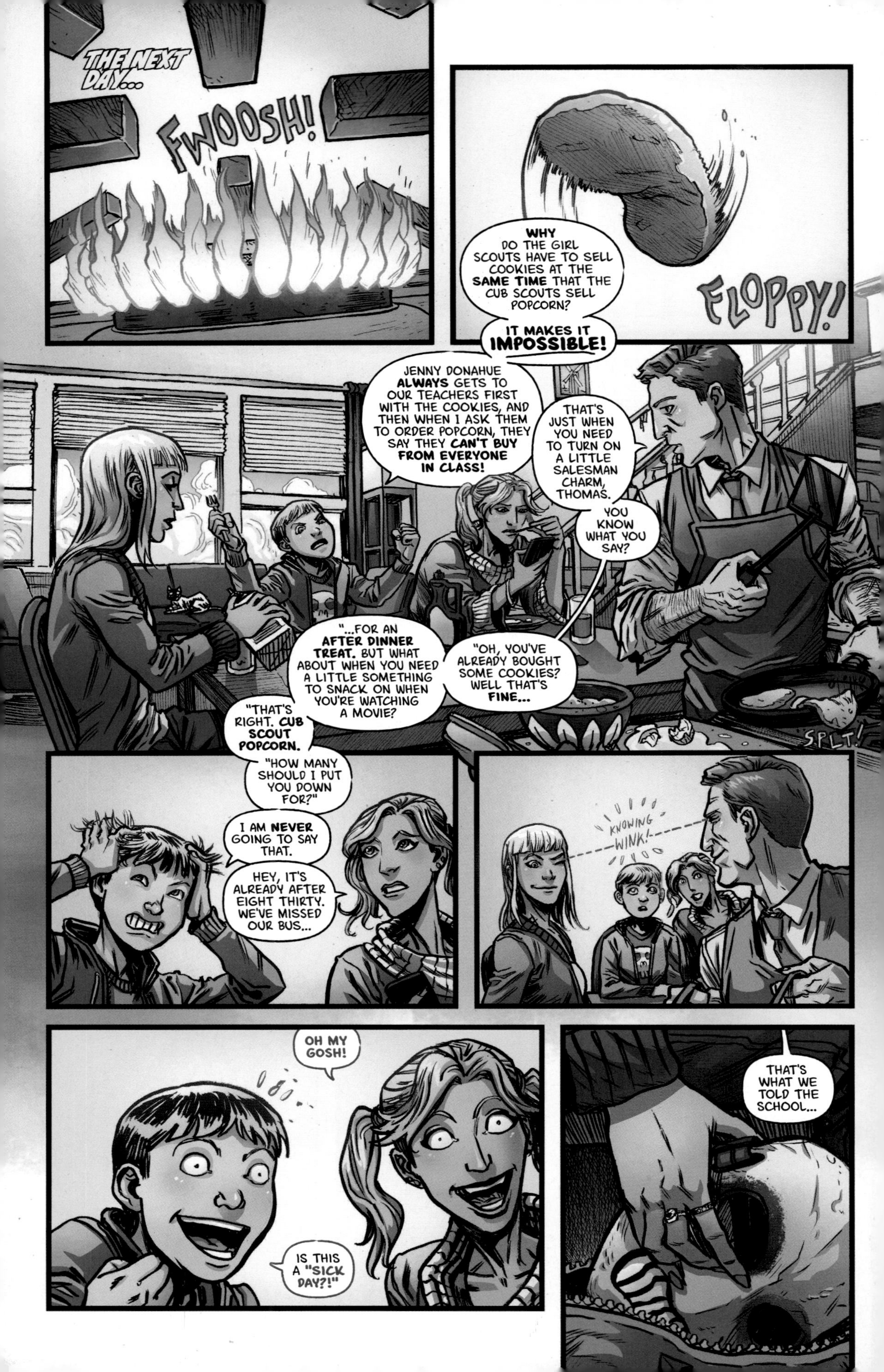
THE NEXT DAY...
FWOOSH!
WHY DO THE GIRL SCOUTS HAVE TO SELL COOKIES AT THE SAME TIME THAT THE CUB SCOUTS SELL POPCORN?
FLOPPY!
IT MAKES IT IMPOSSIBLE!
JENNY DONAHUE ALWAYS GETS TO OUR TEACHERS FIRST WITH THE COOKIES, AND THEN WHEN I ASK THEM TO ORDER POPCORN, THEY SAY THEY CAN'T BUY FROM EVERYONE IN CLASS!
THAT'S JUST WHEN YOU NEED TO TURN ON A LITTLE SALESMAN CHARM, THOMAS.
YOU KNOW WHAT YOU SAY?
"OH, YOU'VE ALREADY BOUGHT SOME COOKIES? WELL THAT'S FINE...
"...FOR AN AFTER DINNER TREAT. BUT WHAT ABOUT WHEN YOU NEED A LITTLE SOMETHING TO SNACK ON WHEN YOU'RE WATCHING A MOVIE?
"THAT'S RIGHT. CUB SCOUT POPCORN.
SPLT!
"HOW MANY SHOULD I PUT YOU DOWN FOR?"
I AM NEVER GOING TO SAY THAT.
HEY, IT'S ALREADY AFTER EIGHT THIRTY. WE'VE MISSED OUR BUS...
KNOWING WINK!
OH MY GOSH!
IS THIS A "SICK DAY?!"
THAT'S WHAT WE TOLD THE SCHOOL...

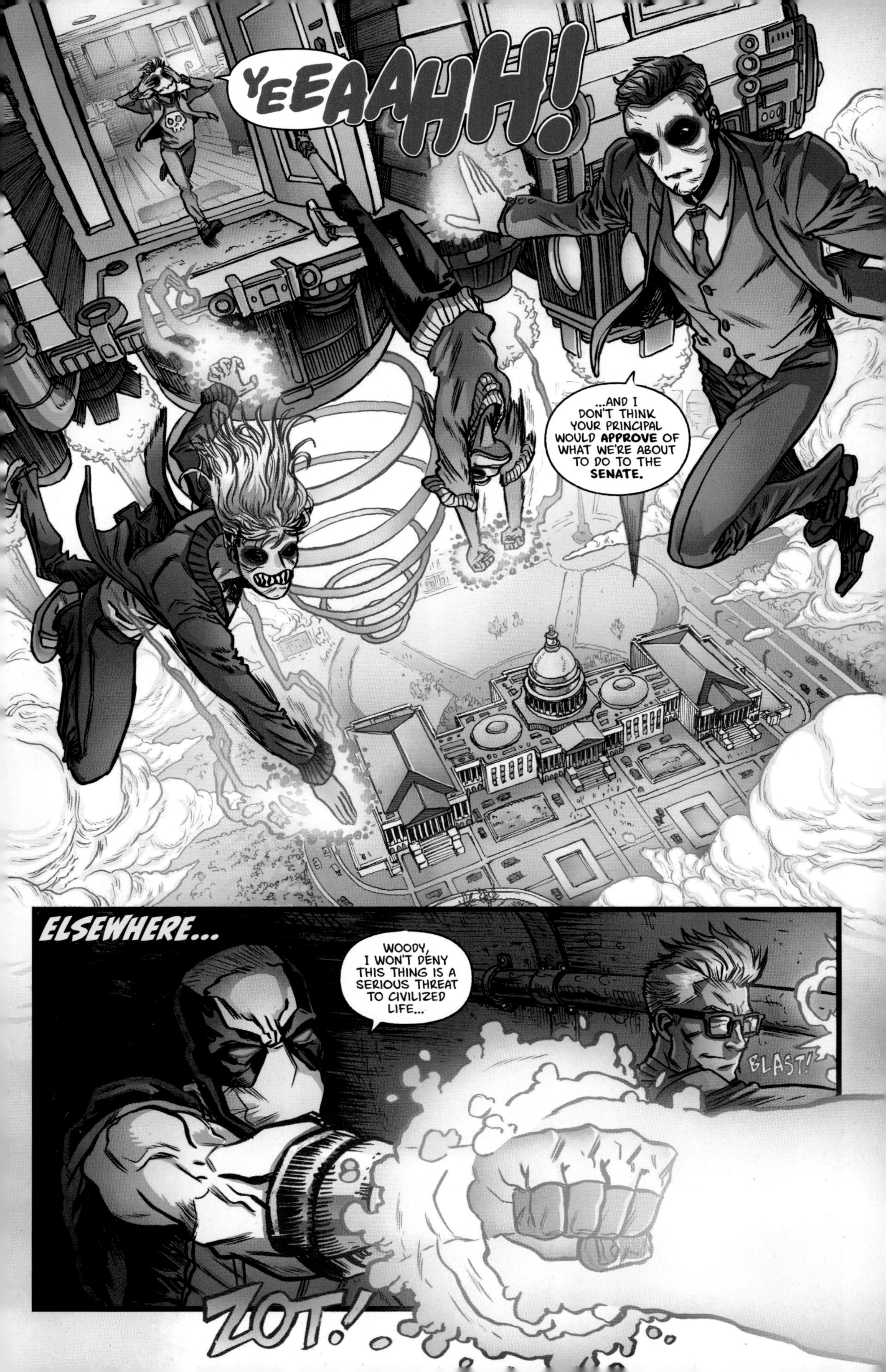
YEEAAHH!
...AND I DON'T THINK YOUR PRINCIPAL WOULD **APPROVE** OF WHAT WE'RE ABOUT TO DO TO THE **SENATE.**
ELSEWHERE...
WOODY, I WON'T DENY THIS THING IS A SERIOUS THREAT TO CIVILIZED LIFE...
BLAST!
ZOT!

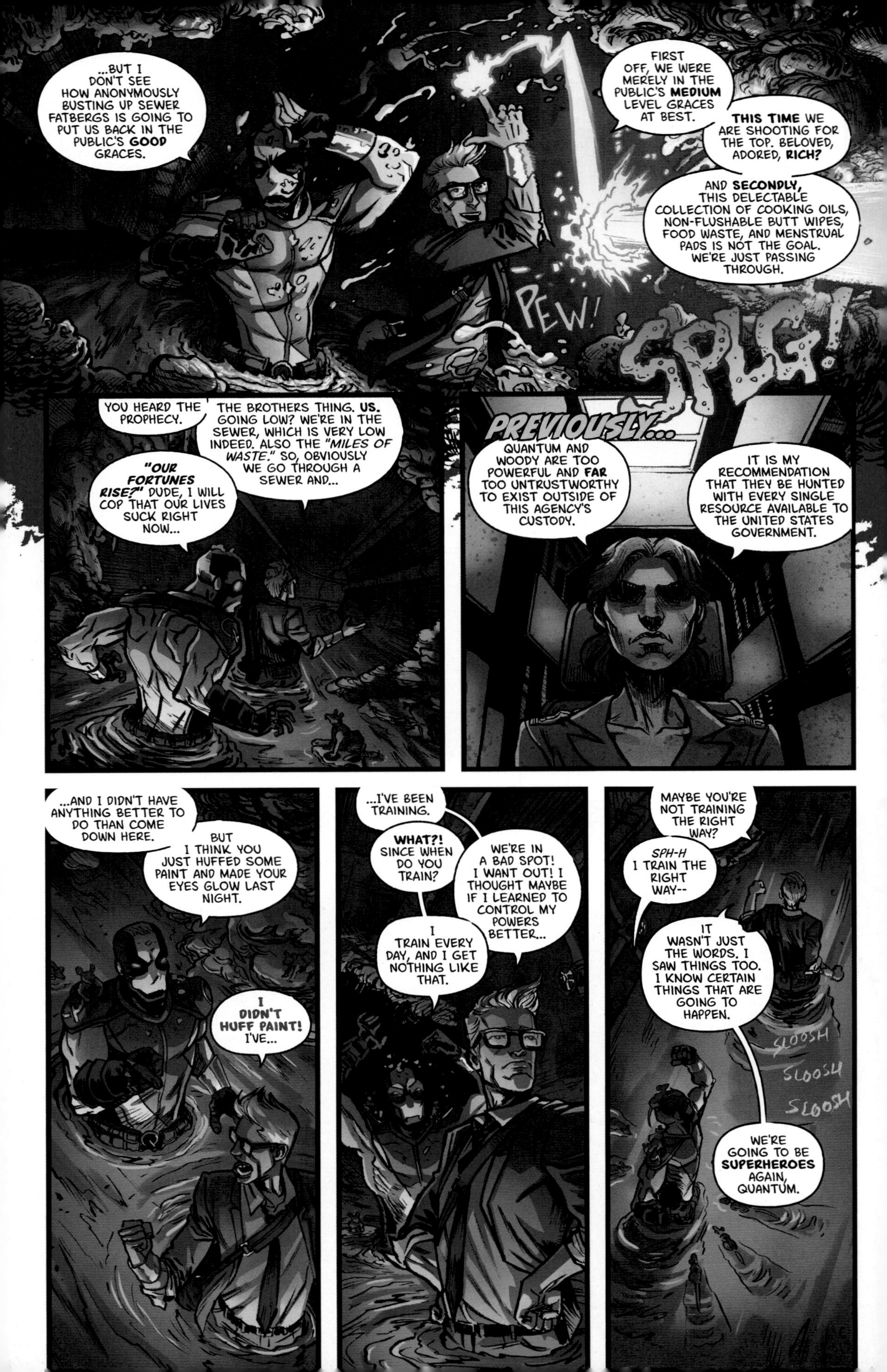
...BUT I DON'T SEE HOW ANONYMOUSLY BUSTING UP SEWER FATBERGS IS GOING TO PUT US BACK IN THE PUBLIC'S GOOD GRACES.
FIRST OFF, WE WERE MERELY IN THE PUBLIC'S MEDIUM LEVEL GRACES AT BEST.
THIS TIME WE ARE SHOOTING FOR THE TOP. BELOVED, ADORED, RICH?
AND SECONDLY, THIS DELECTABLE COLLECTION OF COOKING OILS, NON-FLUSHABLE BUTT WIPES, FOOD WASTE, AND MENSTRUAL PADS IS NOT THE GOAL. WE'RE JUST PASSING THROUGH.
PEW!
SPLG!
YOU HEARD THE PROPHECY.
THE BROTHERS THING. US. GOING LOW? WE'RE IN THE SEWER, WHICH IS VERY LOW INDEED. ALSO THE "MILES OF WASTE." SO, OBVIOUSLY WE GO THROUGH A SEWER AND...
"OUR FORTUNES RISE?" DUDE, I WILL COP THAT OUR LIVES SUCK RIGHT NOW...
PREVIOUSLY...
QUANTUM AND WOODY ARE TOO POWERFUL AND FAR TOO UNTRUSTWORTHY TO EXIST OUTSIDE OF THIS AGENCY'S CUSTODY.
IT IS MY RECOMMENDATION THAT THEY BE HUNTED WITH EVERY SINGLE RESOURCE AVAILABLE TO THE UNITED STATES GOVERNMENT.
...AND I DIDN'T HAVE ANYTHING BETTER TO DO THAN COME DOWN HERE.
BUT I THINK YOU JUST HUFFED SOME PAINT AND MADE YOUR EYES GLOW LAST NIGHT.
I DIDN'T HUFF PAINT! I'VE...
...I'VE BEEN TRAINING.
WHAT?! SINCE WHEN DO YOU TRAIN?
WE'RE IN A BAD SPOT! I WANT OUT! I THOUGHT MAYBE IF I LEARNED TO CONTROL MY POWERS BETTER...
I TRAIN EVERY DAY, AND I GET NOTHING LIKE THAT.
MAYBE YOU'RE NOT TRAINING THE RIGHT WAY?
SPH-H I TRAIN THE RIGHT WAY--
IT WASN'T JUST THE WORDS. I SAW THINGS TOO. I KNOW CERTAIN THINGS THAT ARE GOING TO HAPPEN.
SLOOSH
SLOOSH
SLOOSH
WE'RE GOING TO BE SUPERHEROES AGAIN, QUANTUM.

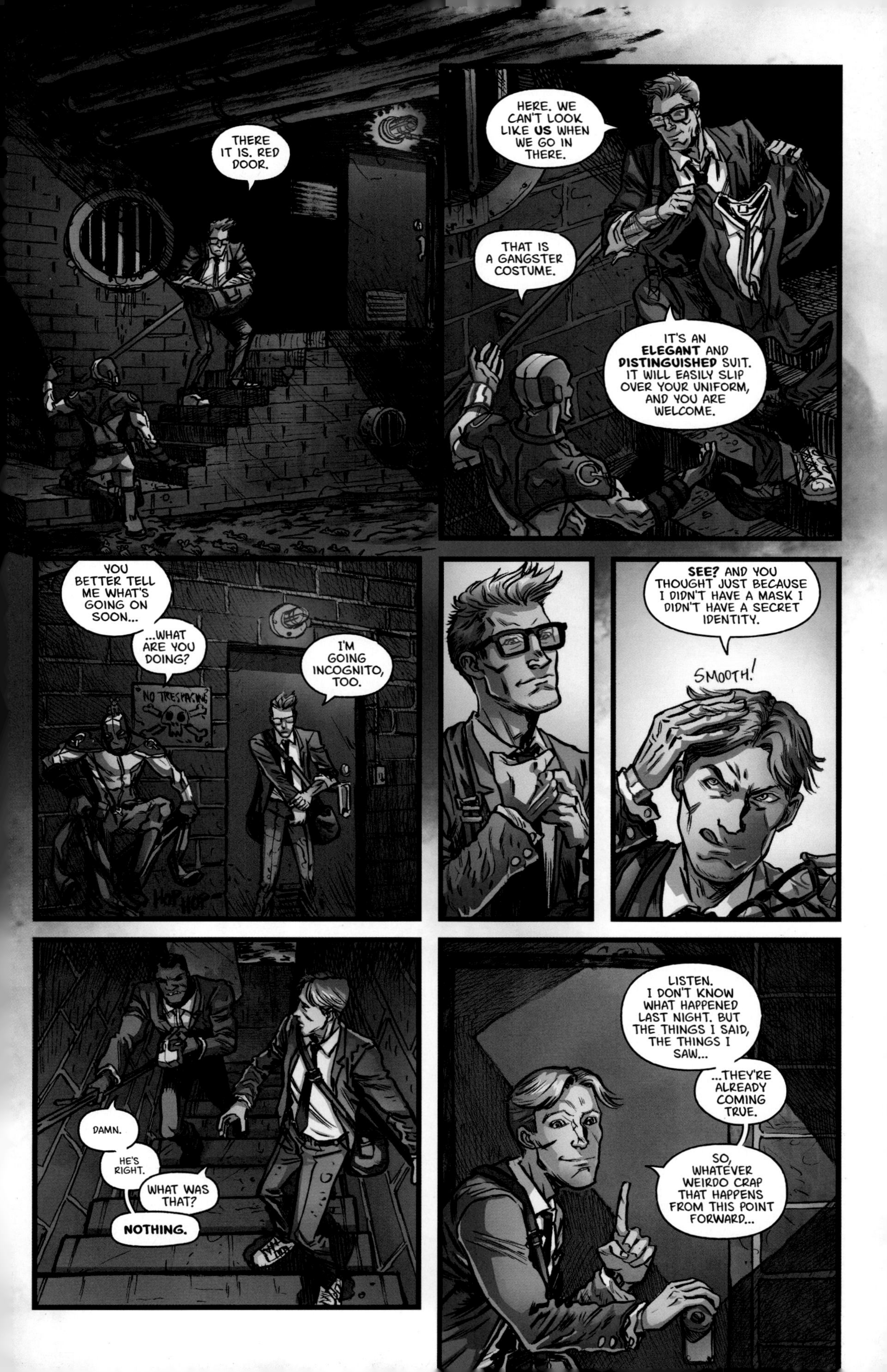
THERE IT IS. RED DOOR.
HERE. WE CAN'T LOOK LIKE **US** WHEN WE GO IN THERE.
THAT IS A GANGSTER COSTUME.
IT'S AN **ELEGANT** AND **DISTINGUISHED** SUIT. IT WILL EASILY SLIP OVER YOUR UNIFORM, AND YOU ARE WELCOME.
YOU BETTER TELL ME WHAT'S GOING ON SOON...
...WHAT ARE YOU DOING?
NO TRESPASSING
I'M GOING INCOGNITO, TOO.
HOP HOP
SEE? AND YOU THOUGHT JUST BECAUSE I DIDN'T HAVE A MASK I DIDN'T HAVE A SECRET IDENTITY.
SMOOTH!
DAMN.
HE'S RIGHT.
WHAT WAS THAT?
NOTHING.
LISTEN. I DON'T KNOW WHAT HAPPENED LAST NIGHT. BUT THE THINGS I SAID, THE THINGS I SAW...
...THEY'RE ALREADY COMING TRUE.
SO, WHATEVER WEIRDO CRAP THAT HAPPENS FROM THIS POINT FORWARD...

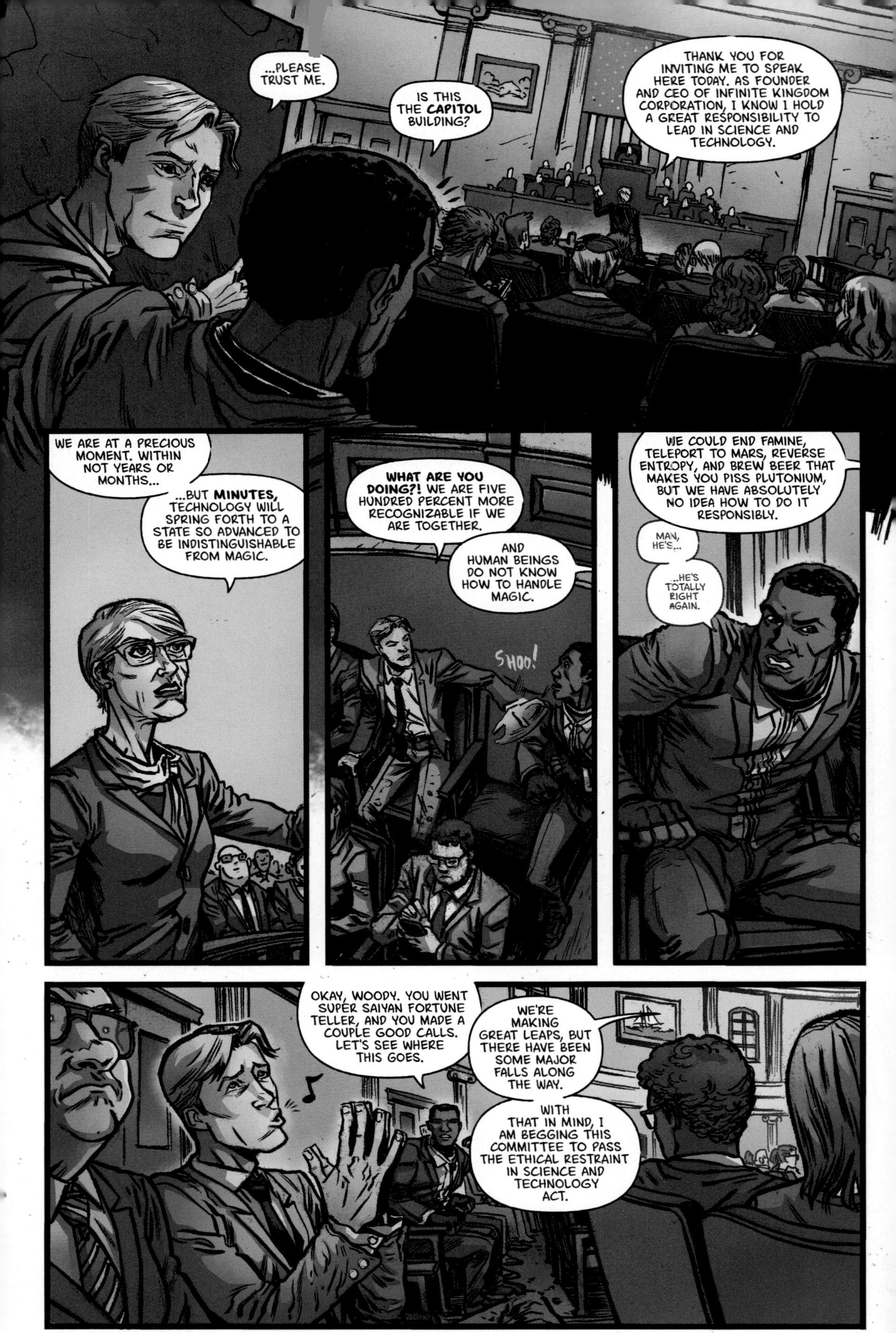

...PLEASE TRUST ME.
IS THIS THE **CAPITOL** BUILDING?
THANK YOU FOR INVITING ME TO SPEAK HERE TODAY. AS FOUNDER AND CEO OF INFINITE KINGDOM CORPORATION, I KNOW I HOLD A GREAT RESPONSIBILITY TO LEAD IN SCIENCE AND TECHNOLOGY.
WE ARE AT A PRECIOUS MOMENT. WITHIN NOT YEARS OR MONTHS...
...BUT **MINUTES**, TECHNOLOGY WILL SPRING FORTH TO A STATE SO ADVANCED TO BE INDISTINGUISHABLE FROM MAGIC.
WHAT ARE YOU DOING?! WE ARE FIVE HUNDRED PERCENT MORE RECOGNIZABLE IF WE ARE TOGETHER.
AND HUMAN BEINGS DO NOT KNOW HOW TO HANDLE MAGIC.
SHOO!
WE COULD END FAMINE, TELEPORT TO MARS, REVERSE ENTROPY, AND BREW BEER THAT MAKES YOU PISS PLUTONIUM, BUT WE HAVE ABSOLUTELY NO IDEA HOW TO DO IT RESPONSIBLY.
MAN, HE'S...
...HE'S TOTALLY RIGHT AGAIN.
OKAY, WOODY. YOU WENT SUPER SAIYAN FORTUNE TELLER, AND YOU MADE A COUPLE GOOD CALLS. LET'S SEE WHERE THIS GOES.
WE'RE MAKING GREAT LEAPS, BUT THERE HAVE BEEN SOME MAJOR FALLS ALONG THE WAY.
WITH THAT IN MIND, I AM BEGGING THIS COMMITTEE TO PASS THE ETHICAL RESTRAINT IN SCIENCE AND TECHNOLOGY ACT.

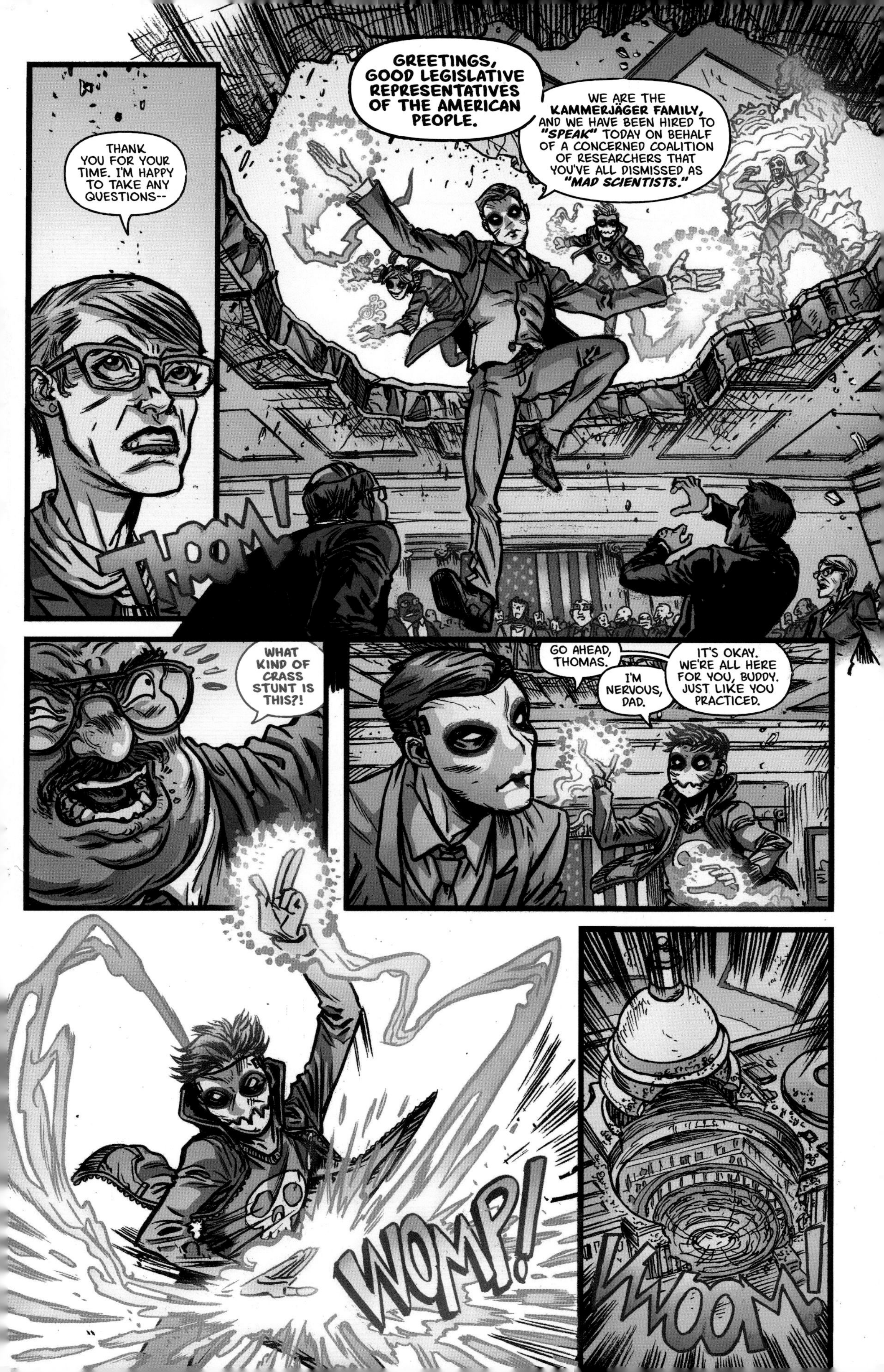

THANK YOU FOR YOUR TIME. I'M HAPPY TO TAKE ANY QUESTIONS--
GREETINGS, GOOD LEGISLATIVE REPRESENTATIVES OF THE AMERICAN PEOPLE.
WE ARE THE KAMMERJÄGER FAMILY, AND WE HAVE BEEN HIRED TO "SPEAK" TODAY ON BEHALF OF A CONCERNED COALITION OF RESEARCHERS THAT YOU'VE ALL DISMISSED AS "MAD SCIENTISTS."
THOOM!
WHAT KIND OF CRASS STUNT IS THIS?!
GO AHEAD, THOMAS.
I'M NERVOUS, DAD.
IT'S OKAY. WE'RE ALL HERE FOR YOU, BUDDY. JUST LIKE YOU PRACTICED.
WOMP!
WHOOM!

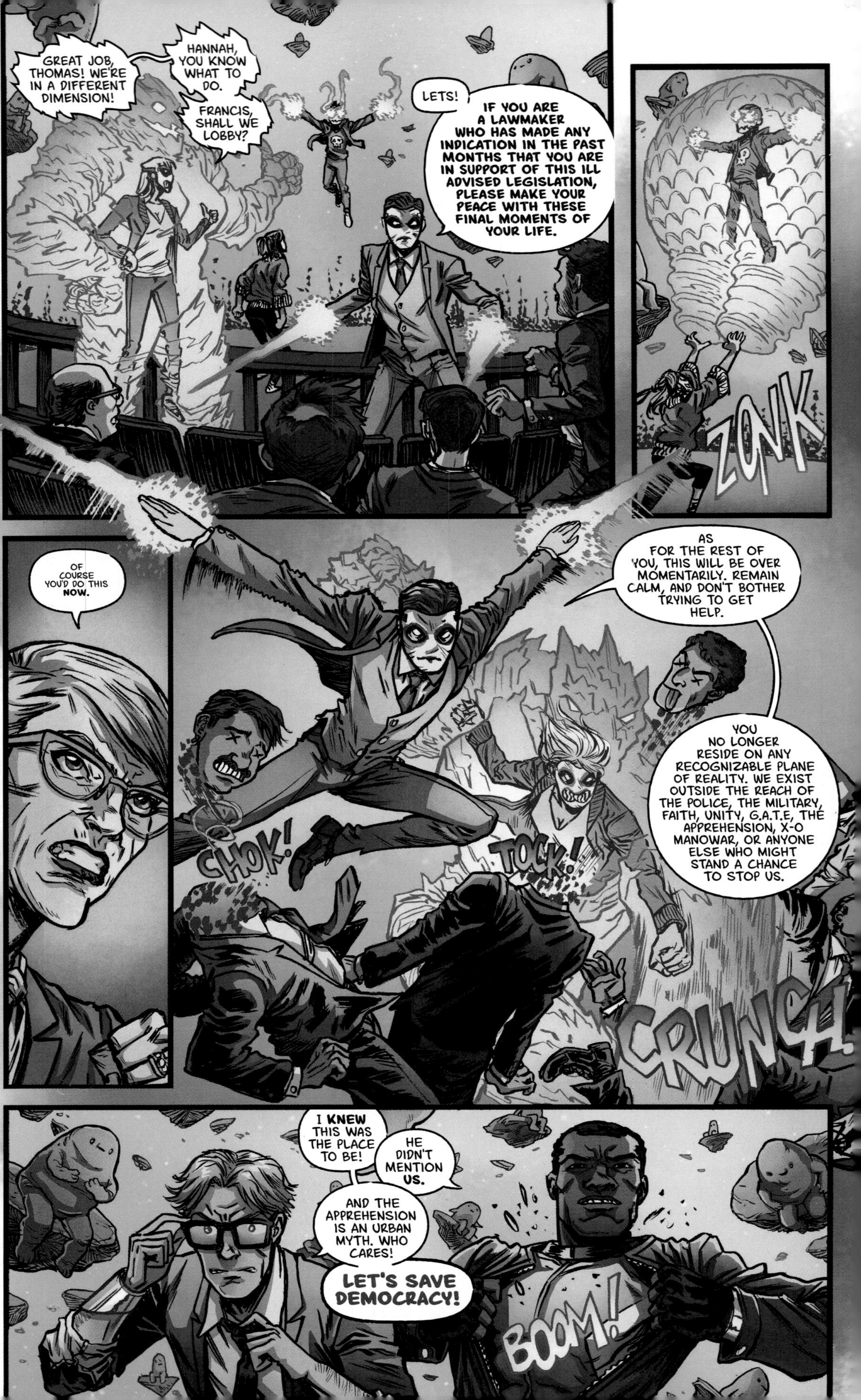

GREAT JOB, THOMAS! WE'RE IN A DIFFERENT DIMENSION!
HANNAH, YOU KNOW WHAT TO DO.
FRANCIS, SHALL WE LOBBY?
LETS!
IF YOU ARE A LAWMAKER WHO HAS MADE ANY INDICATION IN THE PAST MONTHS THAT YOU ARE IN SUPPORT OF THIS ILL ADVISED LEGISLATION, PLEASE MAKE YOUR PEACE WITH THESE FINAL MOMENTS OF YOUR LIFE.
ZONK
OF COURSE YOU'D DO THIS NOW.
AS FOR THE REST OF YOU, THIS WILL BE OVER MOMENTARILY. REMAIN CALM, AND DON'T BOTHER TRYING TO GET HELP.
YOU NO LONGER RESIDE ON ANY RECOGNIZABLE PLANE OF REALITY. WE EXIST OUTSIDE THE REACH OF THE POLICE, THE MILITARY, FAITH, UNITY, G.A.T.E, THE APPREHENSION, X-O MANOWAR, OR ANYONE ELSE WHO MIGHT STAND A CHANCE TO STOP US.
CHOK!
TOCK!
CRUNCH!
I KNEW THIS WAS THE PLACE TO BE!
HE DIDN'T MENTION US.
AND THE APPREHENSION IS AN URBAN MYTH. WHO CARES!
LET'S SAVE DEMOCRACY!
BOOM!

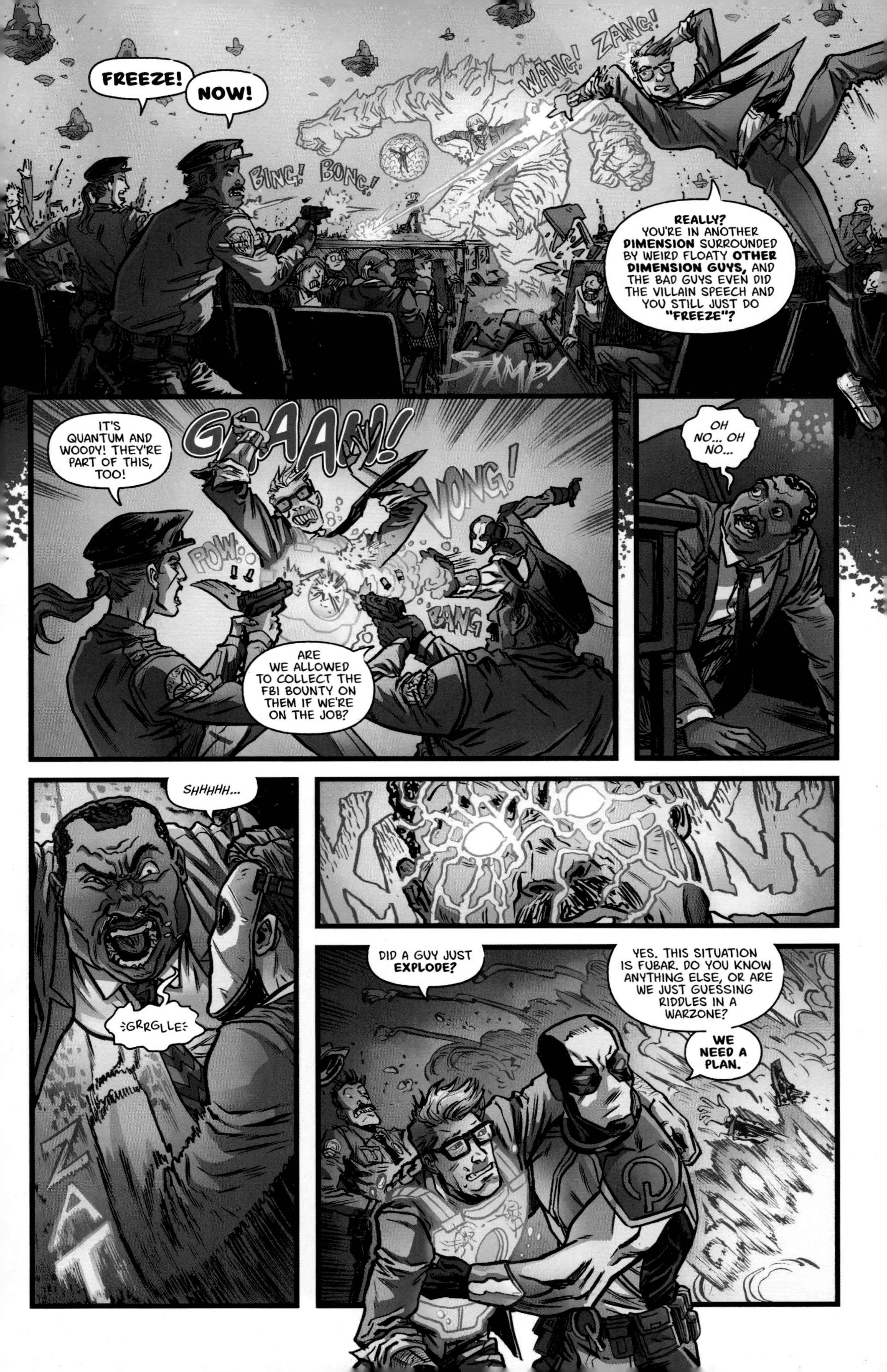
FREEZE!
NOW!
BING! BONG!
WANG! ZANG!
REALLY? YOU'RE IN ANOTHER DIMENSION SURROUNDED BY WEIRD FLOATY OTHER DIMENSION GUYS, AND THE BAD GUYS EVEN DID THE VILLAIN SPEECH AND YOU STILL JUST DO "FREEZE"?
STAMP!
IT'S QUANTUM AND WOODY! THEY'RE PART OF THIS, TOO!
GRAAAM!
VONG!
POW!
BANG
ARE WE ALLOWED TO COLLECT THE FBI BOUNTY ON THEM IF WE'RE ON THE JOB?
OH NO... OH NO...
SHHHHH...
GRRGLLE
DID A GUY JUST EXPLODE?
YES. THIS SITUATION IS FUBAR. DO YOU KNOW ANYTHING ELSE, OR ARE WE JUST GUESSING RIDDLES IN A WARZONE?
WE NEED A PLAN.

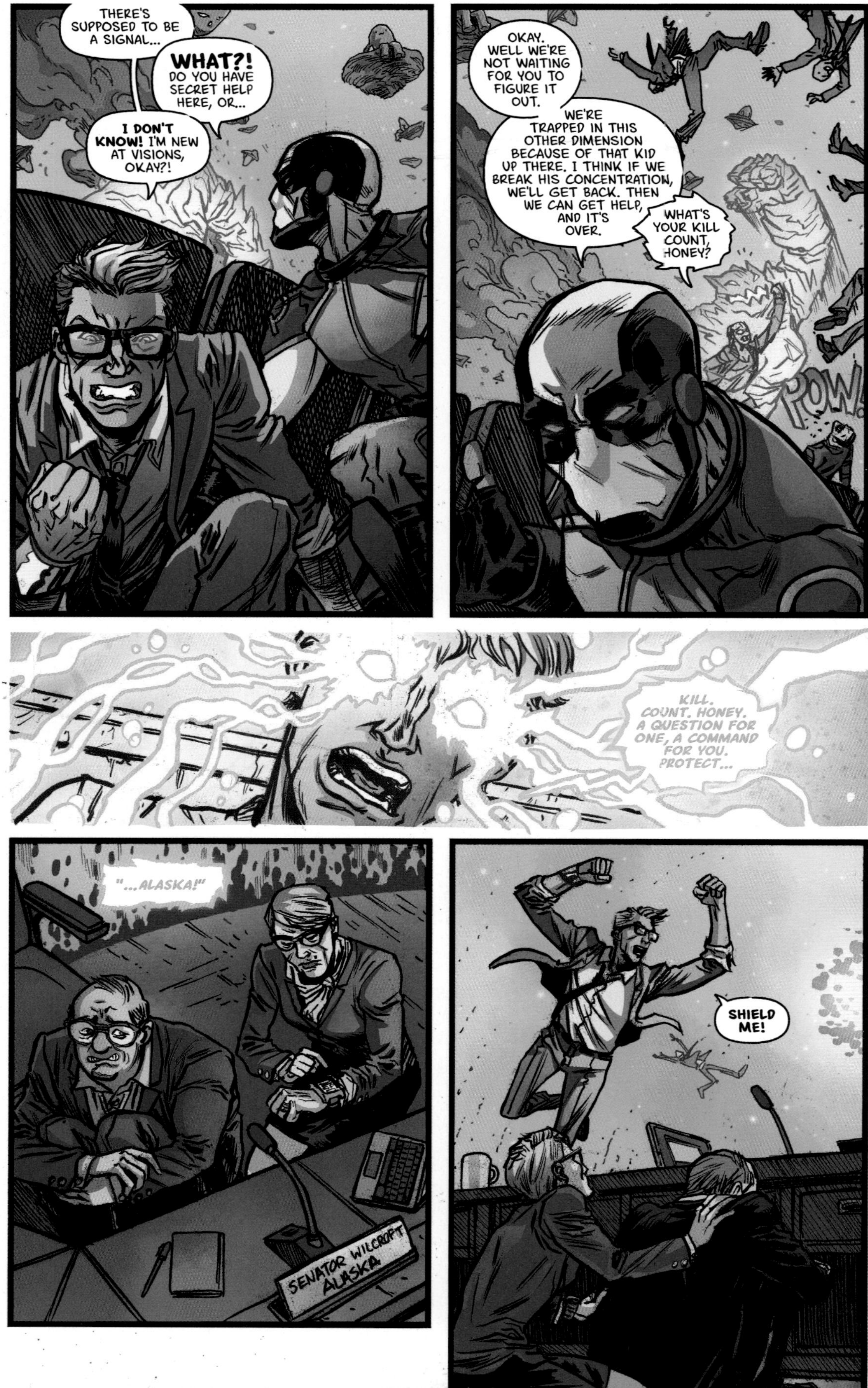

THERE'S SUPPOSED TO BE A SIGNAL...
WHAT?! DO YOU HAVE SECRET HELP HERE, OR...
I DON'T KNOW! I'M NEW AT VISIONS, OKAY?!
OKAY. WELL WE'RE NOT WAITING FOR YOU TO FIGURE IT OUT.
WE'RE TRAPPED IN THIS OTHER DIMENSION BECAUSE OF THAT KID UP THERE. I THINK IF WE BREAK HIS CONCENTRATION, WE'LL GET BACK. THEN WE CAN GET HELP, AND IT'S OVER.
WHAT'S YOUR KILL COUNT, HONEY?
POW!
KILL. COUNT. HONEY. A QUESTION FOR ONE, A COMMAND FOR YOU. PROTECT...
"...ALASKA!"
SENATOR WILCROFT ALASKA
SHIELD ME!

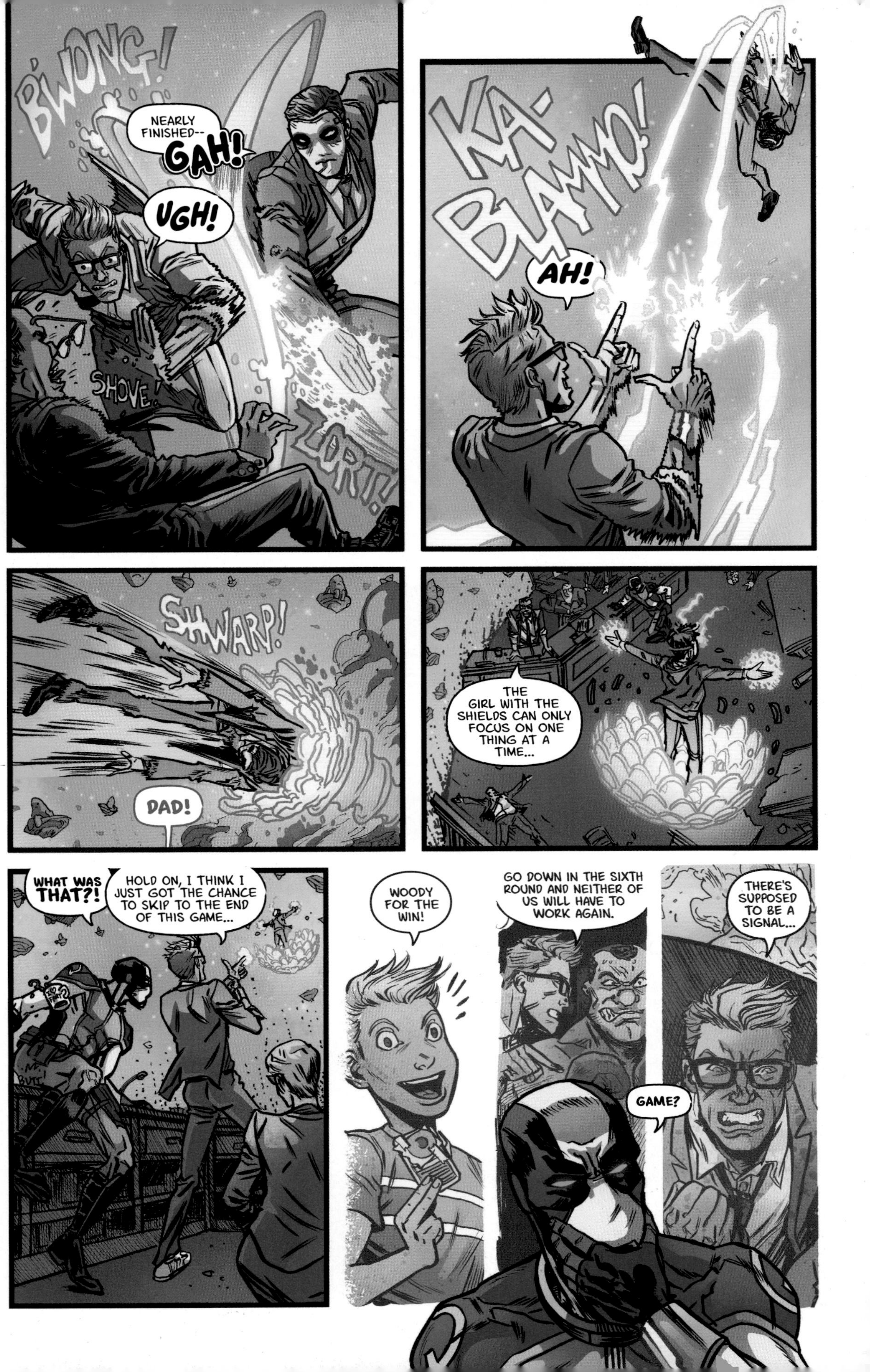
BWONG!
NEARLY FINISHED-- GAH!
UGH!
SHOVE!
ZORT!!
KA-BLAMMO!
AH!
SHWARP!
DAD!
THE GIRL WITH THE SHIELDS CAN ONLY FOCUS ON ONE THING AT A TIME...
WHAT WAS THAT?!
HOLD ON, I THINK I JUST GOT THE CHANCE TO SKIP TO THE END OF THIS GAME...
WOODY FOR THE WIN!
GO DOWN IN THE SIXTH ROUND AND NEITHER OF US WILL HAVE TO WORK AGAIN.
THERE'S SUPPOSED TO BE A SIGNAL...
GAME?

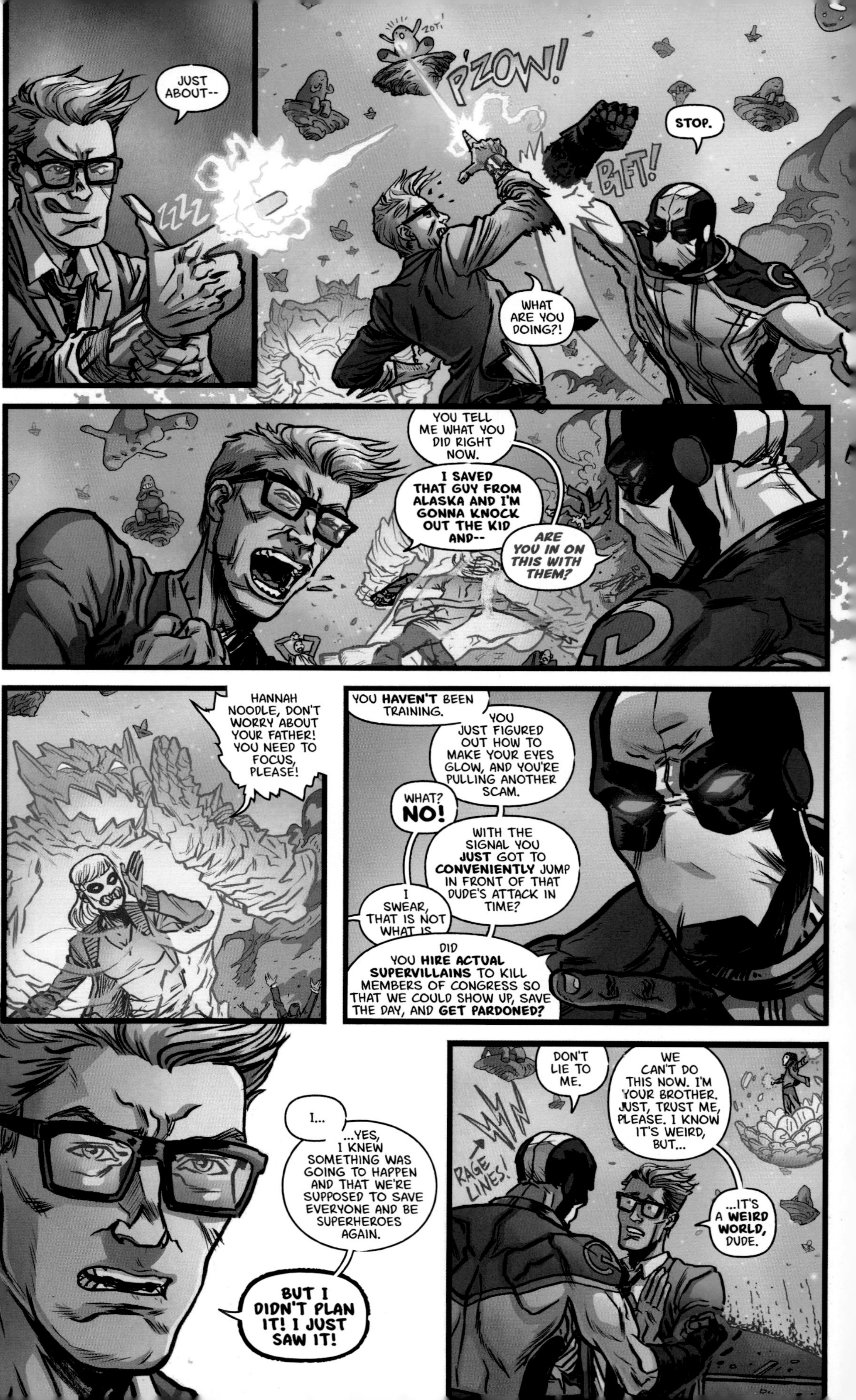

JUST ABOUT--
ZZZZ
ZOT!
P'ZOW!
STOP.
BIFT!
WHAT ARE YOU DOING?!
YOU TELL ME WHAT YOU DID RIGHT NOW.
I SAVED THAT GUY FROM ALASKA AND I'M GONNA KNOCK OUT THE KID AND--
ARE YOU IN ON THIS WITH THEM?
HANNAH NOODLE, DON'T WORRY ABOUT YOUR FATHER! YOU NEED TO FOCUS, PLEASE!
YOU HAVEN'T BEEN TRAINING.
YOU JUST FIGURED OUT HOW TO MAKE YOUR EYES GLOW, AND YOU'RE PULLING ANOTHER SCAM.
WHAT? NO!
WITH THE SIGNAL YOU JUST GOT TO CONVENIENTLY JUMP IN FRONT OF THAT DUDE'S ATTACK IN TIME?
I SWEAR, THAT IS NOT WHAT IS
DID YOU HIRE ACTUAL SUPERVILLAINS TO KILL MEMBERS OF CONGRESS SO THAT WE COULD SHOW UP, SAVE THE DAY, AND GET PARDONED?
I...
...YES, I KNEW SOMETHING WAS GOING TO HAPPEN AND THAT WE'RE SUPPOSED TO SAVE EVERYONE AND BE SUPERHEROES AGAIN.
BUT I DIDN'T PLAN IT! I JUST SAW IT!
DON'T LIE TO ME.
RAGE LINES!
WE CAN'T DO THIS NOW. I'M YOUR BROTHER. JUST, TRUST ME, PLEASE. I KNOW IT'S WEIRD, BUT...
...IT'S A WEIRD WORLD, DUDE.

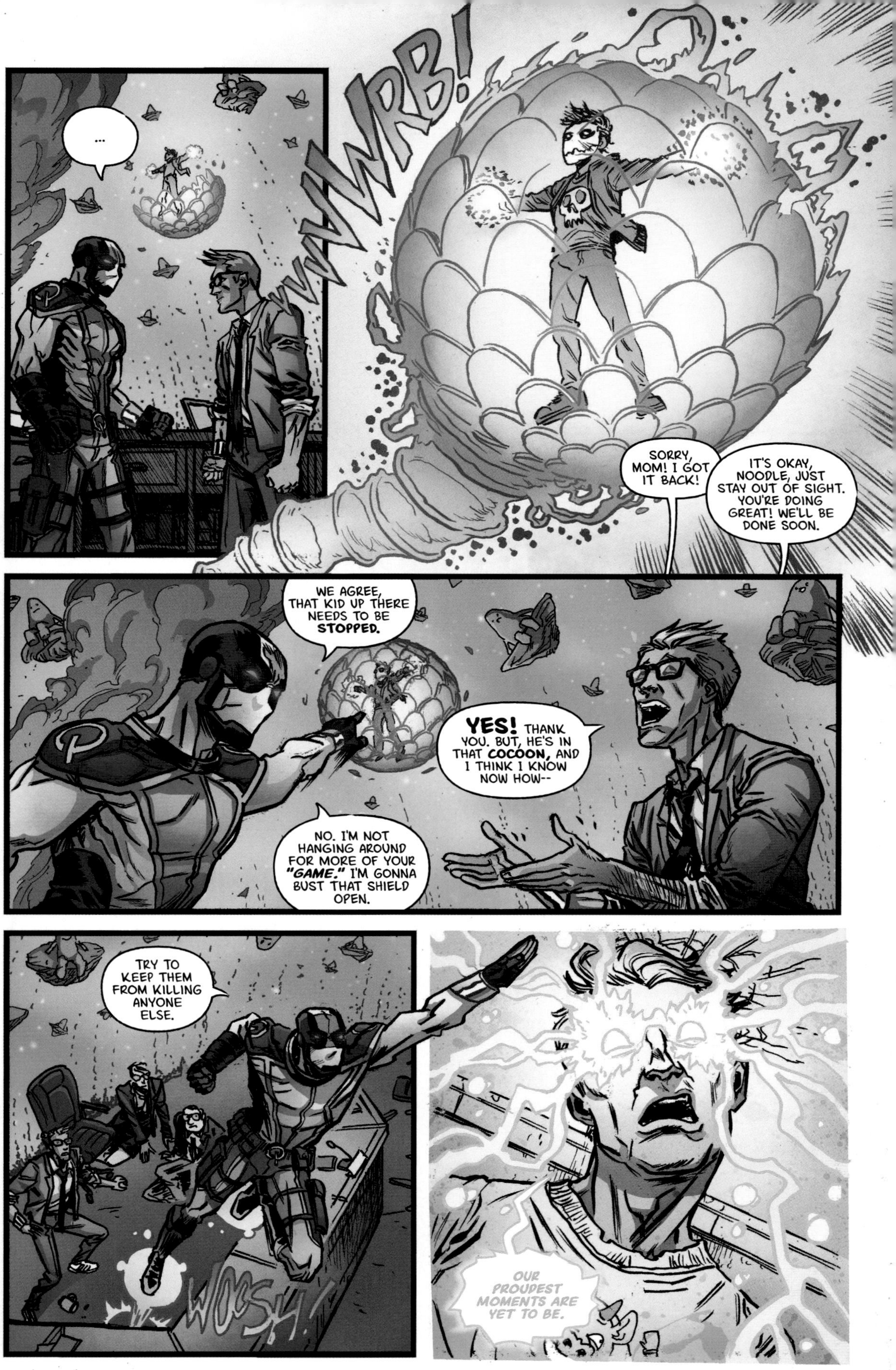
...
VVVVWRB!
SORRY, MOM! I GOT IT BACK!
IT'S OKAY, NOODLE, JUST STAY OUT OF SIGHT. YOU'RE DOING GREAT! WE'LL BE DONE SOON.
WE AGREE, THAT KID UP THERE NEEDS TO BE **STOPPED.**
YES! THANK YOU. BUT, HE'S IN THAT **COCOON,** AND I THINK I KNOW NOW HOW--
NO. I'M NOT HANGING AROUND FOR MORE OF YOUR ***"GAME."*** I'M GONNA BUST THAT SHIELD OPEN.
TRY TO KEEP THEM FROM KILLING ANYONE ELSE.
WOOSH!
OUR PROUDEST MOMENTS ARE YET TO BE.

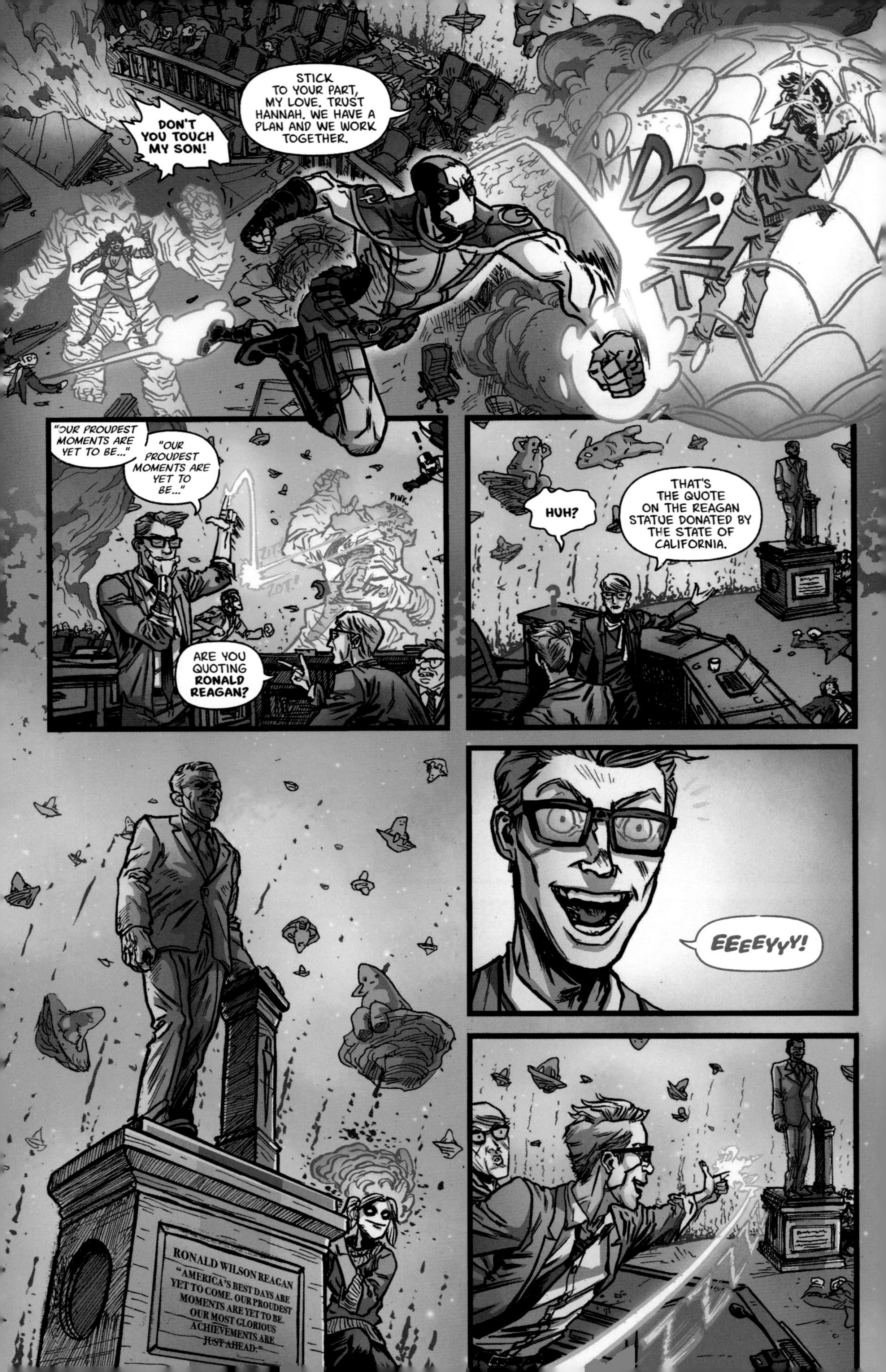
DON'T YOU TOUCH MY SON!
STICK TO YOUR PART, MY LOVE. TRUST HANNAH. WE HAVE A PLAN AND WE WORK TOGETHER.
DOOM
"OUR PROUDEST MOMENTS ARE YET TO BE..."
"OUR PROUDEST MOMENTS ARE YET TO BE..."
PINK!
ZOT!
ARE YOU QUOTING RONALD REAGAN?
HUH?
THAT'S THE QUOTE ON THE REAGAN STATUE DONATED BY THE STATE OF CALIFORNIA.
RONALD WILSON REAGAN
"AMERICA'S BEST DAYS ARE YET TO COME. OUR PROUDEST MOMENTS ARE YET TO BE. OUR MOST GLORIOUS ACHIEVEMENTS ARE JUST AHEAD."
EEEEYYY!

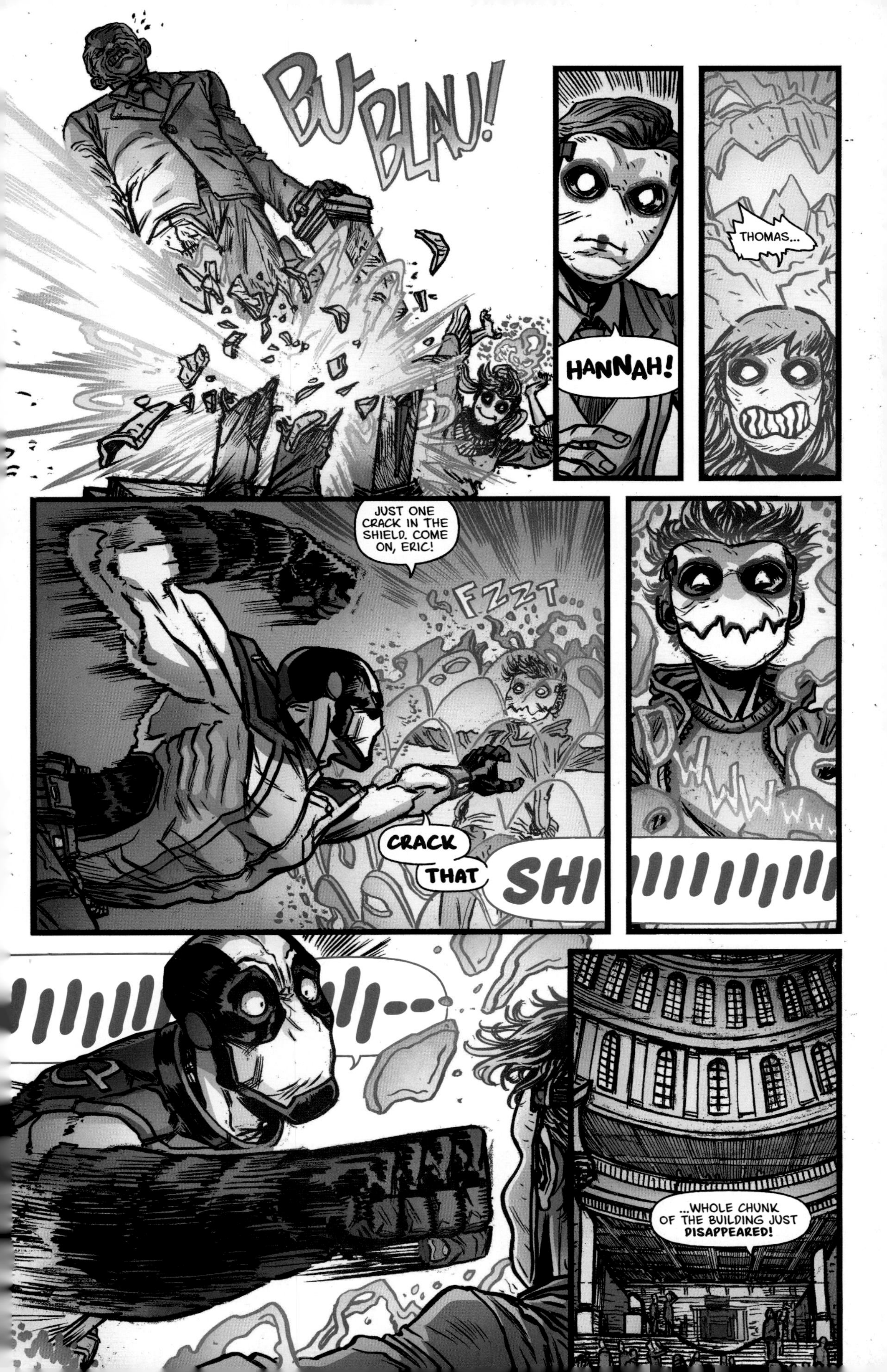
BU-BLAU!
HANNAH!
THOMAS...
JUST ONE CRACK IN THE SHIELD. COME ON, ERIC!
FZZT...
CRACK
THAT
SHIIIIIIIIIIIIIII
IIIIIIIIIIIIII--..
...WHOLE CHUNK OF THE BUILDING JUST DISAPPEARED!

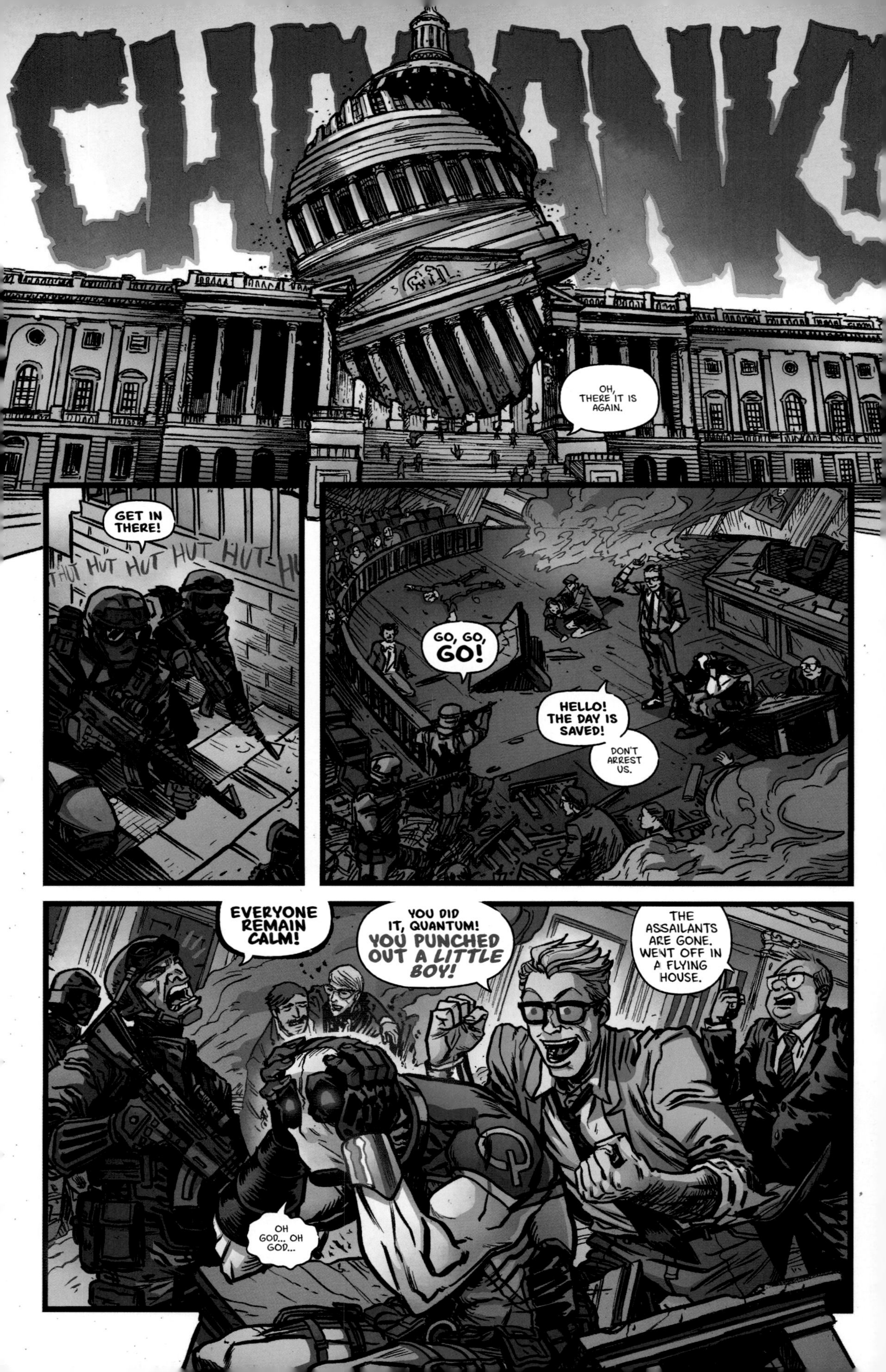
OH, THERE IT IS AGAIN.
GET IN THERE!
HUT HUT HUT HUT HUT-
GO, GO, GO!
HELLO! THE DAY IS SAVED!
DON'T ARREST US.
EVERYONE REMAIN CALM!
YOU DID IT, QUANTUM! YOU PUNCHED OUT A LITTLE BOY!
THE ASSAILANTS ARE GONE. WENT OFF IN A FLYING HOUSE.
OH GOD... OH GOD...

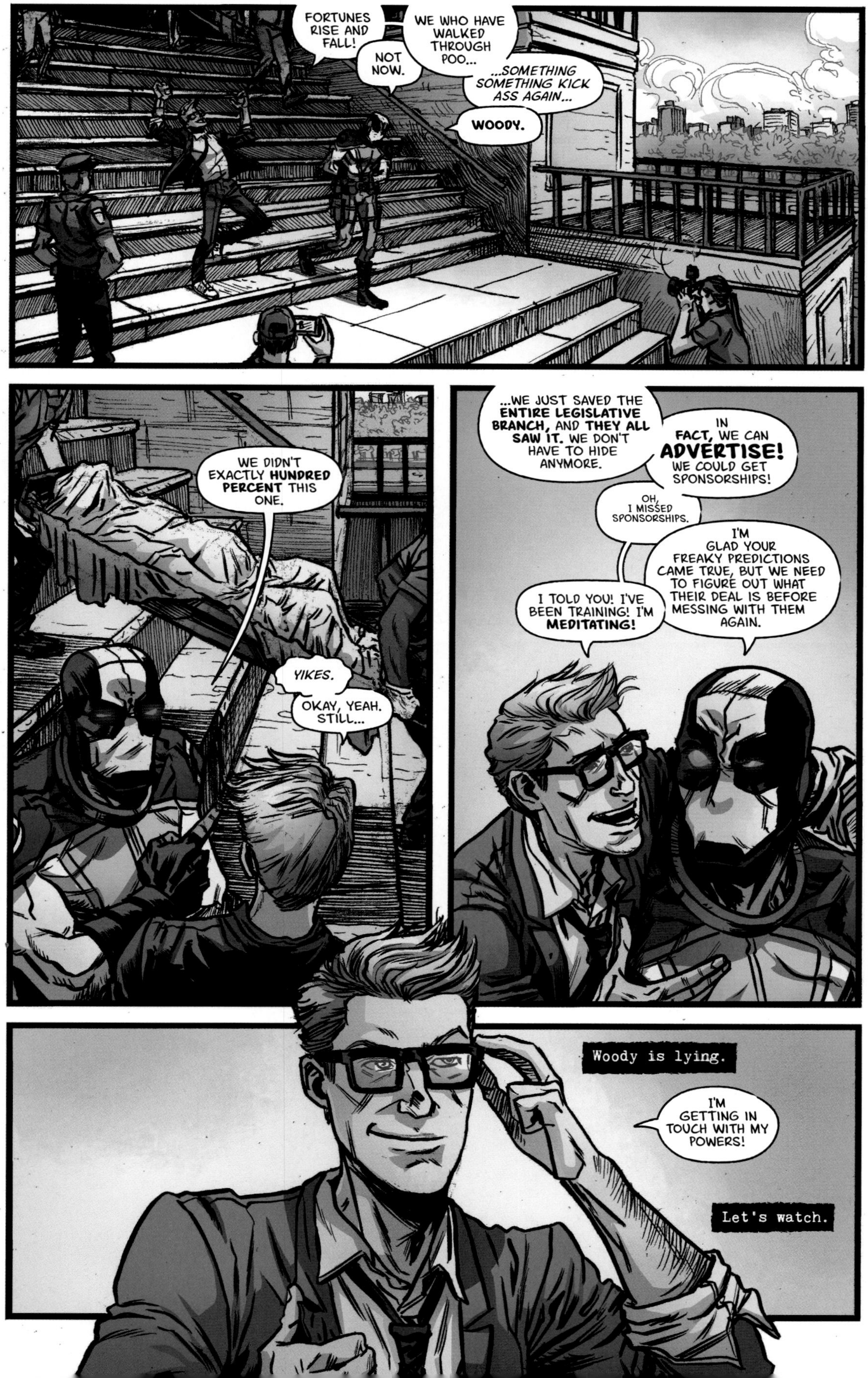
FORTUNES RISE AND FALL!
WE WHO HAVE WALKED THROUGH POO...
NOT NOW.
...SOMETHING SOMETHING KICK ASS AGAIN...
WOODY.
WE DIDN'T EXACTLY HUNDRED PERCENT THIS ONE.
YIKES.
OKAY, YEAH. STILL...
...WE JUST SAVED THE ENTIRE LEGISLATIVE BRANCH, AND THEY ALL SAW IT. WE DON'T HAVE TO HIDE ANYMORE.
IN FACT, WE CAN ADVERTISE! WE COULD GET SPONSORSHIPS!
OH, I MISSED SPONSORSHIPS.
I'M GLAD YOUR FREAKY PREDICTIONS CAME TRUE, BUT WE NEED TO FIGURE OUT WHAT THEIR DEAL IS BEFORE MESSING WITH THEM AGAIN.
I TOLD YOU! I'VE BEEN TRAINING! I'M MEDITATING!
Woody is lying.
I'M GETTING IN TOUCH WITH MY POWERS!
Let's watch.

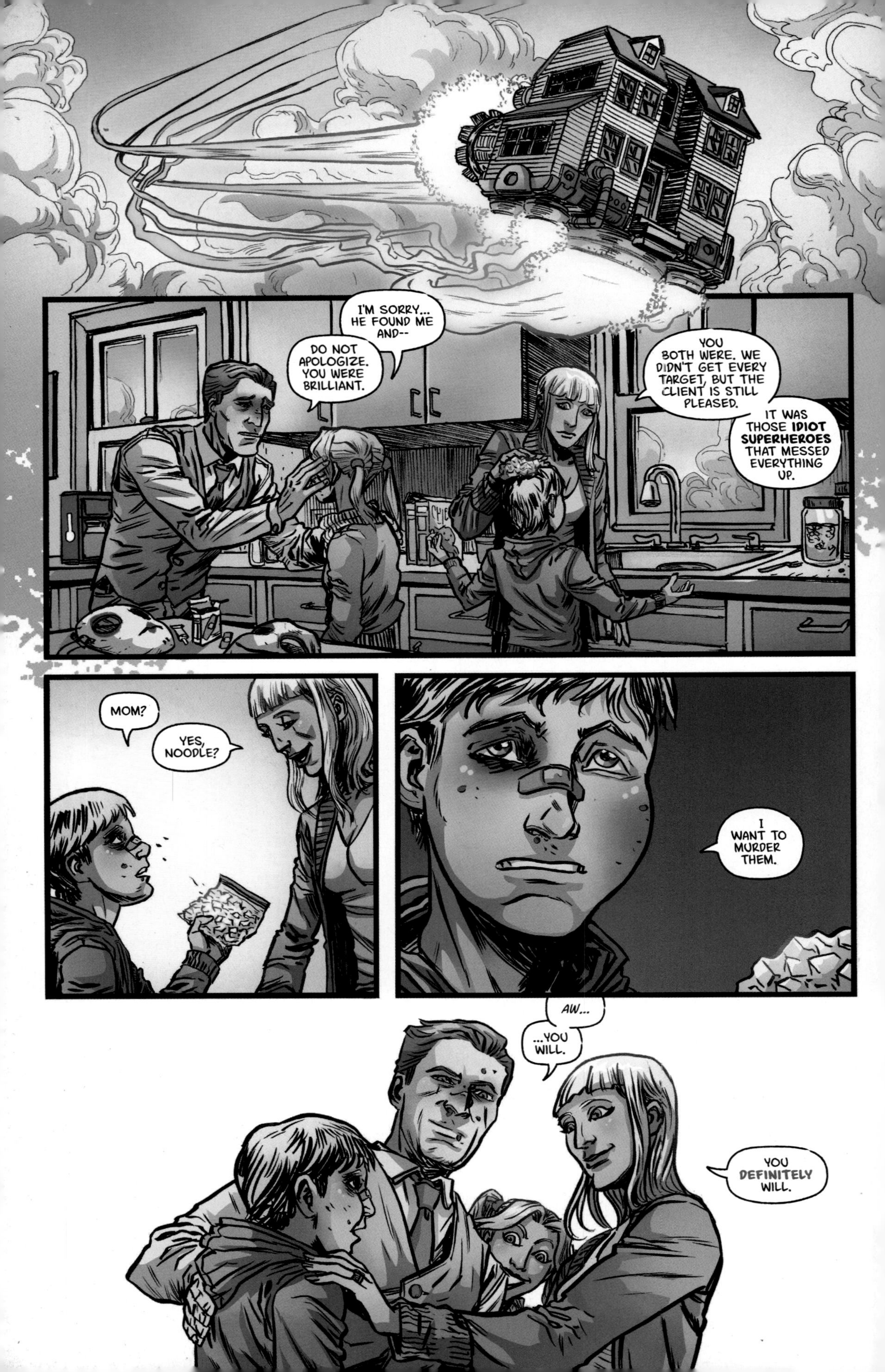

DO NOT APOLOGIZE. YOU WERE BRILLIANT.
I'M SORRY... HE FOUND ME AND--
YOU BOTH WERE. WE DIDN'T GET EVERY TARGET, BUT THE CLIENT IS STILL PLEASED.
IT WAS THOSE **IDIOT SUPERHEROES** THAT MESSED EVERYTHING UP.
MOM?
YES, NOODLE?
I WANT TO MURDER THEM.
AW...
...YOU WILL.
YOU **DEFINITELY** WILL.

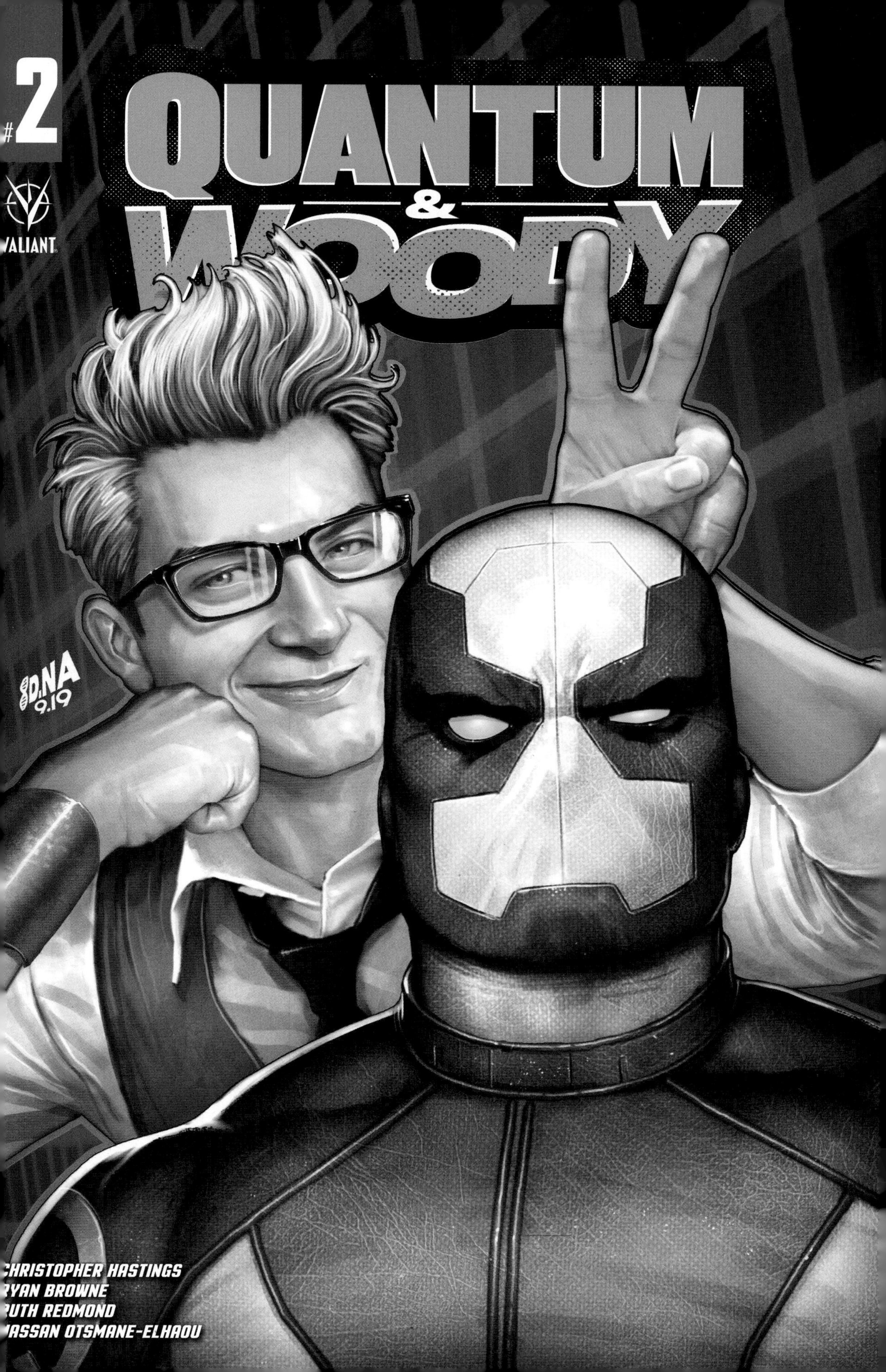
#2
QUANTUM & WOODY
VALIANT
D.NA 9.19
CHRISTOPHER HASTINGS
RYAN BROWNE
RUTH REDMOND
HASSAN OTSMANE-ELHAOU

VOICE IT

Search

White_Chocolate
101k Cheers

v/DListDisasters Posted by OhThatTyler 9 hours ago

31.2k

SPOTTED: Quantum & Woody at Scene of Capitol Attack

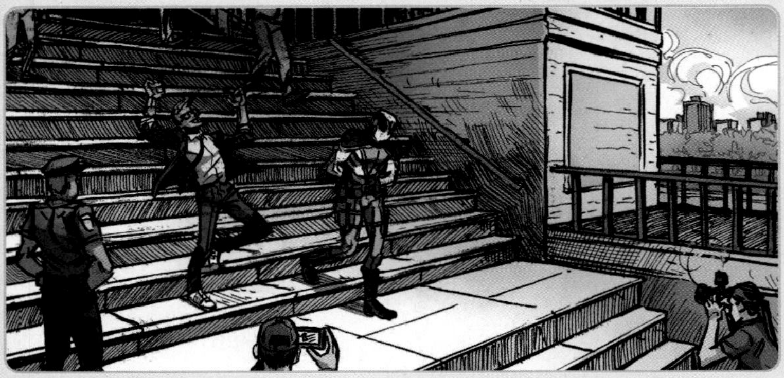

237 Comments · Share · Hide

"Say Something!"

B U I

VOICE IT

OhThatTyler - 20.1k cheers - 9 hours ago
I don't kno if they were behind it, or what, but weren't theez guys wanted fugitives? How r they just walking around in front of the capitol building?
Reply Report

White_Chocolate - 27.5k cheers - 9 hours ago
Behind it? Like we were behind your mo
Reply Report

White_Chocolate - 9.8k cheers - 9 hours ago
Shoot. I posted that too soon. How do you edit again?
Reply Report

HeroesStan - 8.7k cheers - 8 hours ago
Witnesses at the scene reported that Quantum & Woody were rescuing people.
Reply Report

White_Chocolate - 7.4k cheers - 8 hours ago
Just like i said we would, @BlackMamba! My predictions are real! WE CAN BE HEROES!!!!!!1!
Reply Report

BlackMamba - 6.9k cheers - 8 hours ago
Woody, can you try "predicting" what happens when you keep posting like this?
Reply Report

White_Chocolate - 5.2k cheers - 7 hours ago
we get that sweet sweet endorsement money?
Reply Report

Black Mamba - 4.1k cheers - 7 hours ago
Reply Report

White_Chocolate - 2.3k cheers - 6 hours ago
i knew u were gonna say that!!
Reply Report

BrainWise - 1.7k cheers - 4 hours ago
World's Worst Superhero Team.
Reply Report

X-POST_BOT - 6.3k cheers - 9 hours ago
This post has been cross-posted to v/DangerousMorons.
Reply Report

v/DListDisasters

704 ONLINE | 186K MEMBERS

The "Who's Who" of internet fame -- A place to follow celebrities even TNZ thinks aren't worth their time! Find your cult following here!

SUBSCRIBE

CREDITS

Writer...**Christopher Hastings**
Artist...**Ryan Browne**
Colorist...**Ruth Redmond**
Letterer...**Hassan Otsmane-Elhaou**
Cover Artist...**David Nakayama**
Assistant Editor...**Drew Baumgartner**
Editor...**Heather Antos**

TRENDING COMMUNITIES

v/ValiantComicFans 167k members JOIN
v/legionofthunder 33k members JOIN
v/MythosOrMadScience 22k members JOIN
v/deadsidedeadbeats 4k members JOIN

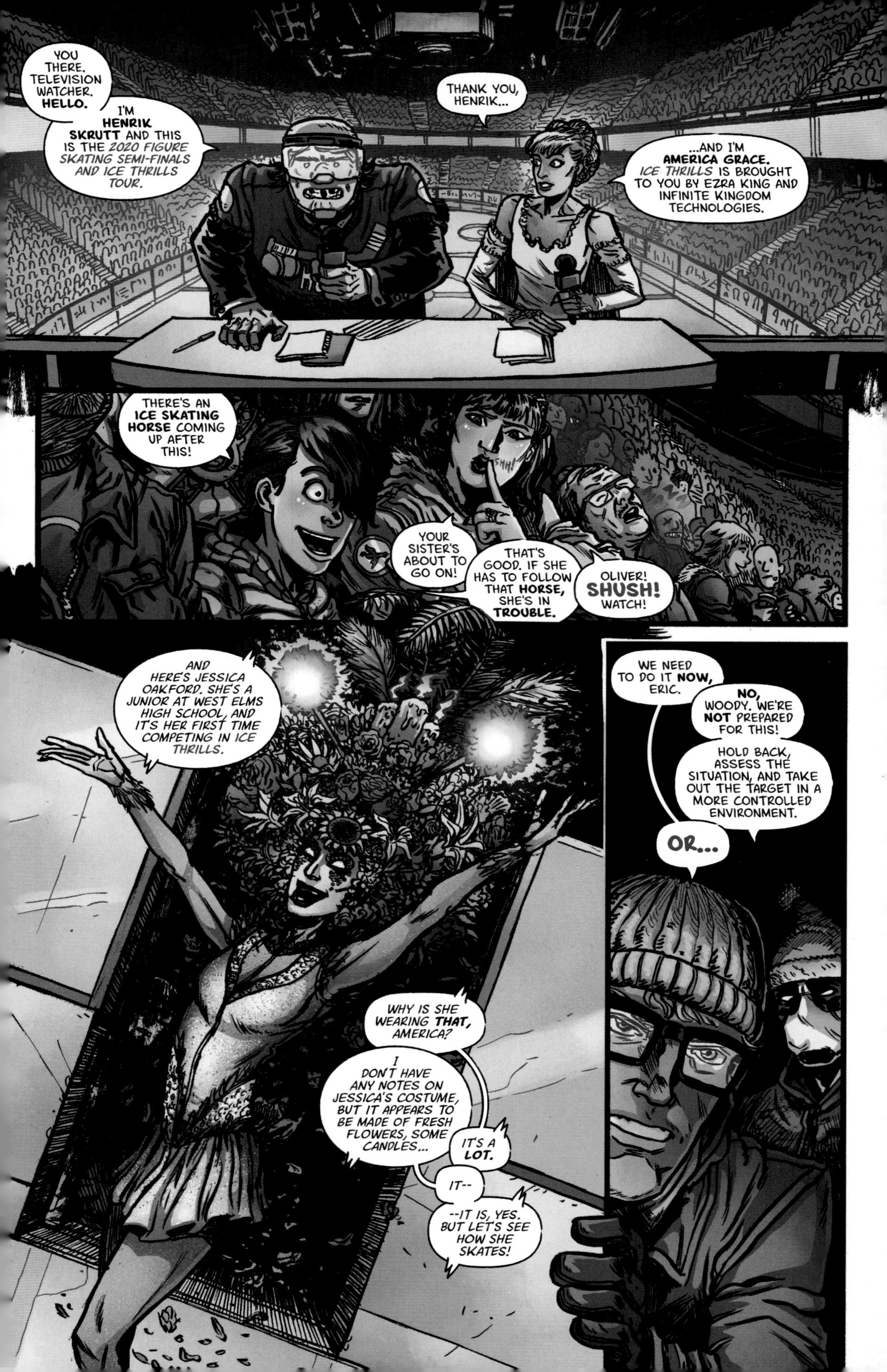
YOU THERE. TELEVISION WATCHER. HELLO.
I'M HENRIK SKRUTT AND THIS IS THE 2020 FIGURE SKATING SEMI-FINALS AND ICE THRILLS TOUR.
THANK YOU, HENRIK...
...AND I'M AMERICA GRACE. ICE THRILLS IS BROUGHT TO YOU BY EZRA KING AND INFINITE KINGDOM TECHNOLOGIES.
THERE'S AN ICE SKATING HORSE COMING UP AFTER THIS!
YOUR SISTER'S ABOUT TO GO ON!
THAT'S GOOD. IF SHE HAS TO FOLLOW THAT HORSE, SHE'S IN TROUBLE.
OLIVER! SHUSH! WATCH!
AND HERE'S JESSICA OAKFORD. SHE'S A JUNIOR AT WEST ELMS HIGH SCHOOL, AND IT'S HER FIRST TIME COMPETING IN ICE THRILLS.
WHY IS SHE WEARING THAT, AMERICA?
I DON'T HAVE ANY NOTES ON JESSICA'S COSTUME, BUT IT APPEARS TO BE MADE OF FRESH FLOWERS, SOME CANDLES...
IT'S A LOT.
IT--
--IT IS, YES. BUT LET'S SEE HOW SHE SKATES!
WE NEED TO DO IT NOW, ERIC.
NO, WOODY. WE'RE NOT PREPARED FOR THIS!
HOLD BACK, ASSESS THE SITUATION, AND TAKE OUT THE TARGET IN A MORE CONTROLLED ENVIRONMENT.
OR...

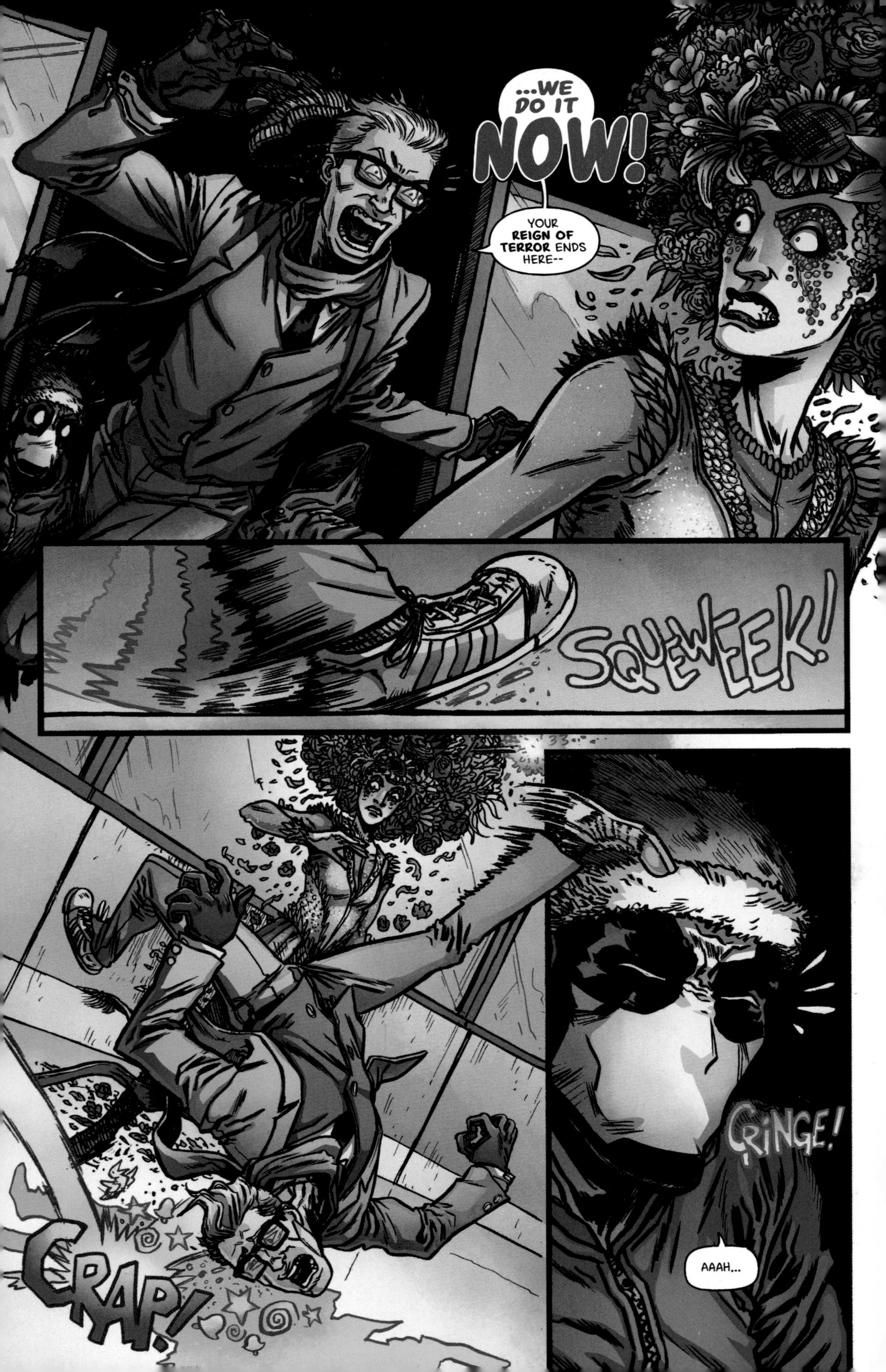
...WE DO IT NOW!
YOUR REIGN OF TERROR ENDS HERE--
SQUEWEEK!
CRAP!
CRINGE!
AAAH...

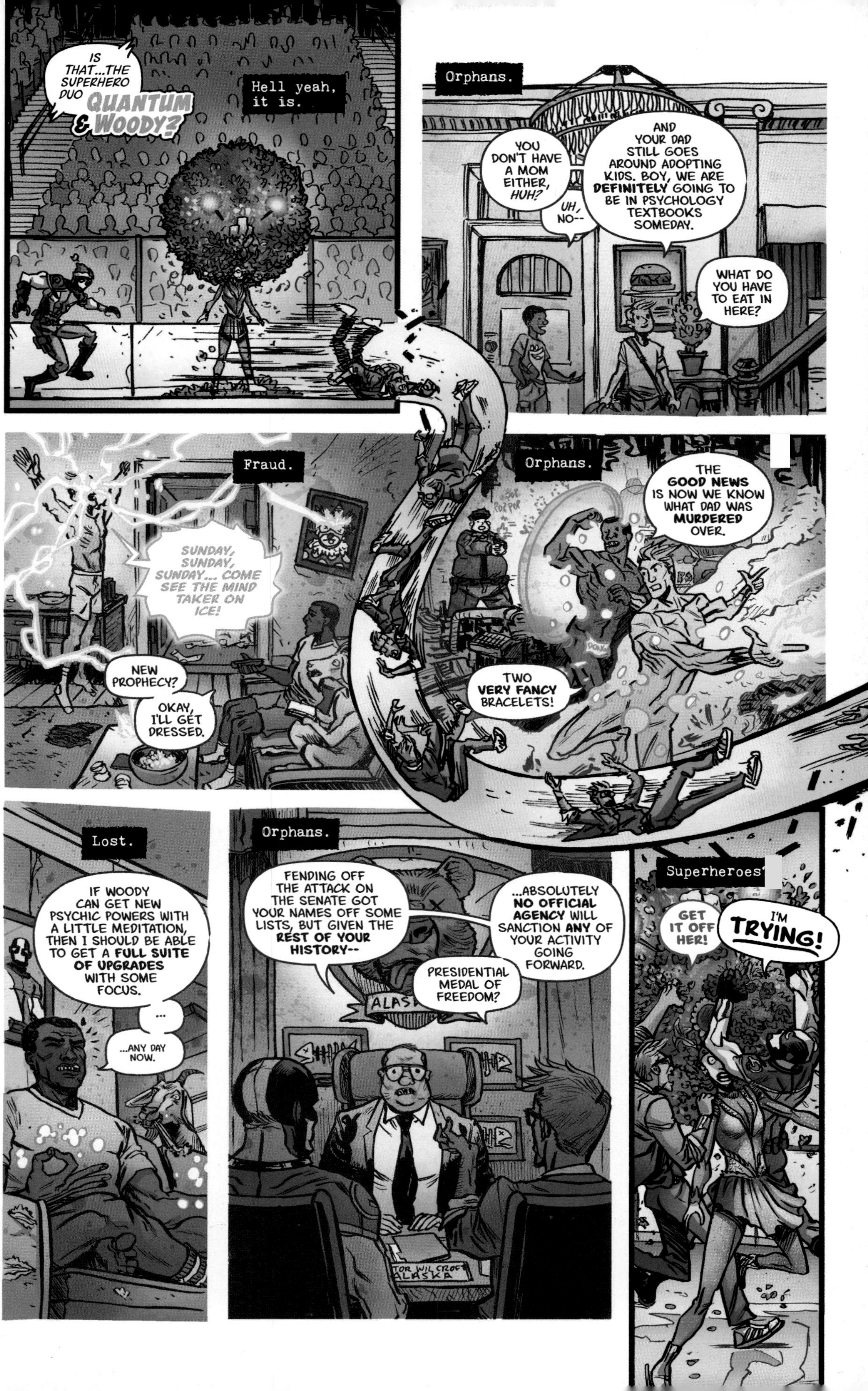
IS THAT...THE SUPERHERO DUO QUANTUM & WOODY?
Hell yeah, it is.
Orphans.
YOU DON'T HAVE A MOM EITHER, HUH?
UH, NO--
AND YOUR DAD STILL GOES AROUND ADOPTING KIDS. BOY, WE ARE DEFINITELY GOING TO BE IN PSYCHOLOGY TEXTBOOKS SOMEDAY.
WHAT DO YOU HAVE TO EAT IN HERE?
Fraud.
SUNDAY, SUNDAY, SUNDAY... COME SEE THE MIND TAKER ON ICE!
NEW PROPHECY?
OKAY, I'LL GET DRESSED.
Orphans.
THE GOOD NEWS IS NOW WE KNOW WHAT DAD WAS MURDERED OVER.
TWO VERY FANCY BRACELETS!
Lost.
IF WOODY CAN GET NEW PSYCHIC POWERS WITH A LITTLE MEDITATION, THEN I SHOULD BE ABLE TO GET A FULL SUITE OF UPGRADES WITH SOME FOCUS.
...
...ANY DAY NOW.
Orphans.
FENDING OFF THE ATTACK ON THE SENATE GOT YOUR NAMES OFF SOME LISTS, BUT GIVEN THE REST OF YOUR HISTORY--
...ABSOLUTELY NO OFFICIAL AGENCY WILL SANCTION ANY OF YOUR ACTIVITY GOING FORWARD.
PRESIDENTIAL MEDAL OF FREEDOM?
Superheroes?
GET IT OFF HER!
I'M TRYING!

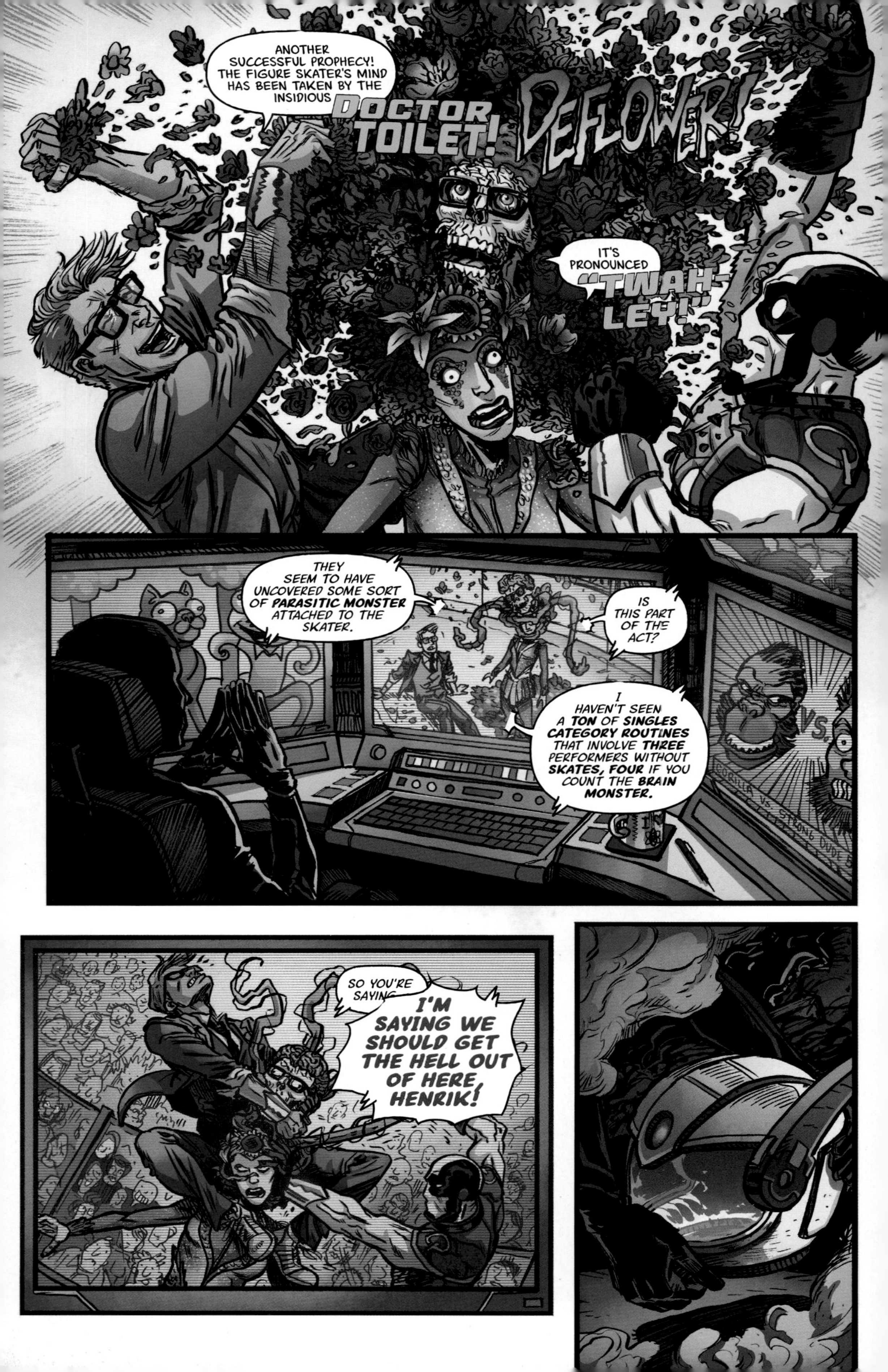
ANOTHER SUCCESSFUL PROPHECY! THE FIGURE SKATER'S MIND HAS BEEN TAKEN BY THE INSIDIOUS DOCTOR TOILET!
DEFLOWER!
IT'S PRONOUNCED "TWAH-LEY!"
THEY SEEM TO HAVE UNCOVERED SOME SORT OF PARASITIC MONSTER ATTACHED TO THE SKATER.
IS THIS PART OF THE ACT?
I HAVEN'T SEEN A TON OF SINGLES CATEGORY ROUTINES THAT INVOLVE THREE PERFORMERS WITHOUT SKATES, FOUR IF YOU COUNT THE BRAIN MONSTER.
VS.
SO YOU'RE SAYING—
I'M SAYING WE SHOULD GET THE HELL OUT OF HERE, HENRIK!

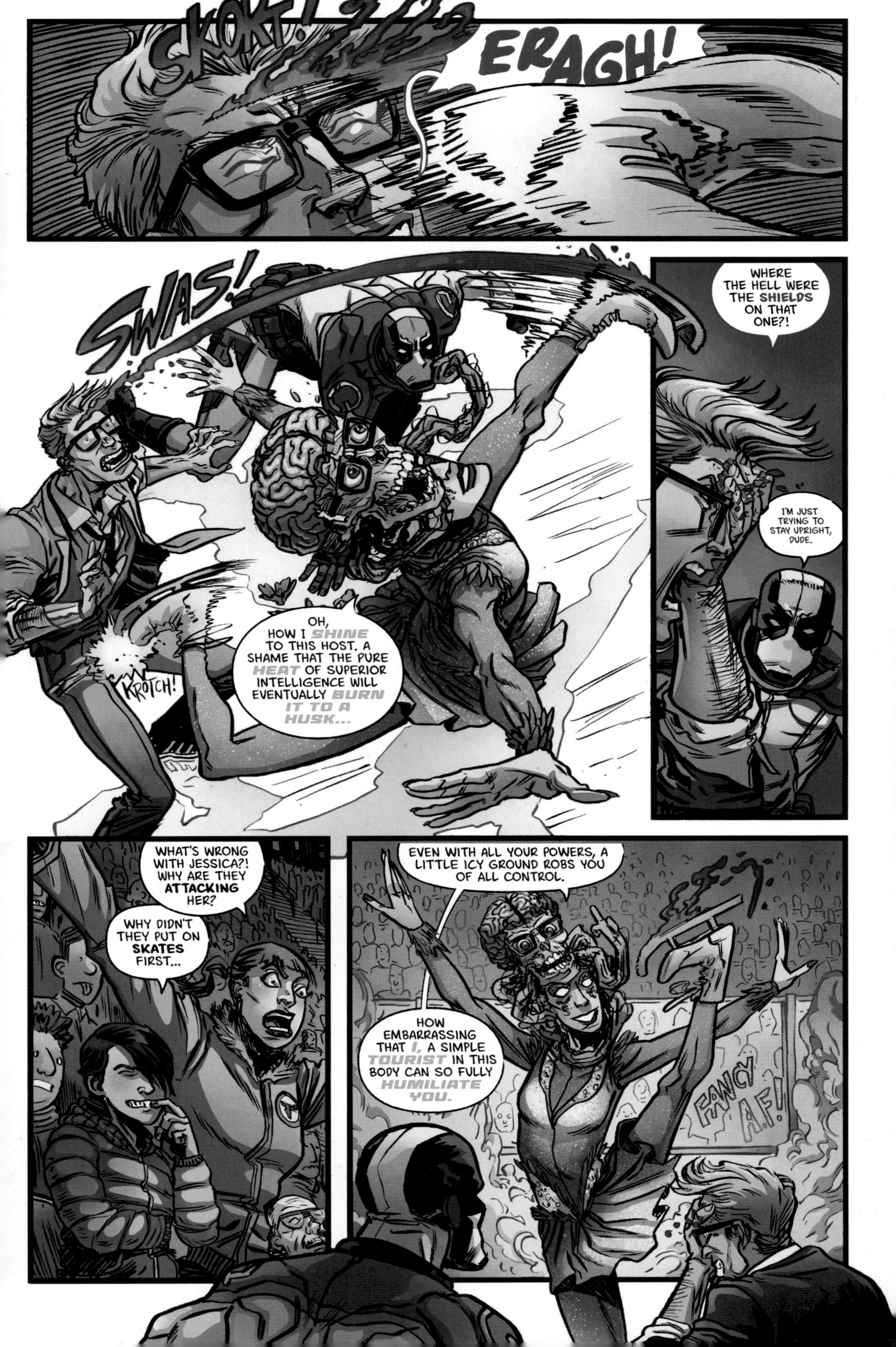
SKORT!
ERAGH!
SWAS!
WHERE THE HELL WERE THE SHIELDS ON THAT ONE?!
I'M JUST TRYING TO STAY UPRIGHT, DUDE.
OH, HOW I SHINE TO THIS HOST. A SHAME THAT THE PURE HEAT OF SUPERIOR INTELLIGENCE WILL EVENTUALLY BURN IT TO A HUSK...
KROTCH!
WHAT'S WRONG WITH JESSICA?! WHY ARE THEY ATTACKING HER?
WHY DIDN'T THEY PUT ON SKATES FIRST...
EVEN WITH ALL YOUR POWERS, A LITTLE ICY GROUND ROBS YOU OF ALL CONTROL.
HOW EMBARRASSING THAT I, A SIMPLE TOURIST IN THIS BODY CAN SO FULLY HUMILIATE YOU.
FANCY A.F.!

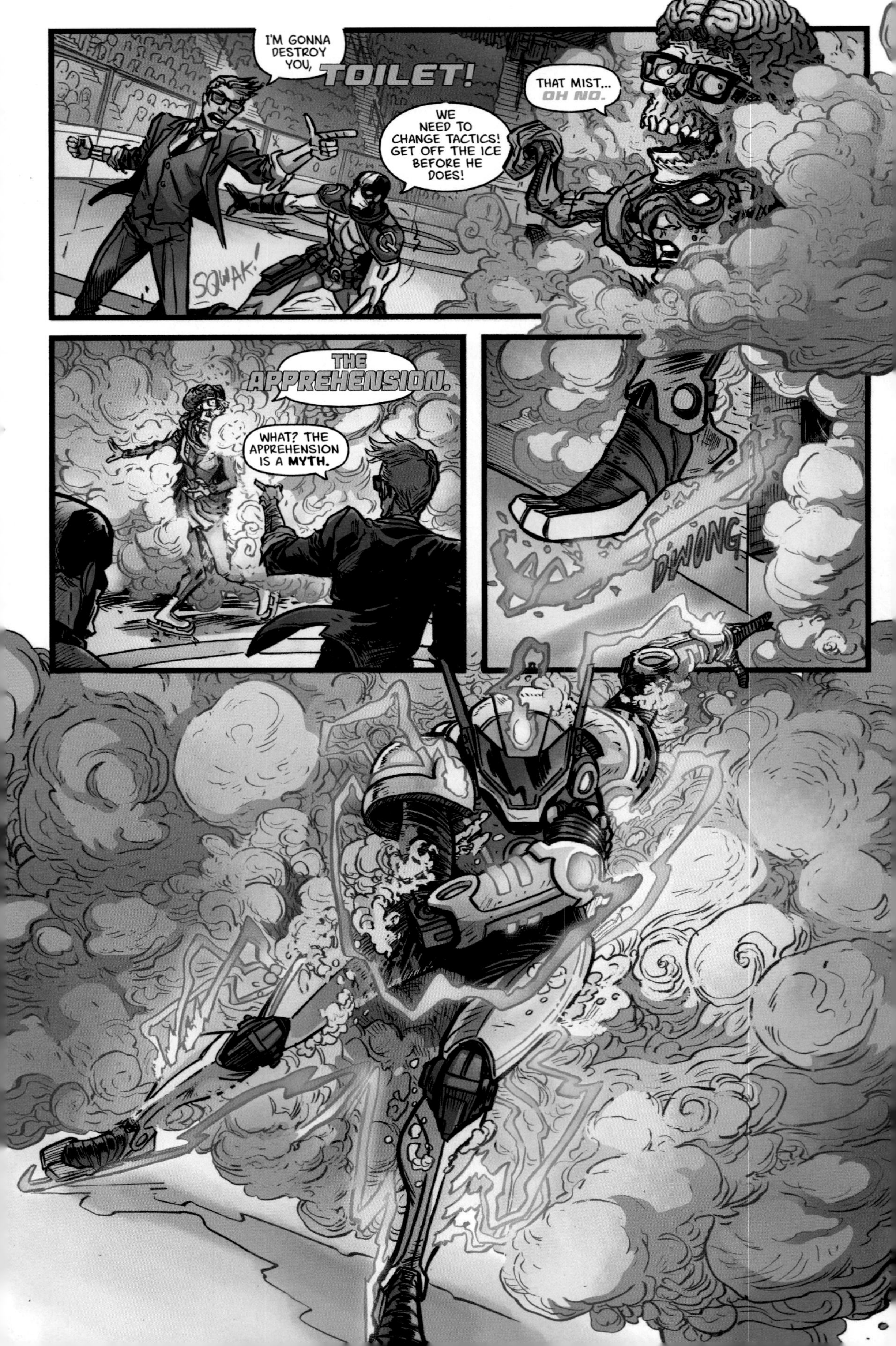
I'M GONNA DESTROY YOU, TOILET!
WE NEED TO CHANGE TACTICS! GET OFF THE ICE BEFORE HE DOES!
THAT MIST... OH NO.
SQWAK!
THE APPREHENSION.
WHAT? THE APPREHENSION IS A MYTH.
DWONG

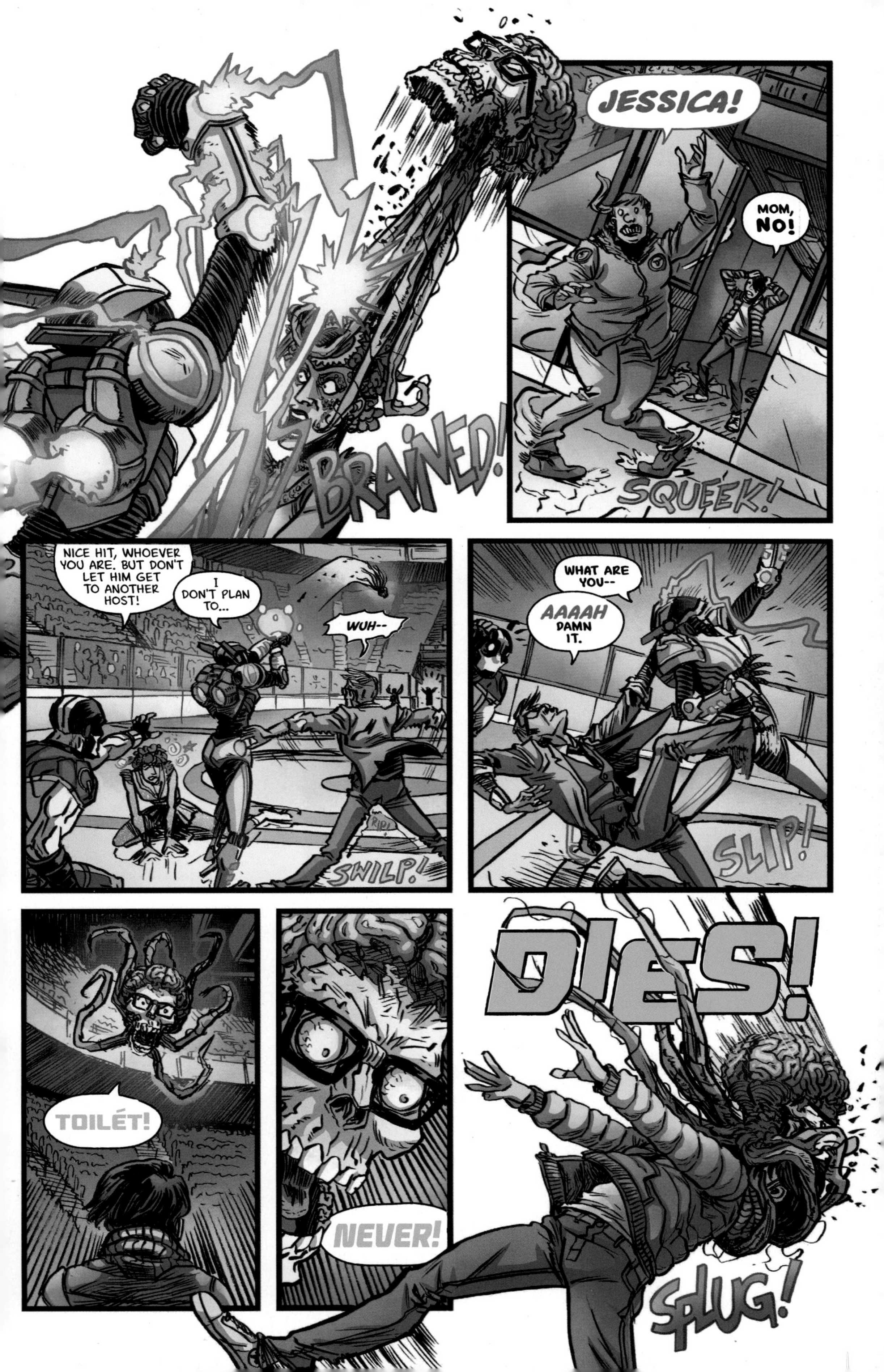
BRAINED!
JESSICA!
MOM, NO!
SQUEEK!
NICE HIT, WHOEVER YOU ARE. BUT DON'T LET HIM GET TO ANOTHER HOST!
I DON'T PLAN TO...
WUH--
RIP!
SWILP!
WHAT ARE YOU--
AAAAH DAMN IT.
SLIP!
TOILÉT!
NEVER!
DIES!
SPLUG!

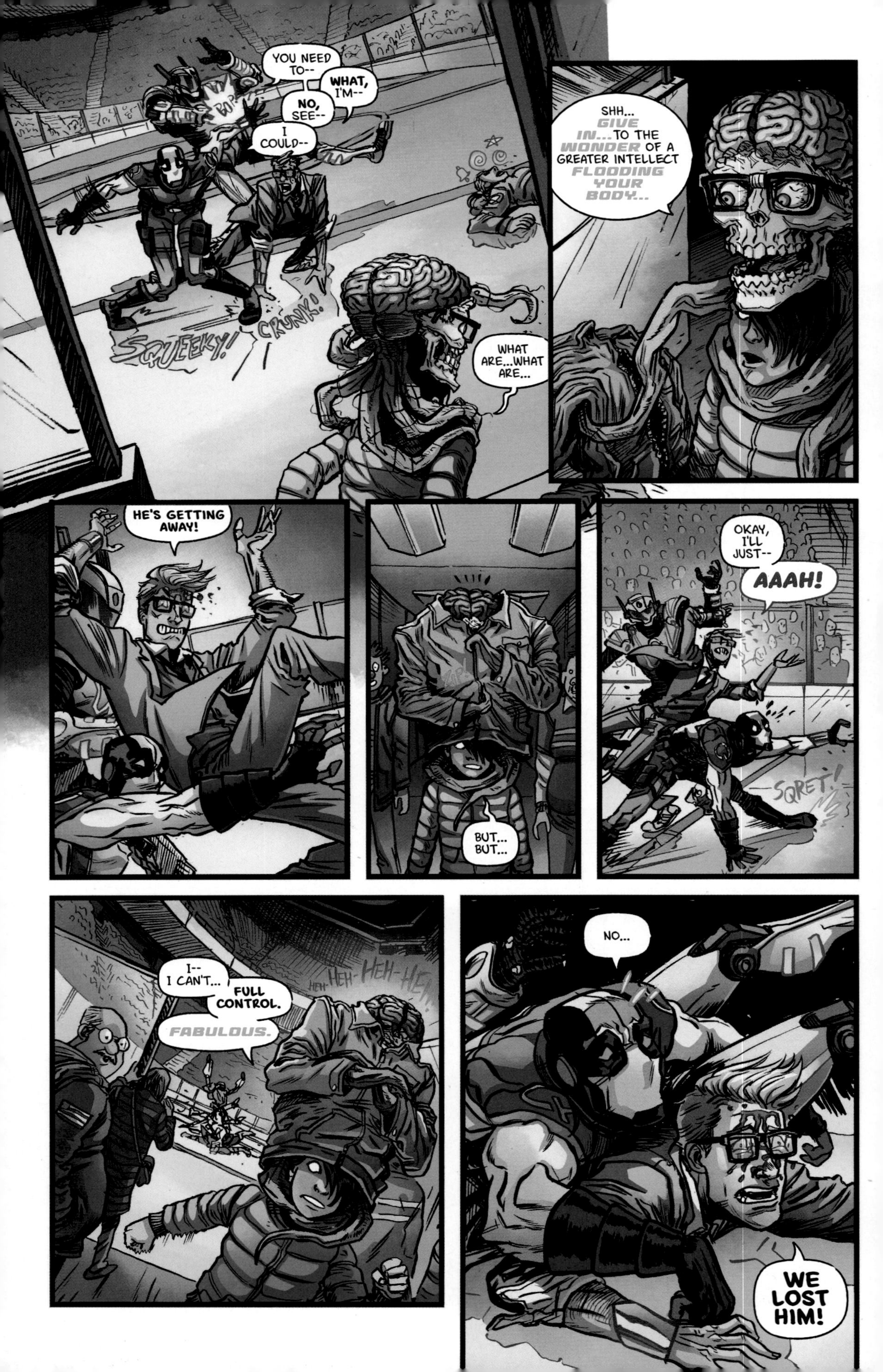

YOU NEED TO--
WHAT, I'M--
NO, SEE--
I COULD--
SQUEEKY!
CRUNK!
WHAT ARE...WHAT ARE...
SHH... GIVE IN... TO THE WONDER OF A GREATER INTELLECT FLOODING YOUR BODY...
HE'S GETTING AWAY!
BUT... BUT...
OKAY, I'LL JUST--
AAAH!
SQRET!
I-- I CAN'T...
FULL CONTROL.
FABULOUS.
HEH-HEH-HEH-HEH
NO...
WE LOST HIM!

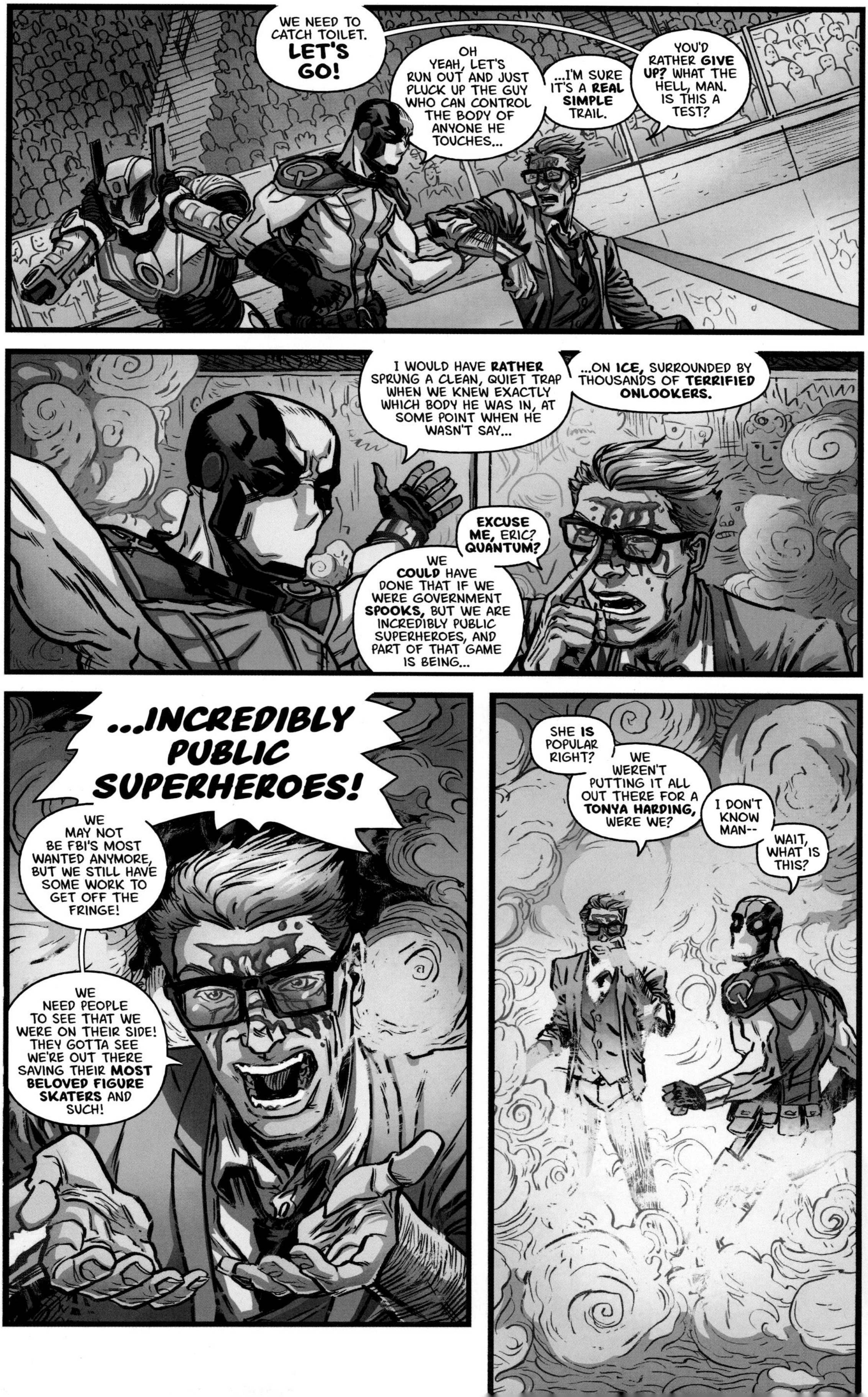
WE NEED TO CATCH TOILET. LET'S GO!
OH YEAH, LET'S RUN OUT AND JUST PLUCK UP THE GUY WHO CAN CONTROL THE BODY OF ANYONE HE TOUCHES...
...I'M SURE IT'S A REAL SIMPLE TRAIL.
YOU'D RATHER GIVE UP? WHAT THE HELL, MAN. IS THIS A TEST?
I WOULD HAVE RATHER SPRUNG A CLEAN, QUIET TRAP WHEN WE KNEW EXACTLY WHICH BODY HE WAS IN, AT SOME POINT WHEN HE WASN'T SAY...
...ON ICE, SURROUNDED BY THOUSANDS OF TERRIFIED ONLOOKERS.
EXCUSE ME, ERIC? QUANTUM?
WE COULD HAVE DONE THAT IF WE WERE GOVERNMENT SPOOKS, BUT WE ARE INCREDIBLY PUBLIC SUPERHEROES, AND PART OF THAT GAME IS BEING...
...INCREDIBLY PUBLIC SUPERHEROES!
WE MAY NOT BE FBI'S MOST WANTED ANYMORE, BUT WE STILL HAVE SOME WORK TO GET OFF THE FRINGE!
WE NEED PEOPLE TO SEE THAT WE WERE ON THEIR SIDE! THEY GOTTA SEE WE'RE OUT THERE SAVING THEIR MOST BELOVED FIGURE SKATERS AND SUCH!
SHE IS POPULAR RIGHT?
WE WEREN'T PUTTING IT ALL OUT THERE FOR A TONYA HARDING, WERE WE?
I DON'T KNOW MAN--
WAIT, WHAT IS THIS?

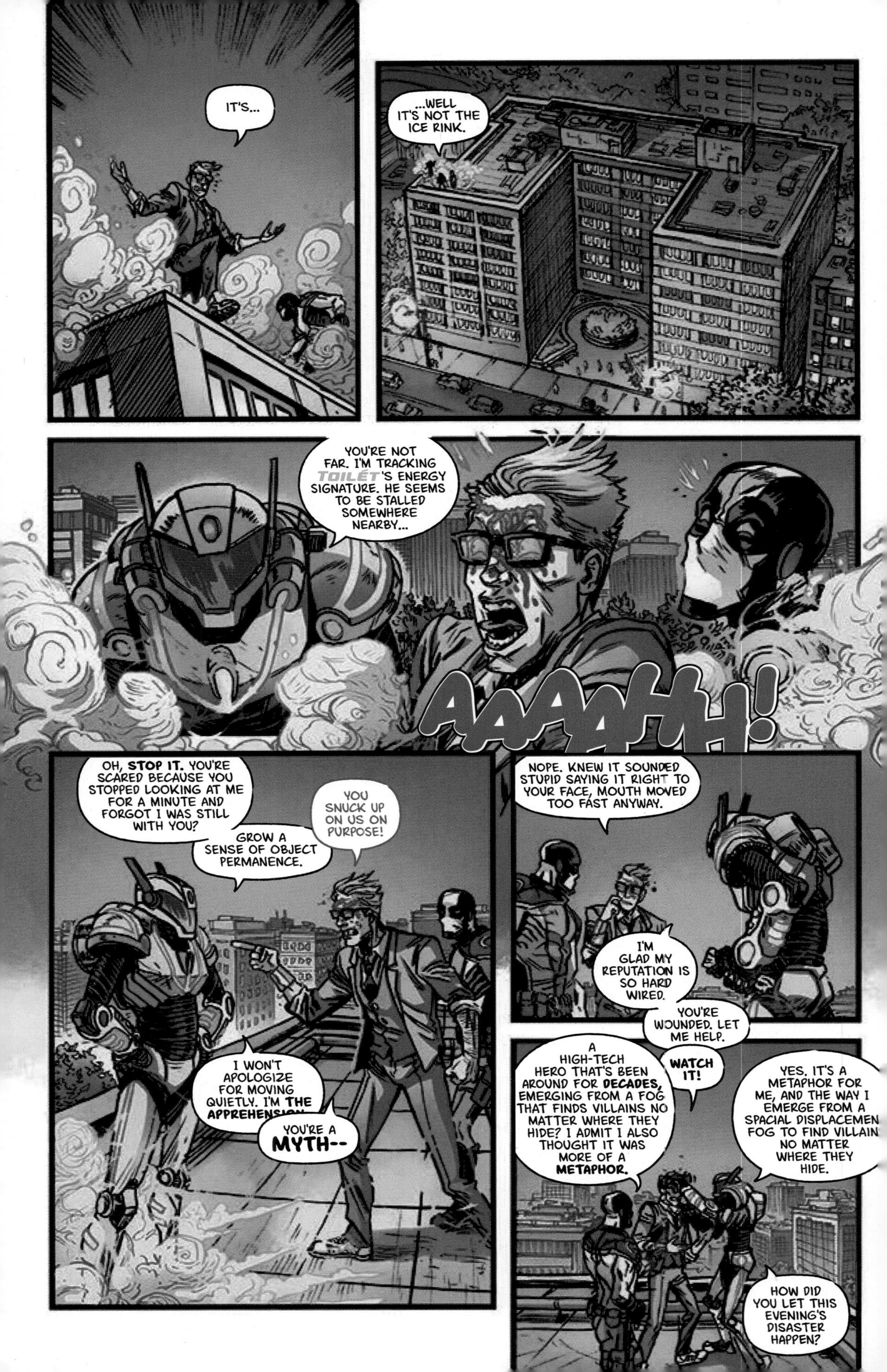
IT'S...
...WELL IT'S NOT THE ICE RINK.
YOU'RE NOT FAR. I'M TRACKING TOILÉT'S ENERGY SIGNATURE. HE SEEMS TO BE STALLED SOMEWHERE NEARBY...
AAAAHH!
OH, STOP IT. YOU'RE SCARED BECAUSE YOU STOPPED LOOKING AT ME FOR A MINUTE AND FORGOT I WAS STILL WITH YOU?
GROW A SENSE OF OBJECT PERMANENCE.
YOU SNUCK UP ON US ON PURPOSE!
I WON'T APOLOGIZE FOR MOVING QUIETLY. I'M THE APPREHENSION
YOU'RE A MYTH--
NOPE. KNEW IT SOUNDED STUPID SAYING IT RIGHT TO YOUR FACE, MOUTH MOVED TOO FAST ANYWAY.
I'M GLAD MY REPUTATION IS SO HARD WIRED.
YOU'RE WOUNDED. LET ME HELP.
WATCH IT!
A HIGH-TECH HERO THAT'S BEEN AROUND FOR DECADES, EMERGING FROM A FOG THAT FINDS VILLAINS NO MATTER WHERE THEY HIDE? I ADMIT I ALSO THOUGHT IT WAS MORE OF A METAPHOR.
YES, IT'S A METAPHOR FOR ME, AND THE WAY I EMERGE FROM A SPACIAL DISPLACEMEN FOG TO FIND VILLAIN NO MATTER WHERE THEY HIDE.
HOW DID YOU LET THIS EVENING'S DISASTER HAPPEN?

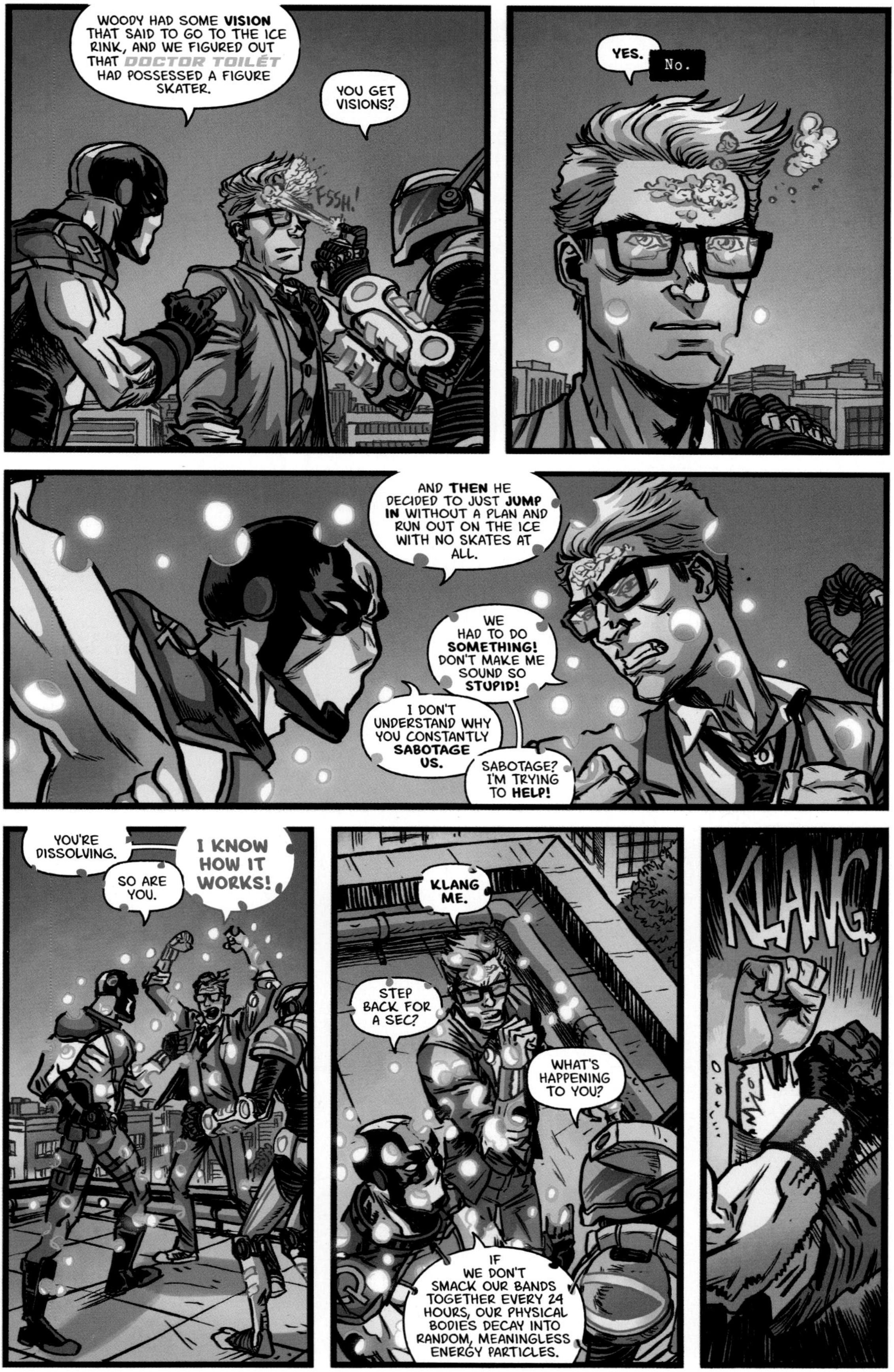
WOODY HAD SOME VISION THAT SAID TO GO TO THE ICE RINK, AND WE FIGURED OUT THAT DOCTOR TOILÉT HAD POSSESSED A FIGURE SKATER.
YOU GET VISIONS?
FSSH!
YES.
No.
AND THEN HE DECIDED TO JUST JUMP IN WITHOUT A PLAN AND RUN OUT ON THE ICE WITH NO SKATES AT ALL.
WE HAD TO DO SOMETHING! DON'T MAKE ME SOUND SO STUPID!
I DON'T UNDERSTAND WHY YOU CONSTANTLY SABOTAGE US.
SABOTAGE? I'M TRYING TO HELP!
YOU'RE DISSOLVING.
SO ARE YOU.
I KNOW HOW IT WORKS!
KLANG ME.
STEP BACK FOR A SEC?
WHAT'S HAPPENING TO YOU?
IF WE DON'T SMACK OUR BANDS TOGETHER EVERY 24 HOURS, OUR PHYSICAL BODIES DECAY INTO RANDOM, MEANINGLESS ENERGY PARTICLES.
KLANG!

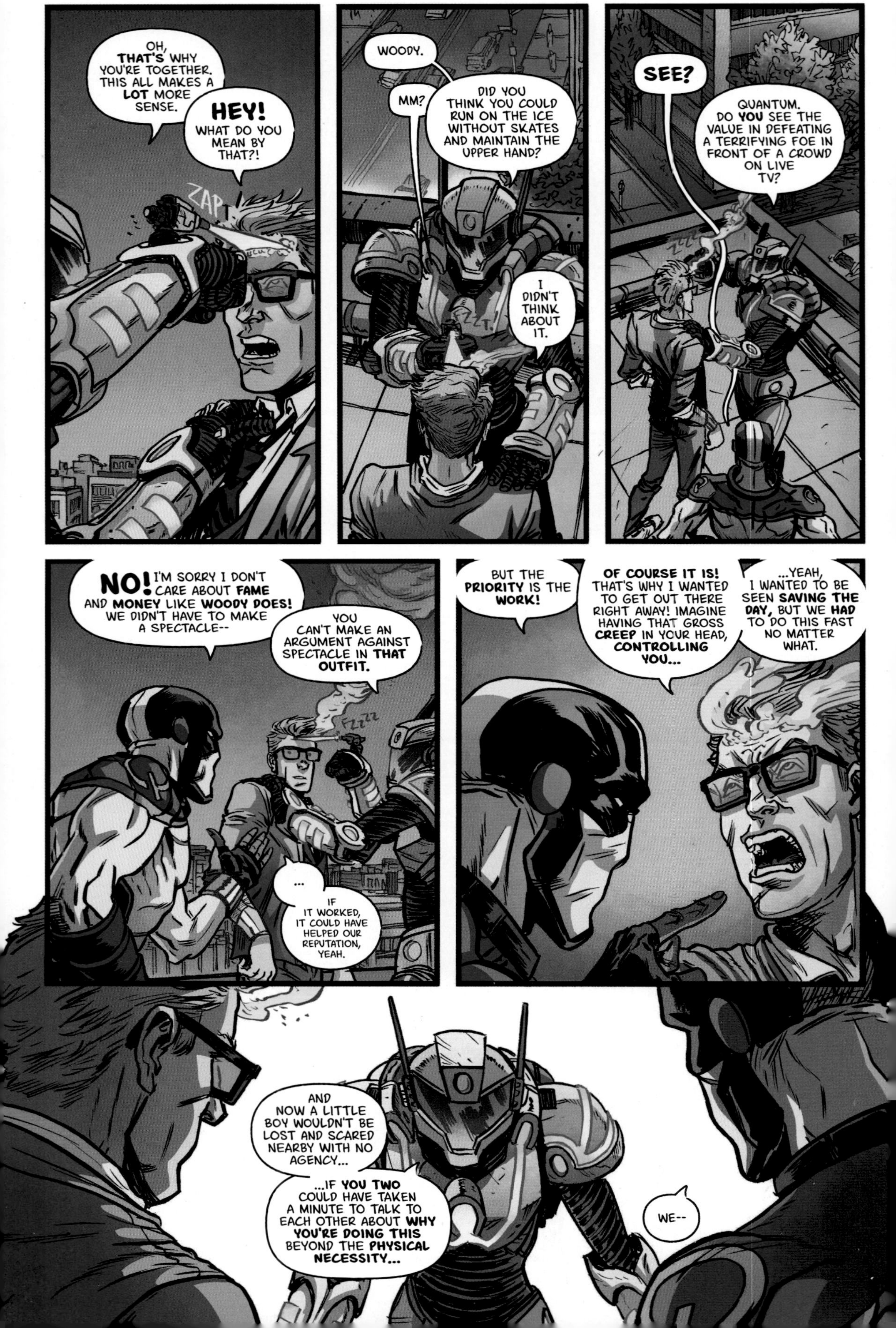
OH, THAT'S WHY YOU'RE TOGETHER. THIS ALL MAKES A LOT MORE SENSE.
HEY! WHAT DO YOU MEAN BY THAT?!
ZAP
WOODY.
MM?
DID YOU THINK YOU COULD RUN ON THE ICE WITHOUT SKATES AND MAINTAIN THE UPPER HAND?
I DIDN'T THINK ABOUT IT.
SEE?
QUANTUM. DO YOU SEE THE VALUE IN DEFEATING A TERRIFYING FOE IN FRONT OF A CROWD ON LIVE TV?
NO! I'M SORRY I DON'T CARE ABOUT FAME AND MONEY LIKE WOODY DOES! WE DIDN'T HAVE TO MAKE A SPECTACLE--
YOU CAN'T MAKE AN ARGUMENT AGAINST SPECTACLE IN THAT OUTFIT.
...
IF IT WORKED, IT COULD HAVE HELPED OUR REPUTATION, YEAH.
BUT THE PRIORITY IS THE WORK!
OF COURSE IT IS! THAT'S WHY I WANTED TO GET OUT THERE RIGHT AWAY! IMAGINE HAVING THAT GROSS CREEP IN YOUR HEAD, CONTROLLING YOU...
...YEAH, I WANTED TO BE SEEN SAVING THE DAY, BUT WE HAD TO DO THIS FAST NO MATTER WHAT.
AND NOW A LITTLE BOY WOULDN'T BE LOST AND SCARED NEARBY WITH NO AGENCY...
...IF YOU TWO COULD HAVE TAKEN A MINUTE TO TALK TO EACH OTHER ABOUT WHY YOU'RE DOING THIS BEYOND THE PHYSICAL NECESSITY...
WE--

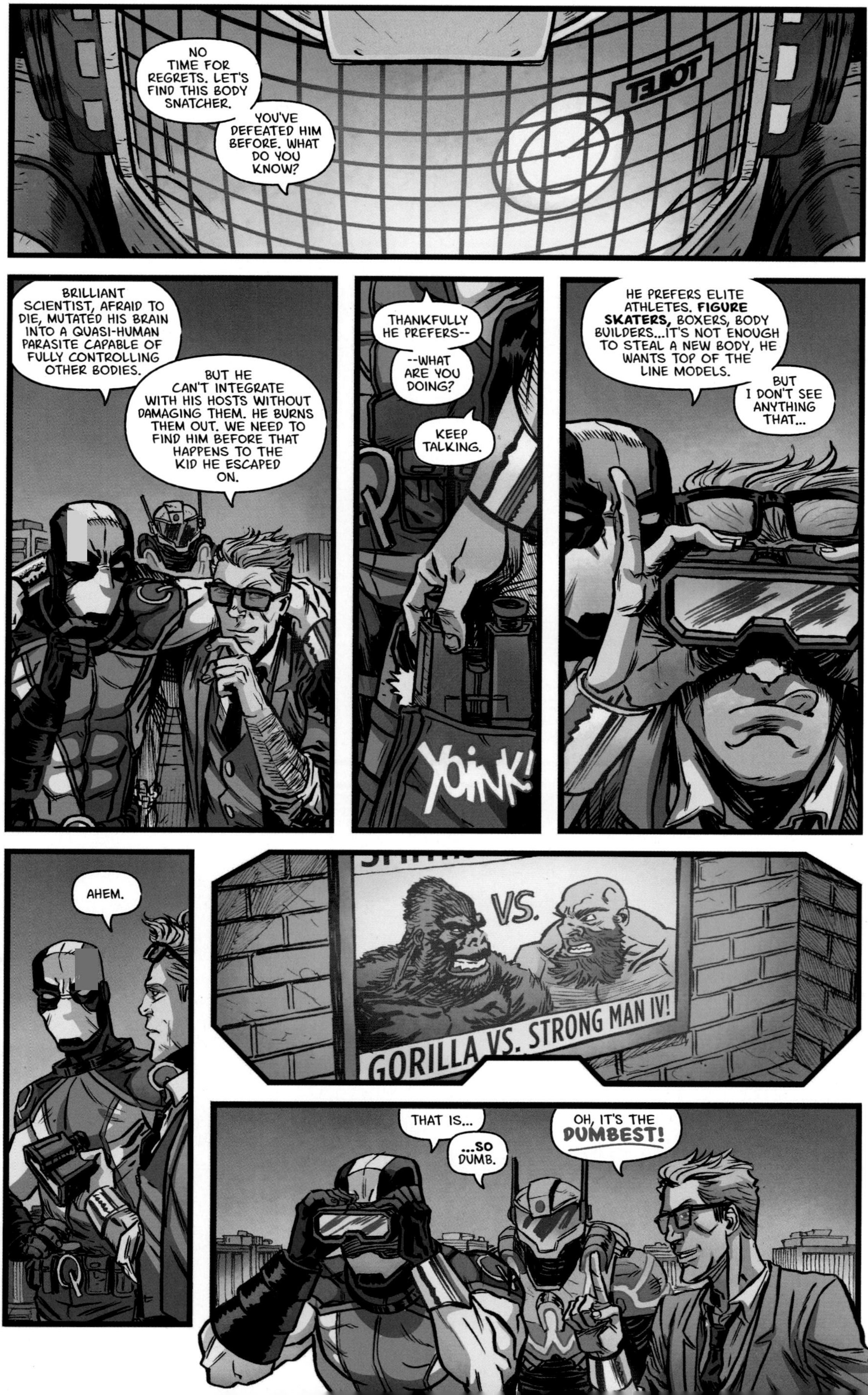
TOILET
NO TIME FOR REGRETS. LET'S FIND THIS BODY SNATCHER.
YOU'VE DEFEATED HIM BEFORE. WHAT DO YOU KNOW?
BRILLIANT SCIENTIST, AFRAID TO DIE, MUTATED HIS BRAIN INTO A QUASI-HUMAN PARASITE CAPABLE OF FULLY CONTROLLING OTHER BODIES.
BUT HE CAN'T INTEGRATE WITH HIS HOSTS WITHOUT DAMAGING THEM. HE BURNS THEM OUT. WE NEED TO FIND HIM BEFORE THAT HAPPENS TO THE KID HE ESCAPED ON.
THANKFULLY HE PREFERS--
--WHAT ARE YOU DOING?
KEEP TALKING.
YOINK!
HE PREFERS ELITE ATHLETES. **FIGURE SKATERS,** BOXERS, BODY BUILDERS...IT'S NOT ENOUGH TO STEAL A NEW BODY, HE WANTS TOP OF THE LINE MODELS.
BUT I DON'T SEE ANYTHING THAT...
AHEM.
VS.
GORILLA VS. STRONG MAN IV!
THAT IS...
...SO DUMB.
OH, IT'S THE DUMBEST!

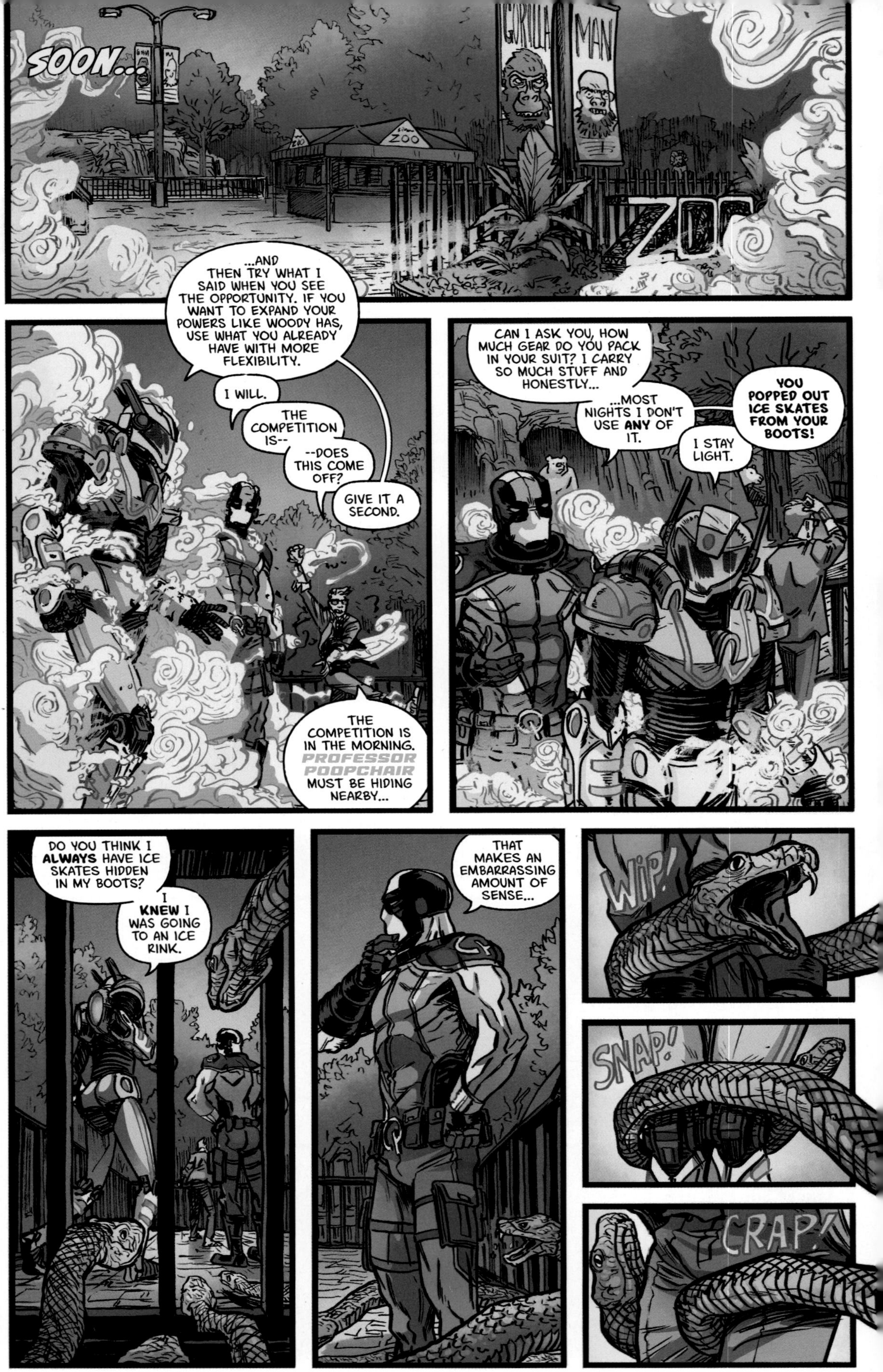
SOON...
GORILLA
MAN
ZOO
ZOO
ZOO
...AND THEN TRY WHAT I SAID WHEN YOU SEE THE OPPORTUNITY. IF YOU WANT TO EXPAND YOUR POWERS LIKE WOODY HAS, USE WHAT YOU ALREADY HAVE WITH MORE FLEXIBILITY.
I WILL.
THE COMPETITION IS--
--DOES THIS COME OFF?
GIVE IT A SECOND.
THE COMPETITION IS IN THE MORNING. PROFESSOR POOPCHAIR MUST BE HIDING NEARBY...
CAN I ASK YOU, HOW MUCH GEAR DO YOU PACK IN YOUR SUIT? I CARRY SO MUCH STUFF AND HONESTLY...
...MOST NIGHTS I DON'T USE ANY OF IT.
I STAY LIGHT.
YOU POPPED OUT ICE SKATES FROM YOUR BOOTS!
DO YOU THINK I ALWAYS HAVE ICE SKATES HIDDEN IN MY BOOTS?
I KNEW I WAS GOING TO AN ICE RINK.
THAT MAKES AN EMBARRASSING AMOUNT OF SENSE...
WIP!
SNAP!
CRAP!

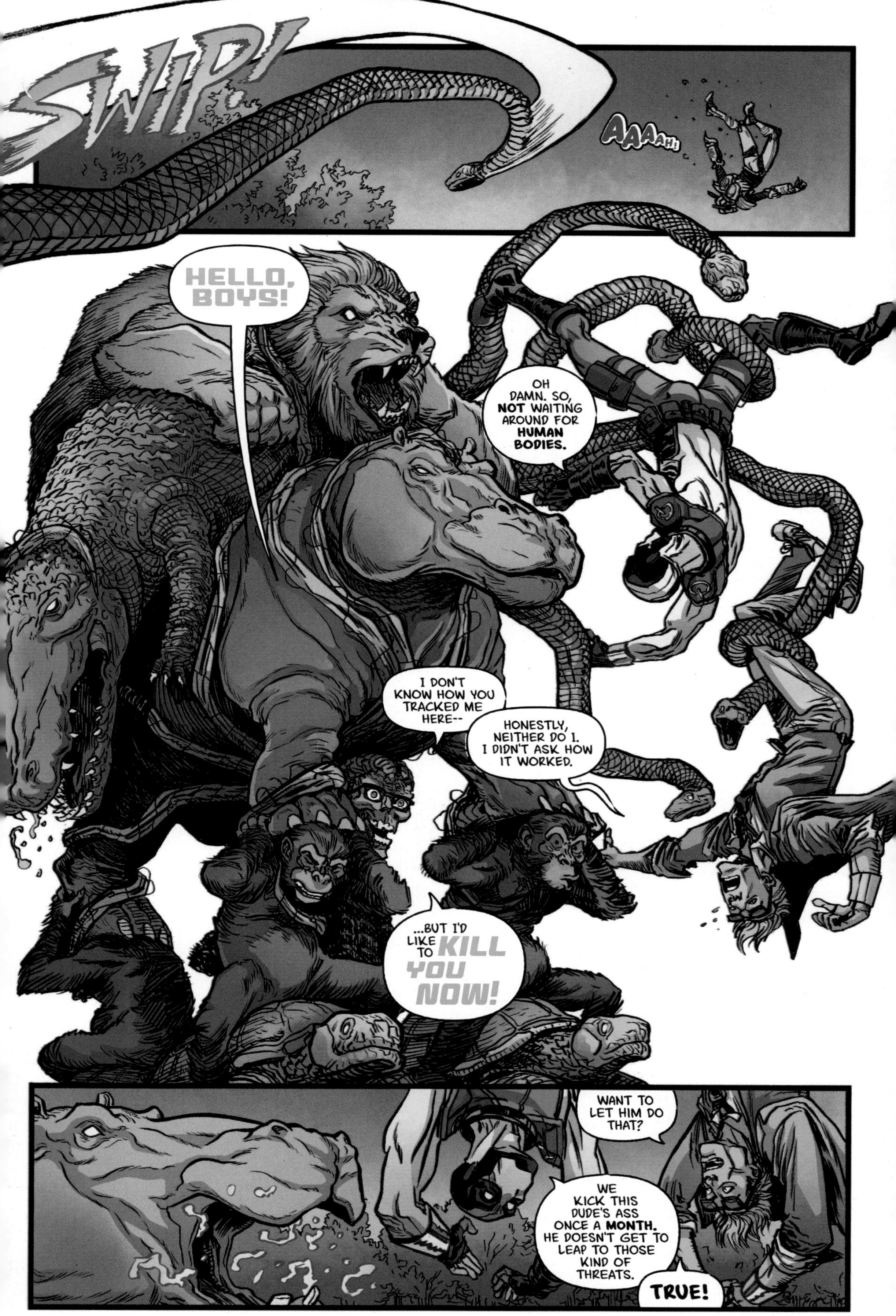
SWIP!
AAAAAH!
HELLO, BOYS!
OH DAMN. SO, NOT WAITING AROUND FOR HUMAN BODIES.
I DON'T KNOW HOW YOU TRACKED ME HERE--
HONESTLY, NEITHER DO I. I DIDN'T ASK HOW IT WORKED.
...BUT I'D LIKE TO KILL YOU NOW!
WANT TO LET HIM DO THAT?
WE KICK THIS DUDE'S ASS ONCE A MONTH. HE DOESN'T GET TO LEAP TO THOSE KIND OF THREATS.
TRUE!

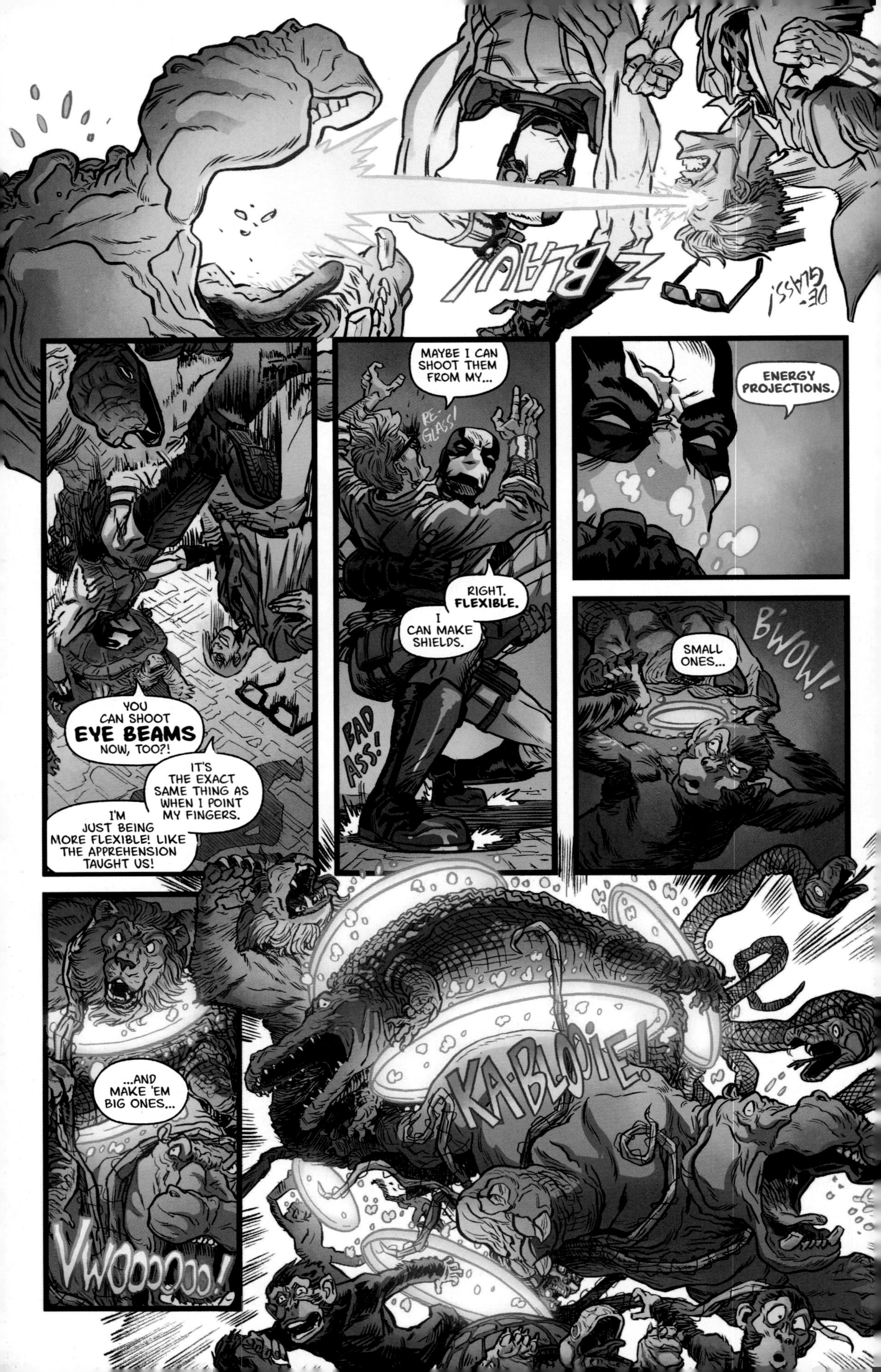
ZBLAV!
DE-GLASS!
YOU CAN SHOOT EYE BEAMS NOW, TOO?!
IT'S THE EXACT SAME THING AS WHEN I POINT MY FINGERS.
I'M JUST BEING MORE FLEXIBLE! LIKE THE APPREHENSION TAUGHT US!
MAYBE I CAN SHOOT THEM FROM MY...
RE-GLASS!
RIGHT. FLEXIBLE.
I CAN MAKE SHIELDS.
BAD ASS!
ENERGY PROJECTIONS.
SMALL ONES...
BWOW!
...AND MAKE 'EM BIG ONES...
VWOOOOOOO!
KA-BLOOIE!

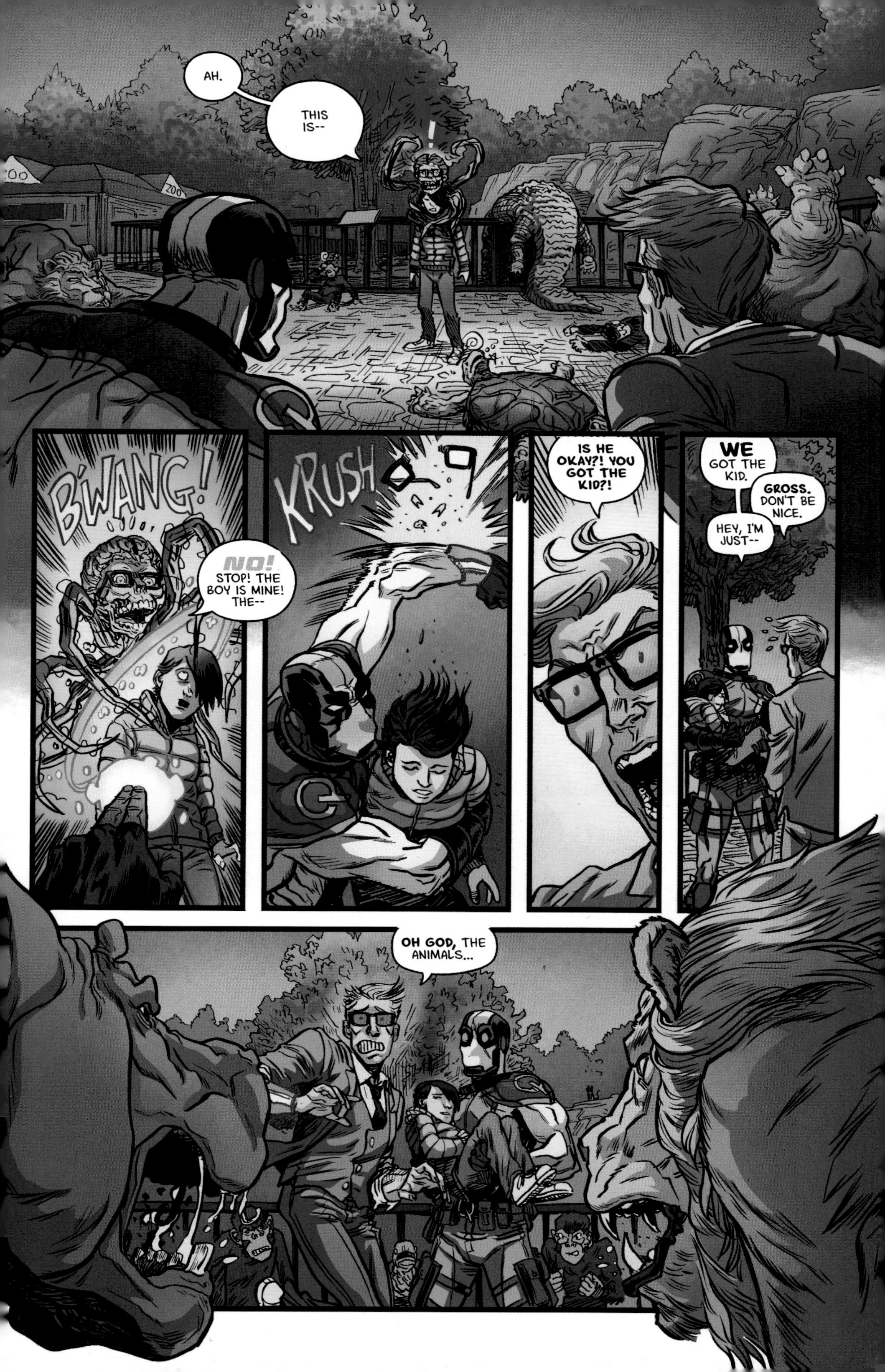
AH.
THIS IS--
ZOO
ZOO
B'WANG!
NO! STOP! THE BOY IS MINE! THE--
KRUSH
IS HE OKAY?! YOU GOT THE KID?!
WE GOT THE KID.
HEY, I'M JUST--
GROSS. DON'T BE NICE.
OH GOD, THE ANIMALS...

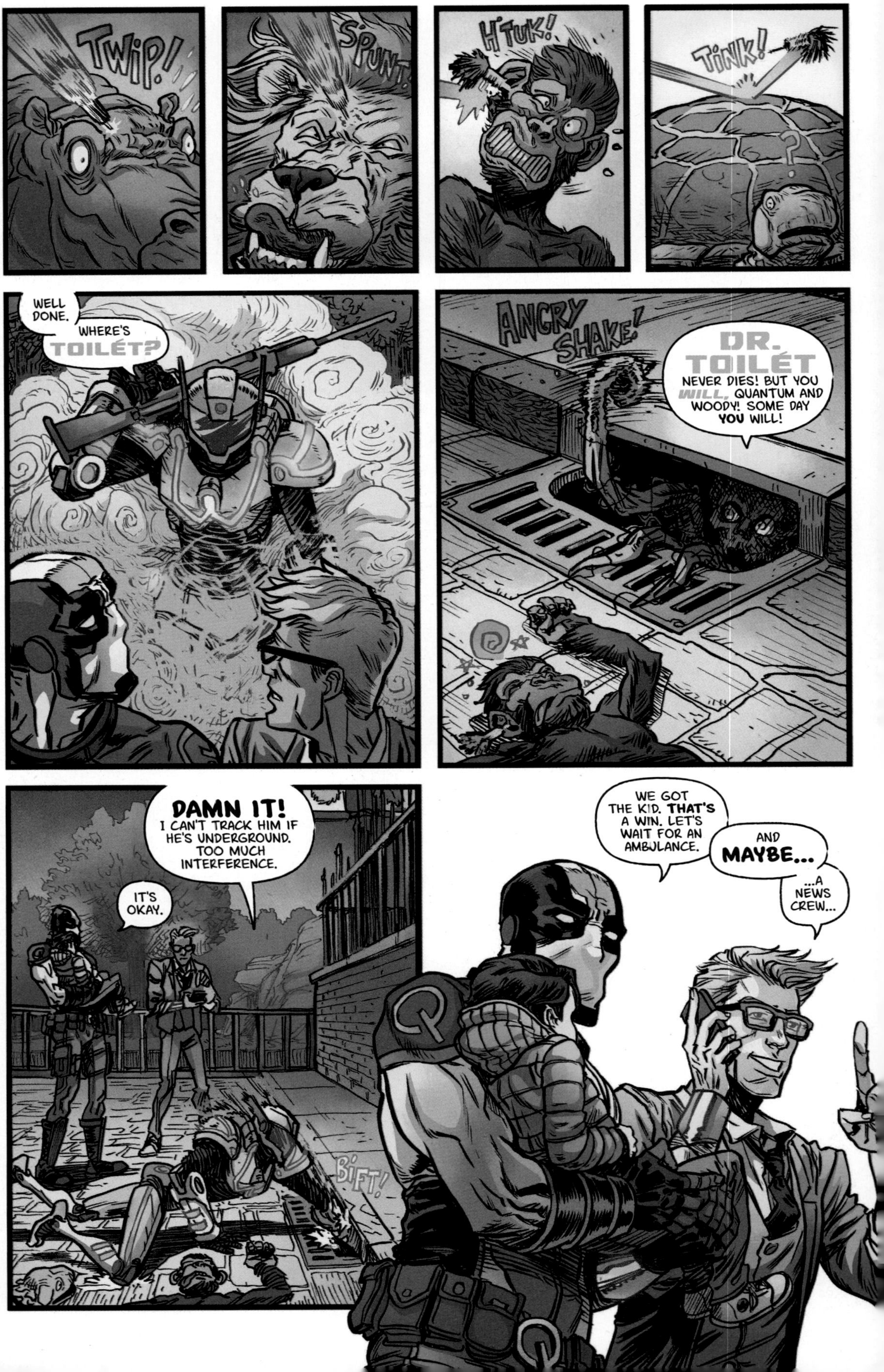
TWIP!
SPUNT!
H'TUK!
TINK!
?
WELL DONE.
WHERE'S TOILÉT?
ANGRY SHAKE!
DR. TOILÉT NEVER DIES! BUT YOU WILL, QUANTUM AND WOODY! SOME DAY YOU WILL!
DAMN IT! I CAN'T TRACK HIM IF HE'S UNDERGROUND. TOO MUCH INTERFERENCE.
IT'S OKAY.
BIFT!
WE GOT THE KID. THAT'S A WIN. LET'S WAIT FOR AN AMBULANCE.
AND MAYBE...
...A NEWS CREW...

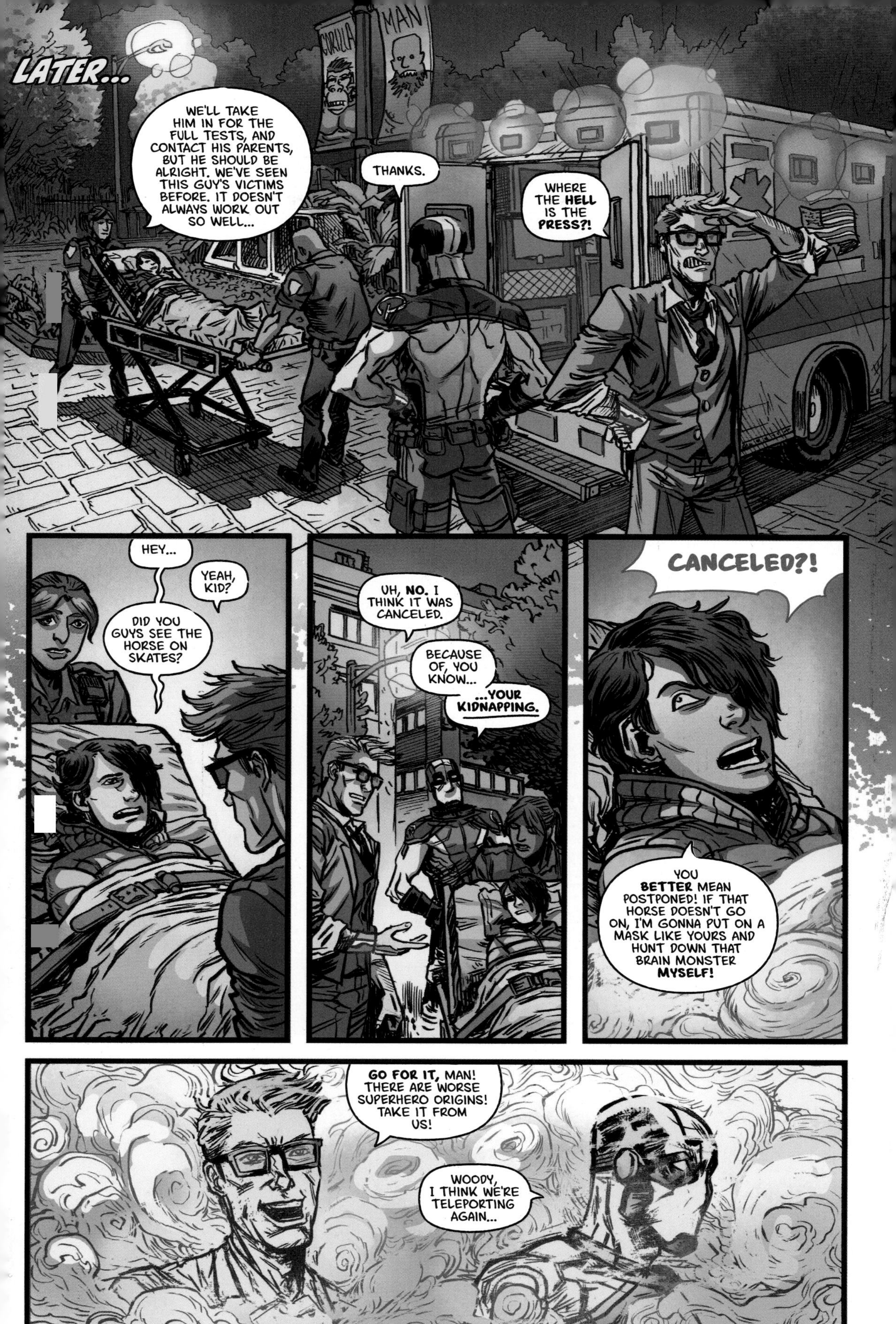
LATER...
GORILLA
MAN
WE'LL TAKE HIM IN FOR THE FULL TESTS, AND CONTACT HIS PARENTS, BUT HE SHOULD BE ALRIGHT. WE'VE SEEN THIS GUY'S VICTIMS BEFORE. IT DOESN'T ALWAYS WORK OUT SO WELL...
THANKS.
WHERE THE HELL IS THE PRESS?!
HEY...
YEAH, KID?
DID YOU GUYS SEE THE HORSE ON SKATES?
UH, NO. I THINK IT WAS CANCELED.
BECAUSE OF, YOU KNOW...
...YOUR KIDNAPPING.
CANCELED?!
YOU BETTER MEAN POSTPONED! IF THAT HORSE DOESN'T GO ON, I'M GONNA PUT ON A MASK LIKE YOURS AND HUNT DOWN THAT BRAIN MONSTER MYSELF!
GO FOR IT, MAN! THERE ARE WORSE SUPERHERO ORIGINS! TAKE IT FROM US!
WOODY, I THINK WE'RE TELEPORTING AGAIN...

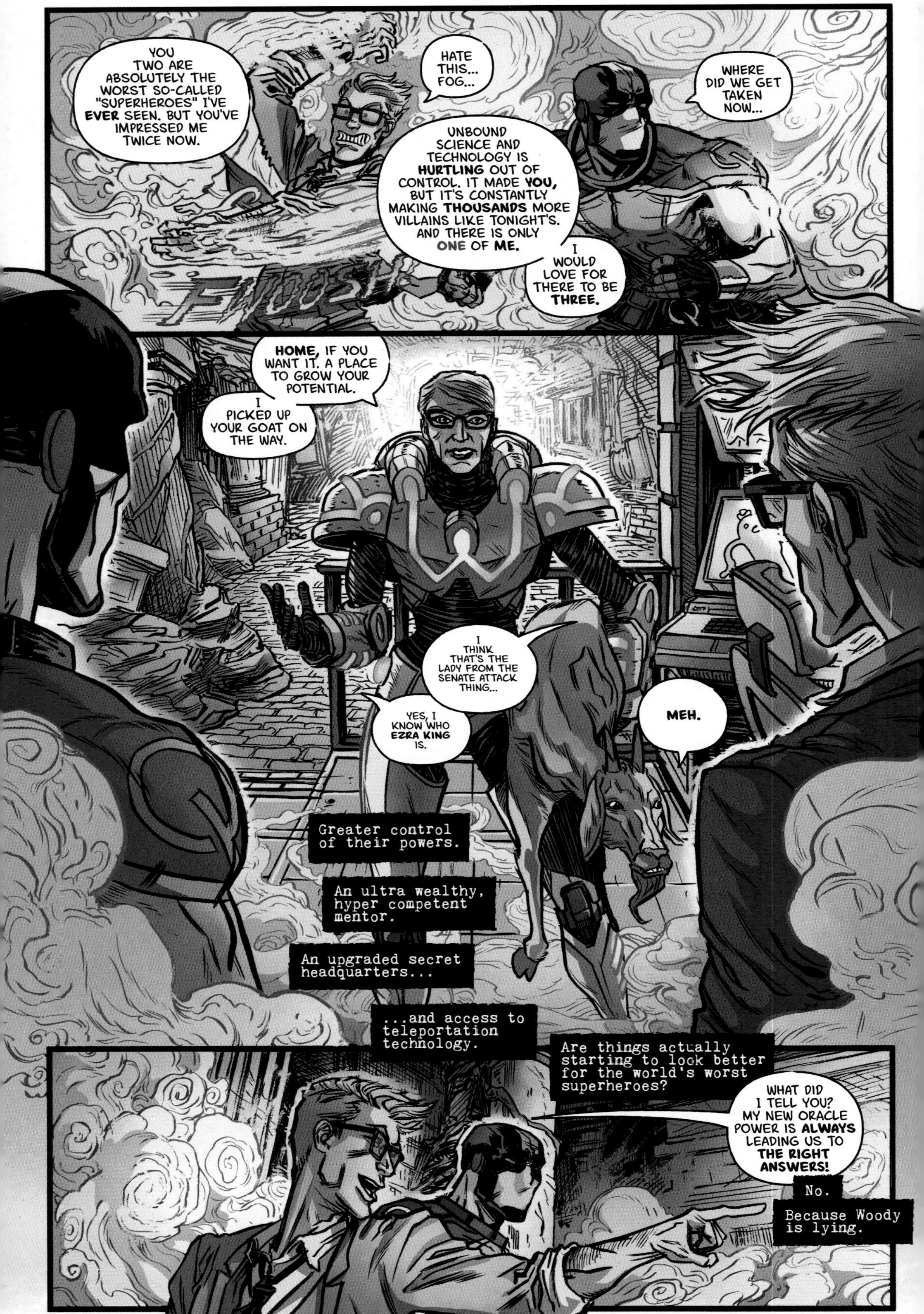

YOU TWO ARE ABSOLUTELY THE WORST SO-CALLED "SUPERHEROES" I'VE EVER SEEN. BUT YOU'VE IMPRESSED ME TWICE NOW.
HATE THIS... FOG...
WHERE DID WE GET TAKEN NOW...
UNBOUND SCIENCE AND TECHNOLOGY IS HURTLING OUT OF CONTROL. IT MADE YOU, BUT IT'S CONSTANTLY MAKING THOUSANDS MORE VILLAINS LIKE TONIGHT'S. AND THERE IS ONLY ONE OF ME.
I WOULD LOVE FOR THERE TO BE THREE.
FWOOSH
HOME, IF YOU WANT IT. A PLACE TO GROW YOUR POTENTIAL.
I PICKED UP YOUR GOAT ON THE WAY.
I THINK THAT'S THE LADY FROM THE SENATE ATTACK THING...
YES, I KNOW WHO EZRA KING IS.
MEH.
Greater control of their powers.
An ultra wealthy, hyper competent mentor.
An upgraded secret headquarters...
...and access to teleportation technology.
Are things actually starting to look better for the world's worst superheroes?
WHAT DID I TELL YOU? MY NEW ORACLE POWER IS ALWAYS LEADING US TO THE RIGHT ANSWERS!
No.
Because Woody is lying.

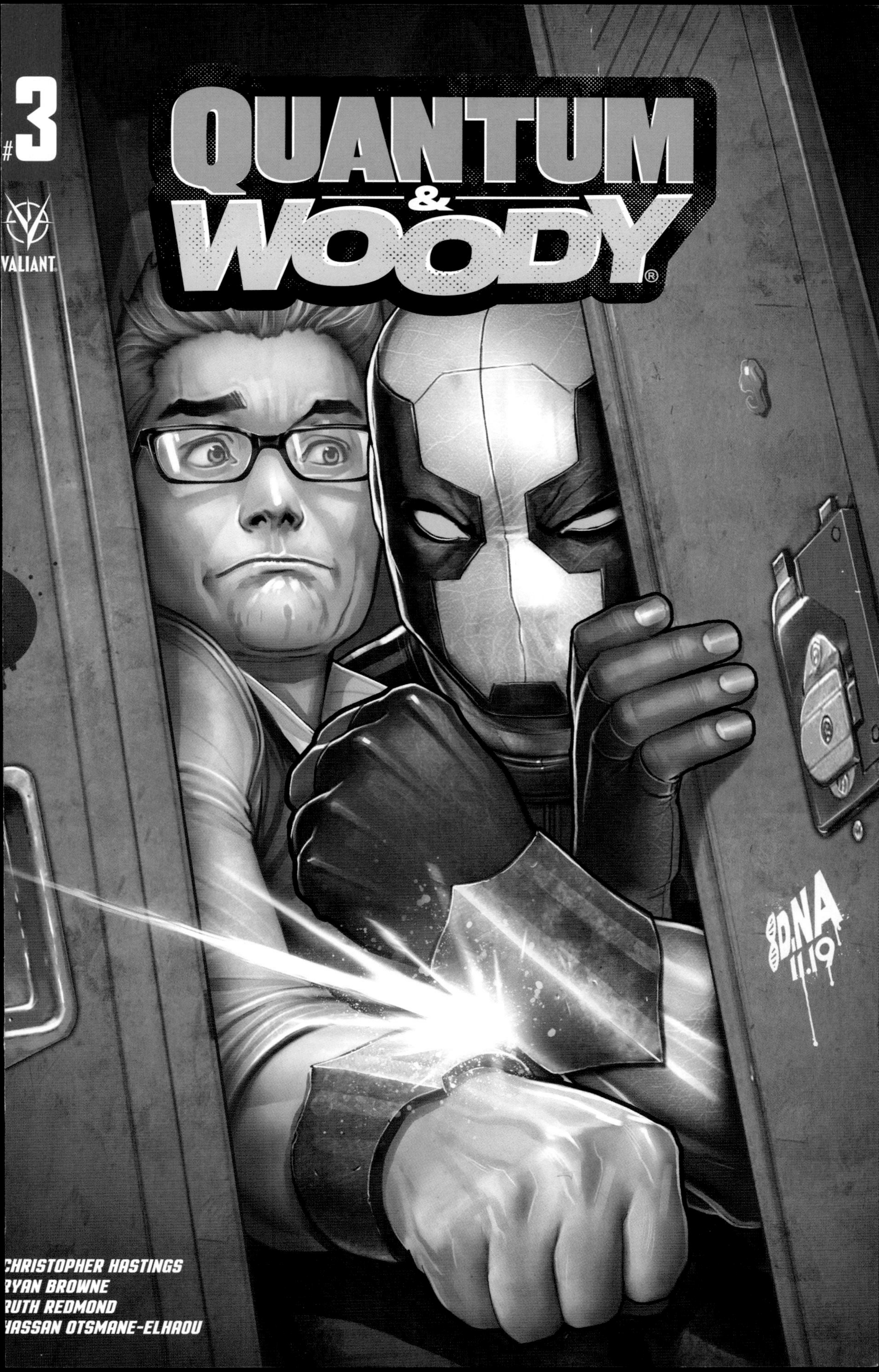
#3
QUANTUM & WOODY®
VALIANT
D.NA 11.19
CHRISTOPHER HASTINGS
RYAN BROWNE
RUTH REDMOND
HASSAN OTSMANE-ELHAOU

VOICE IT

Search

White_Chocolate
145k Cheers

v/DListDisasters Posted by OhThatTyler 6 hours ago

51.8k

SPOTTED: Quantum & Woody with THE APPREHENSION???

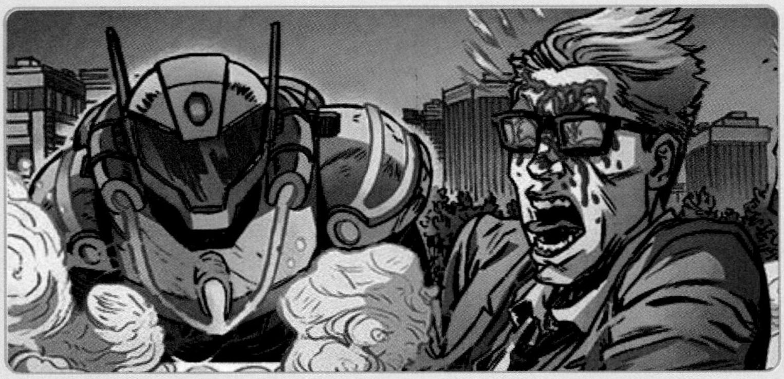

237 Comments Share Hide

"Say Something!"

B U I

VOICE IT

OhThatTyler - 47.2k cheers - 6 hours ago
The Apprehension iz real!!! I knew it!!!!
Reply Report

JayRobArt - 45.3k cheers - 6 hours ago
The Apprehension is a myth.
Reply Report

OhThatTyler - 40k cheers - 5 hours ago
Naw, man. This pic confirms it. Now the only question iz who it could b...my guess iz Ezra King. Shez the only 1 w/ the resources and tech to pull it off!!!
Reply Report

JayRobArt - 37.6k cheers - 5 hours ago
Right. The CEO of a major tech company moonlights as a costumed crimefighter. You're batty.
Reply Report

White_Chocolate - 32.4k cheers - 5 hours ago
THAT'S WHAT I THOUGHT!!!!
Reply Report

BlackMamba - 31.7k cheers - 4 hours ago
Nope. Definitely a myth.
Reply Report

White_Chocolate - 30.1k cheers - 4 hours ago
what are you talking about, dood? we're in her hideout right now. i can see u.
Reply Report

Black Mamba - 29.1k cheers - 4 hours ago
IF* The Apprehension were real, then her hideout would be a *SECRET
Reply Report

White_Chocolate - 27.2k cheers - 4 hours ago
oh i get it! ya, the Apprehension definitely isn't our superhero mom now
Reply Report

Black Mamba - 24.5k cheers - 4 hours ago
Reply Report

JayRobArt - 22.1k cheers - 5 hours ago
#WorldsWorstSuperheroTeam
Reply Report

v/DListDisasters

761 ONLINE | 188K MEMBERS

The "Who's Who" of internet fame -- A place to follow celebrities even TNZ thinks aren't worth their time! Find your cult following here!

SUBSCRIBE

CREDITS

Writer...**Christopher Hastings**
Artist...**Ryan Browne**
Colorist...**Ruth Redmond**
Letterer...**Hassan Otsmane-Elhaou**
Cover Artist...**David Nakayama**
Assistant Editor...**Drew Baumgartner**
Senior Editor...**Heather Antos**

TRENDING COMMUNITIES

v/ValiantComicFans 167k members JOIN
v/legionofthunder 33k members JOIN
v/MythosOrMadScience 22k members JOIN
v/deadsidedeadbeats 4k members JOIN

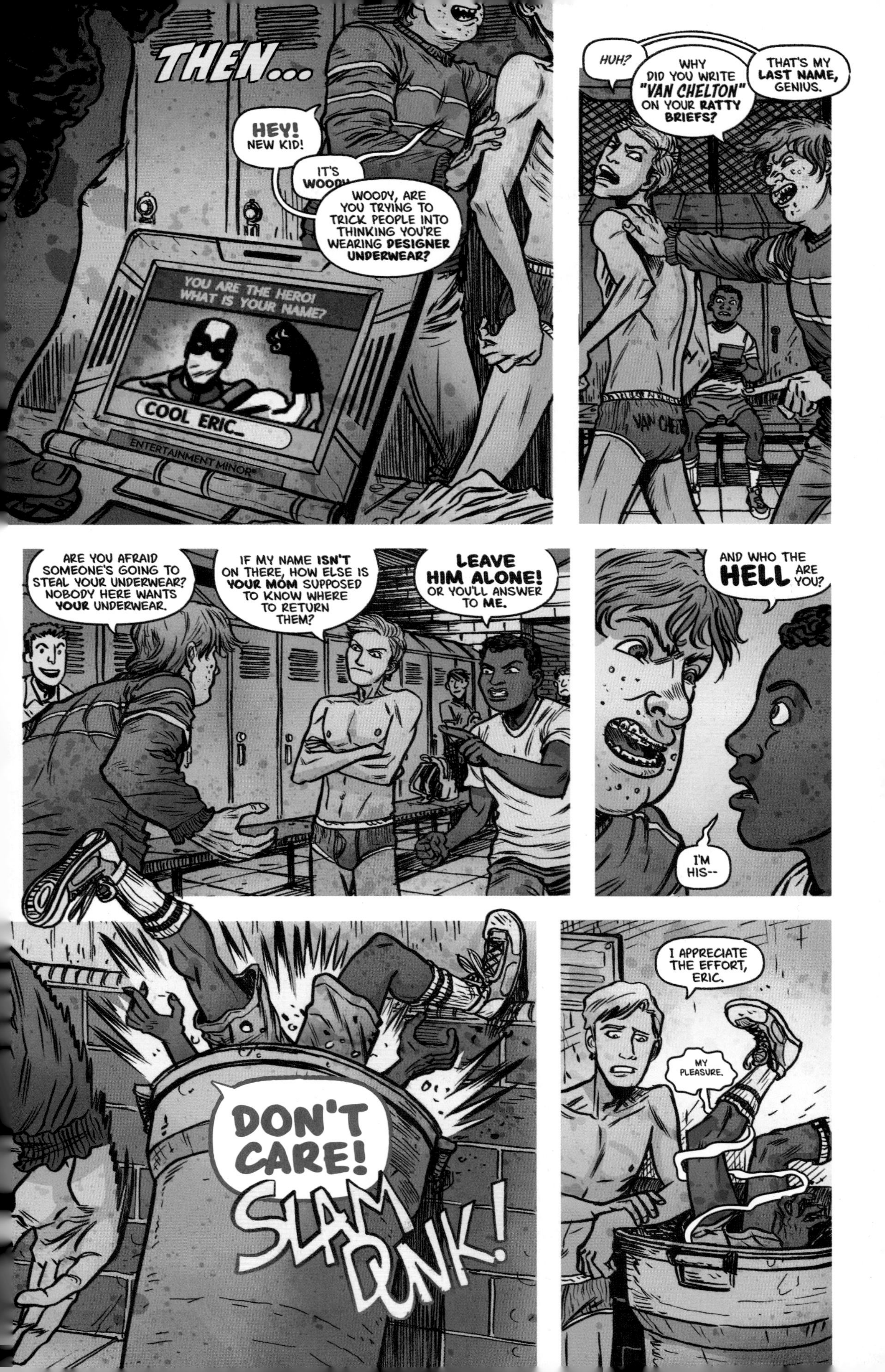
THEN...
HEY! NEW KID!
IT'S WOOD-
WOODY, ARE YOU TRYING TO TRICK PEOPLE INTO THINKING YOU'RE WEARING DESIGNER UNDERWEAR?
YOU ARE THE HERO! WHAT IS YOUR NAME?
COOL ERIC_
ENTERTAINMENT MINOR
HUH?
WHY DID YOU WRITE "VAN CHELTON" ON YOUR RATTY BRIEFS?
THAT'S MY LAST NAME, GENIUS.
ARE YOU AFRAID SOMEONE'S GOING TO STEAL YOUR UNDERWEAR? NOBODY HERE WANTS YOUR UNDERWEAR.
IF MY NAME ISN'T ON THERE, HOW ELSE IS YOUR MOM SUPPOSED TO KNOW WHERE TO RETURN THEM?
LEAVE HIM ALONE! OR YOU'LL ANSWER TO ME.
AND WHO THE HELL ARE YOU?
I'M HIS--
DON'T CARE!
SLAM DUNK!
I APPRECIATE THE EFFORT, ERIC.
MY PLEASURE.

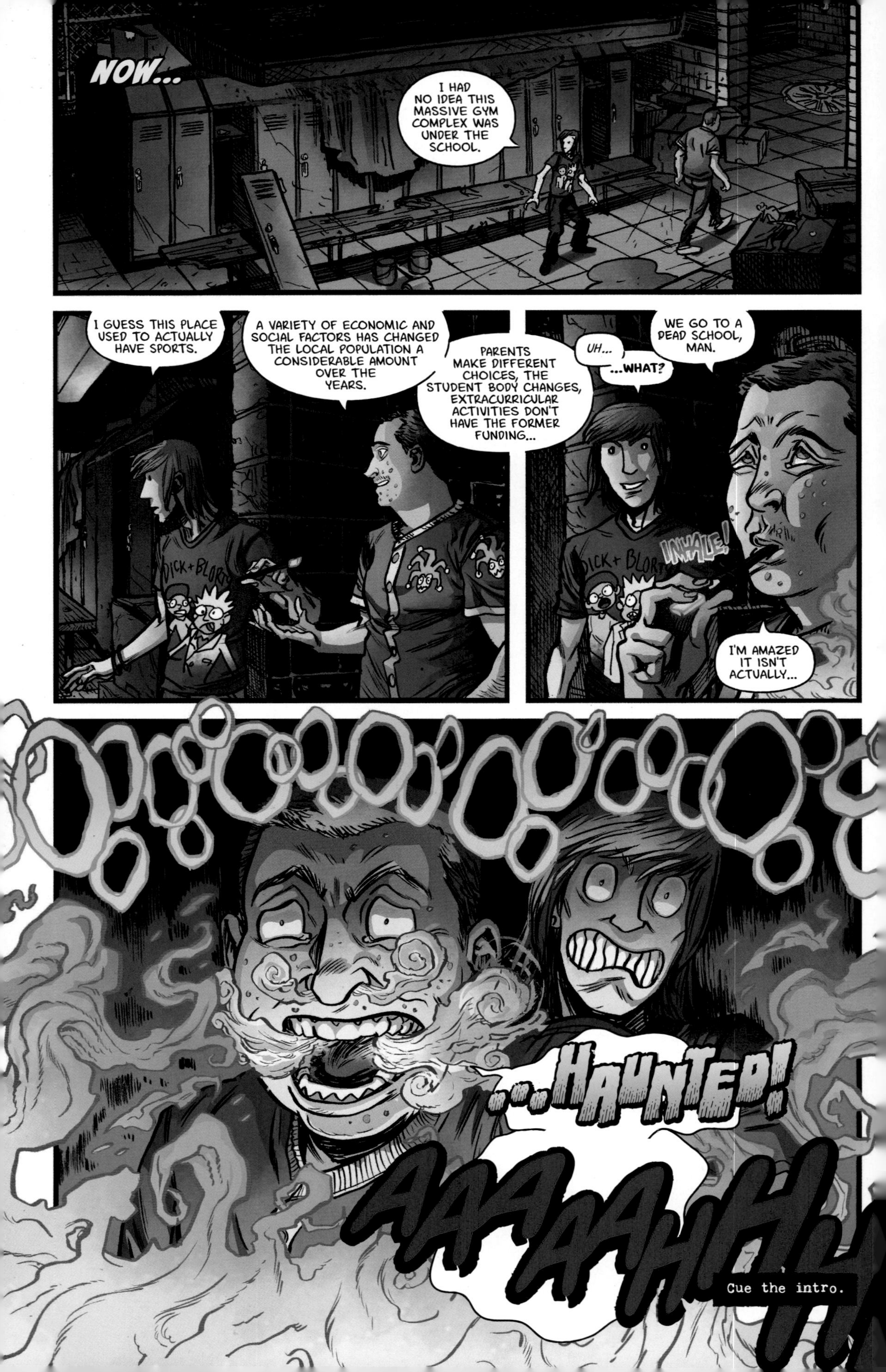
NOW...
I HAD NO IDEA THIS MASSIVE GYM COMPLEX WAS UNDER THE SCHOOL.
I GUESS THIS PLACE USED TO ACTUALLY HAVE SPORTS.
A VARIETY OF ECONOMIC AND SOCIAL FACTORS HAS CHANGED THE LOCAL POPULATION A CONSIDERABLE AMOUNT OVER THE YEARS.
PARENTS MAKE DIFFERENT CHOICES, THE STUDENT BODY CHANGES, EXTRACURRICULAR ACTIVITIES DON'T HAVE THE FORMER FUNDING...
DICK + BLORT
UH...
...WHAT?
WE GO TO A DEAD SCHOOL, MAN.
INHALE!
I'M AMAZED IT ISN'T ACTUALLY...
...HAUNTED!
AAAAAHHH
Cue the intro.

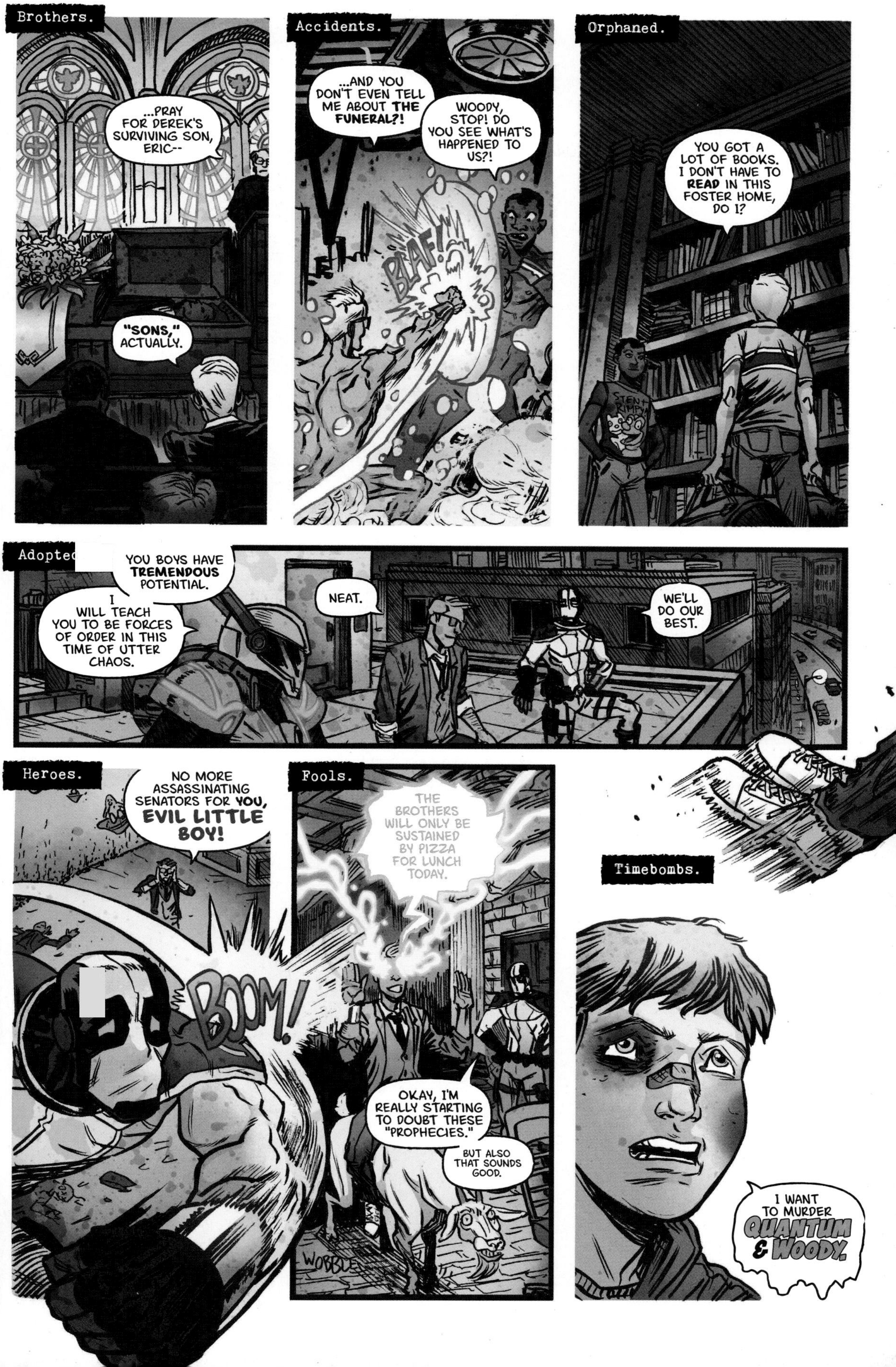
Brothers.
...PRAY FOR DEREK'S SURVIVING SON, ERIC--
"SONS," ACTUALLY.
Accidents.
...AND YOU DON'T EVEN TELL ME ABOUT THE FUNERAL?!
WOODY, STOP! DO YOU SEE WHAT'S HAPPENED TO US?!
BLAF!
Orphaned.
YOU GOT A LOT OF BOOKS. I DON'T HAVE TO READ IN THIS FOSTER HOME, DO I?
Adopte
YOU BOYS HAVE TREMENDOUS POTENTIAL.
I WILL TEACH YOU TO BE FORCES OF ORDER IN THIS TIME OF UTTER CHAOS.
NEAT.
WE'LL DO OUR BEST.
Heroes.
NO MORE ASSASSINATING SENATORS FOR YOU, EVIL LITTLE BOY!
BOOM!
Fools.
THE BROTHERS WILL ONLY BE SUSTAINED BY PIZZA FOR LUNCH TODAY.
OKAY, I'M REALLY STARTING TO DOUBT THESE "PROPHECIES."
BUT ALSO THAT SOUNDS GOOD.
WOBBLE
Timebombs.
I WANT TO MURDER QUANTUM & WOODY.

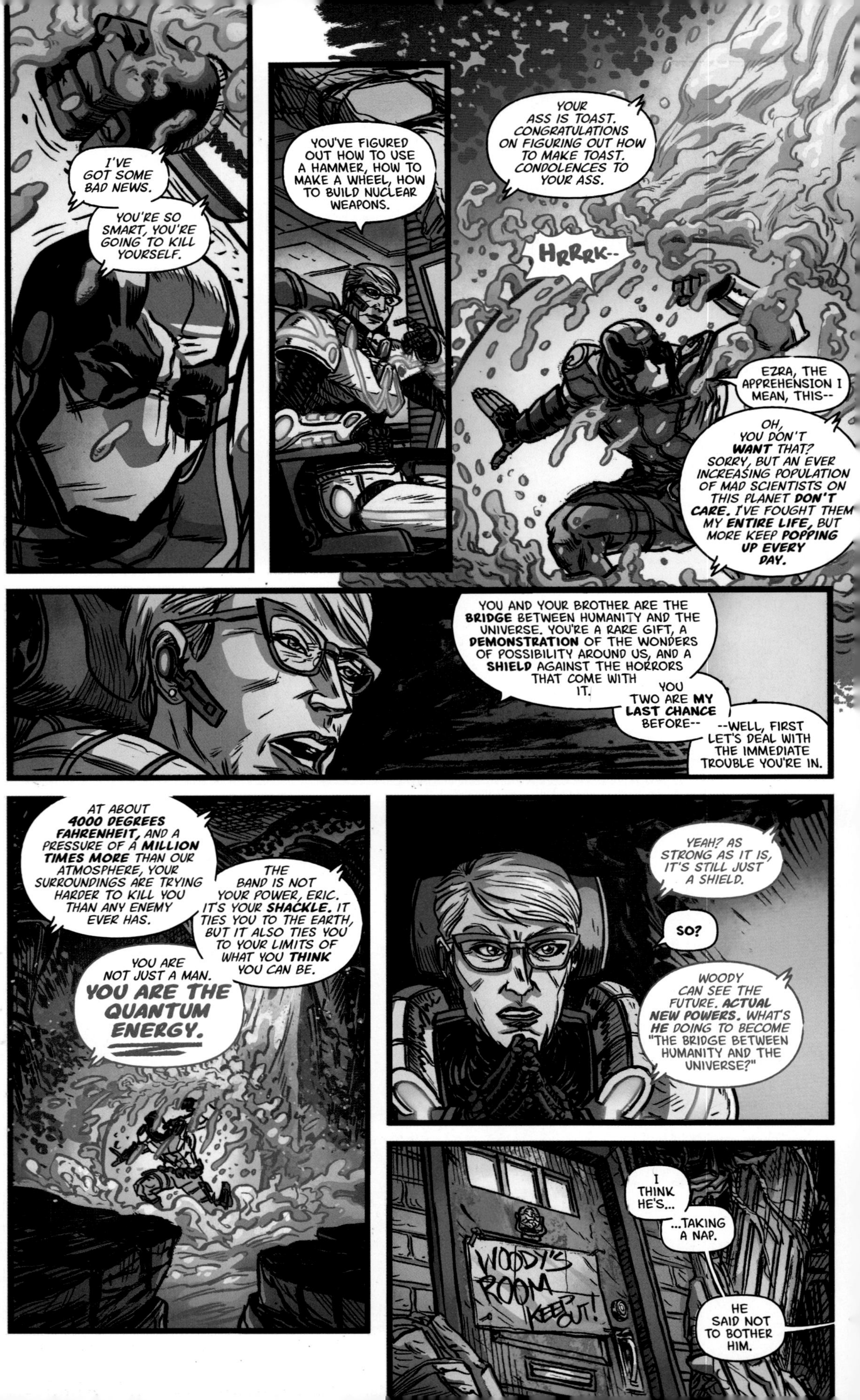

I'VE GOT SOME BAD NEWS.
YOU'RE SO SMART, YOU'RE GOING TO KILL YOURSELF.
YOU'VE FIGURED OUT HOW TO USE A HAMMER, HOW TO MAKE A WHEEL, HOW TO BUILD NUCLEAR WEAPONS.
YOUR ASS IS TOAST. CONGRATULATIONS ON FIGURING OUT HOW TO MAKE TOAST. CONDOLENCES TO YOUR ASS.
HRRRK--
EZRA, THE APPREHENSION I MEAN, THIS--
OH, YOU DON'T WANT THAT? SORRY, BUT AN EVER INCREASING POPULATION OF MAD SCIENTISTS ON THIS PLANET DON'T CARE. I'VE FOUGHT THEM MY ENTIRE LIFE, BUT MORE KEEP POPPING UP EVERY DAY.
YOU AND YOUR BROTHER ARE THE BRIDGE BETWEEN HUMANITY AND THE UNIVERSE. YOU'RE A RARE GIFT, A DEMONSTRATION OF THE WONDERS OF POSSIBILITY AROUND US, AND A SHIELD AGAINST THE HORRORS THAT COME WITH IT.
YOU TWO ARE MY LAST CHANCE BEFORE--
--WELL, FIRST LET'S DEAL WITH THE IMMEDIATE TROUBLE YOU'RE IN.
AT ABOUT 4000 DEGREES FAHRENHEIT, AND A PRESSURE OF A MILLION TIMES MORE THAN OUR ATMOSPHERE, YOUR SURROUNDINGS ARE TRYING HARDER TO KILL YOU THAN ANY ENEMY EVER HAS.
THE BAND IS NOT YOUR POWER, ERIC. IT'S YOUR SHACKLE. IT TIES YOU TO THE EARTH, BUT IT ALSO TIES YOU TO YOUR LIMITS OF WHAT YOU THINK YOU CAN BE.
YOU ARE NOT JUST A MAN. YOU ARE THE QUANTUM ENERGY.
YEAH? AS STRONG AS IT IS, IT'S STILL JUST A SHIELD.
SO?
WOODY CAN SEE THE FUTURE. ACTUAL NEW POWERS. WHAT'S HE DOING TO BECOME "THE BRIDGE BETWEEN HUMANITY AND THE UNIVERSE?"
I THINK HE'S...
...TAKING A NAP.
WOODY'S ROOM KEEP OUT!
HE SAID NOT TO BOTHER HIM.

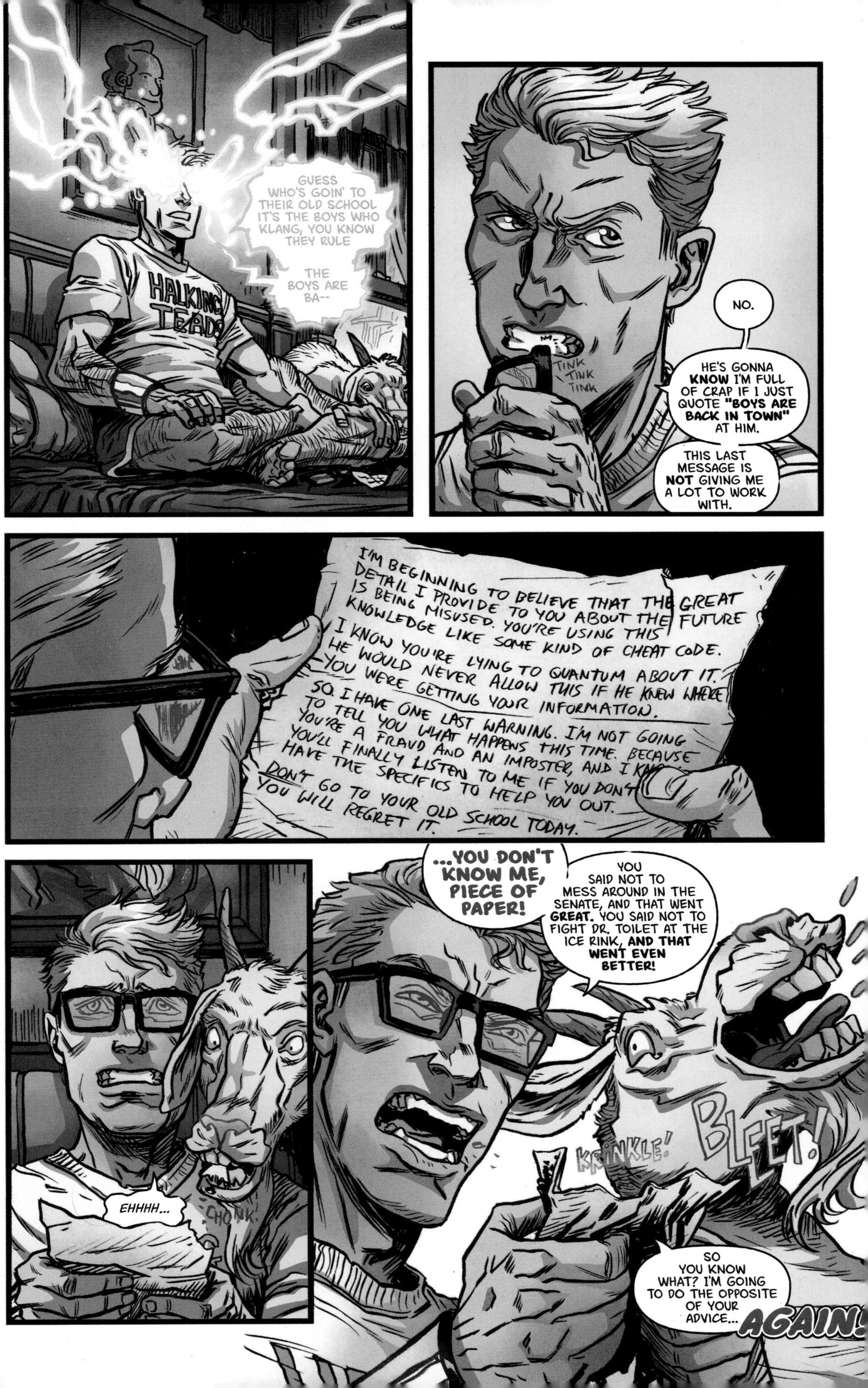
GUESS WHO'S GOIN' TO THEIR OLD SCHOOL IT'S THE BOYS WHO KLANG, YOU KNOW THEY RULE
THE BOYS ARE BA--
HALKING TEADS
NO.
TINK TINK TINK
HE'S GONNA KNOW I'M FULL OF CRAP IF I JUST QUOTE "BOYS ARE BACK IN TOWN" AT HIM.
THIS LAST MESSAGE IS NOT GIVING ME A LOT TO WORK WITH.
I'M BEGINNING TO BELIEVE THAT THE GREAT DETAIL I PROVIDE TO YOU ABOUT THE FUTURE IS BEING MISUSED. YOU'RE USING THIS KNOWLEDGE LIKE SOME KIND OF CHEAT CODE.
I KNOW YOU'RE LYING TO QUANTUM ABOUT IT. HE WOULD NEVER ALLOW THIS IF HE KNEW WHERE YOU WERE GETTING YOUR INFORMATION.
SO. I HAVE ONE LAST WARNING. I'M NOT GOING TO TELL YOU WHAT HAPPENS THIS TIME. BECAUSE YOU'RE A FRAUD AND AN IMPOSTER, AND I KNOW YOU'LL FINALLY LISTEN TO ME IF YOU DON'T HAVE THE SPECIFICS TO HELP YOU OUT.
DON'T GO TO YOUR OLD SCHOOL TODAY. YOU WILL REGRET IT.
EHHHH...
CHOMK
...YOU DON'T KNOW ME, PIECE OF PAPER!
YOU SAID NOT TO MESS AROUND IN THE SENATE, AND THAT WENT GREAT. YOU SAID NOT TO FIGHT DR. TOILET AT THE ICE RINK, AND THAT WENT EVEN BETTER!
KRINKLE!
BLEET!
SO YOU KNOW WHAT? I'M GOING TO DO THE OPPOSITE OF YOUR ADVICE... AGAIN!

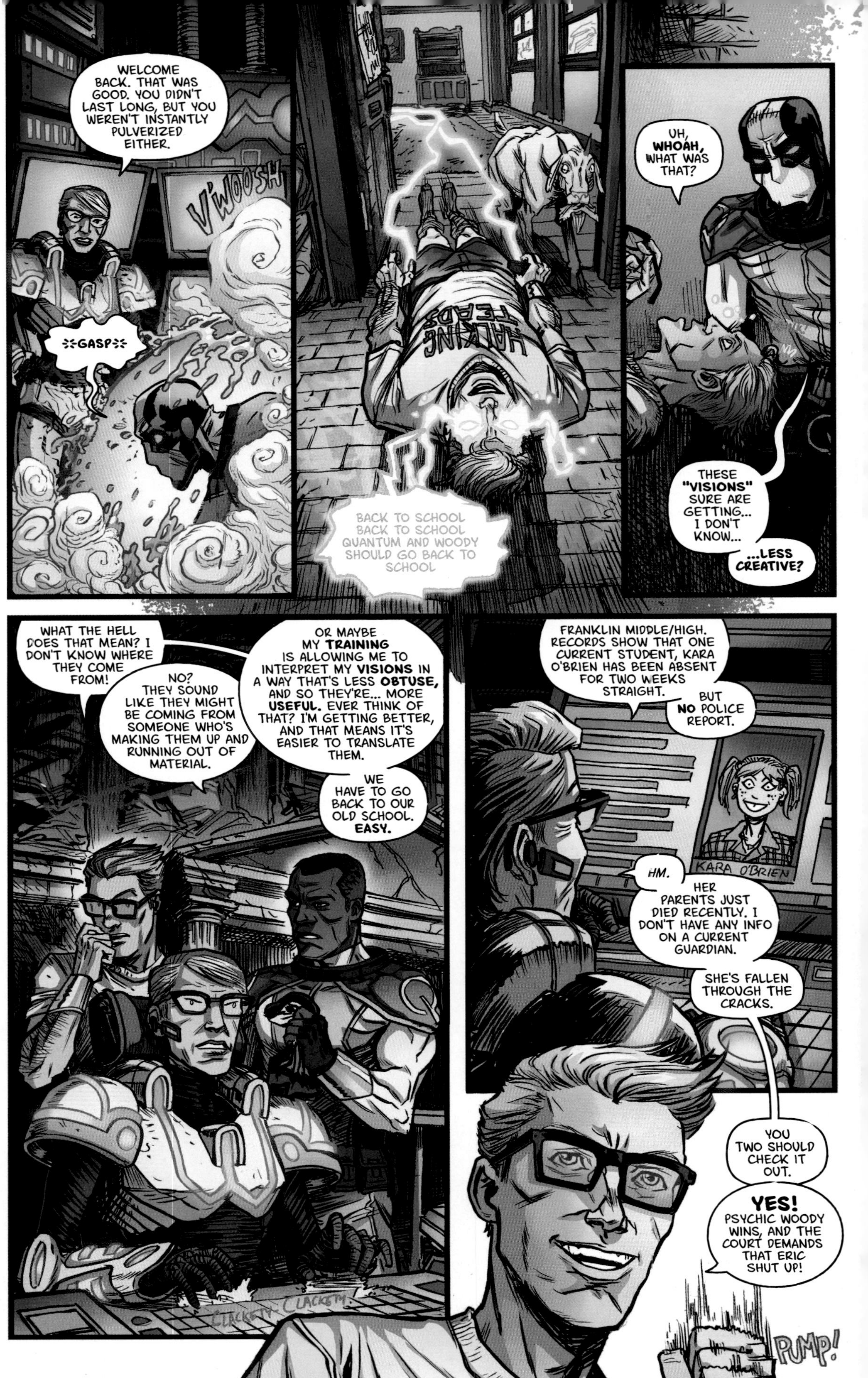
WELCOME BACK. THAT WAS GOOD. YOU DIDN'T LAST LONG, BUT YOU WEREN'T INSTANTLY PULVERIZED EITHER.
V'WOOSH
GASP
BACK TO SCHOOL BACK TO SCHOOL QUANTUM AND WOODY SHOULD GO BACK TO SCHOOL
UH, WHOAH, WHAT WAS THAT?
THESE "VISIONS" SURE ARE GETTING... I DON'T KNOW...
...LESS CREATIVE?
WHAT THE HELL DOES THAT MEAN? I DON'T KNOW WHERE THEY COME FROM!
NO? THEY SOUND LIKE THEY MIGHT BE COMING FROM SOMEONE WHO'S MAKING THEM UP AND RUNNING OUT OF MATERIAL.
OR MAYBE MY TRAINING IS ALLOWING ME TO INTERPRET MY VISIONS IN A WAY THAT'S LESS OBTUSE, AND SO THEY'RE... MORE USEFUL. EVER THINK OF THAT? I'M GETTING BETTER, AND THAT MEANS IT'S EASIER TO TRANSLATE THEM.
WE HAVE TO GO BACK TO OUR OLD SCHOOL. EASY.
CLACKETY-CLACKETY
FRANKLIN MIDDLE/HIGH. RECORDS SHOW THAT ONE CURRENT STUDENT, KARA O'BRIEN HAS BEEN ABSENT FOR TWO WEEKS STRAIGHT.
BUT NO POLICE REPORT.
KARA O'BRIEN
HM.
HER PARENTS JUST DIED RECENTLY. I DON'T HAVE ANY INFO ON A CURRENT GUARDIAN.
SHE'S FALLEN THROUGH THE CRACKS.
YOU TWO SHOULD CHECK IT OUT.
YES! PSYCHIC WOODY WINS, AND THE COURT DEMANDS THAT ERIC SHUT UP!
PUMP!

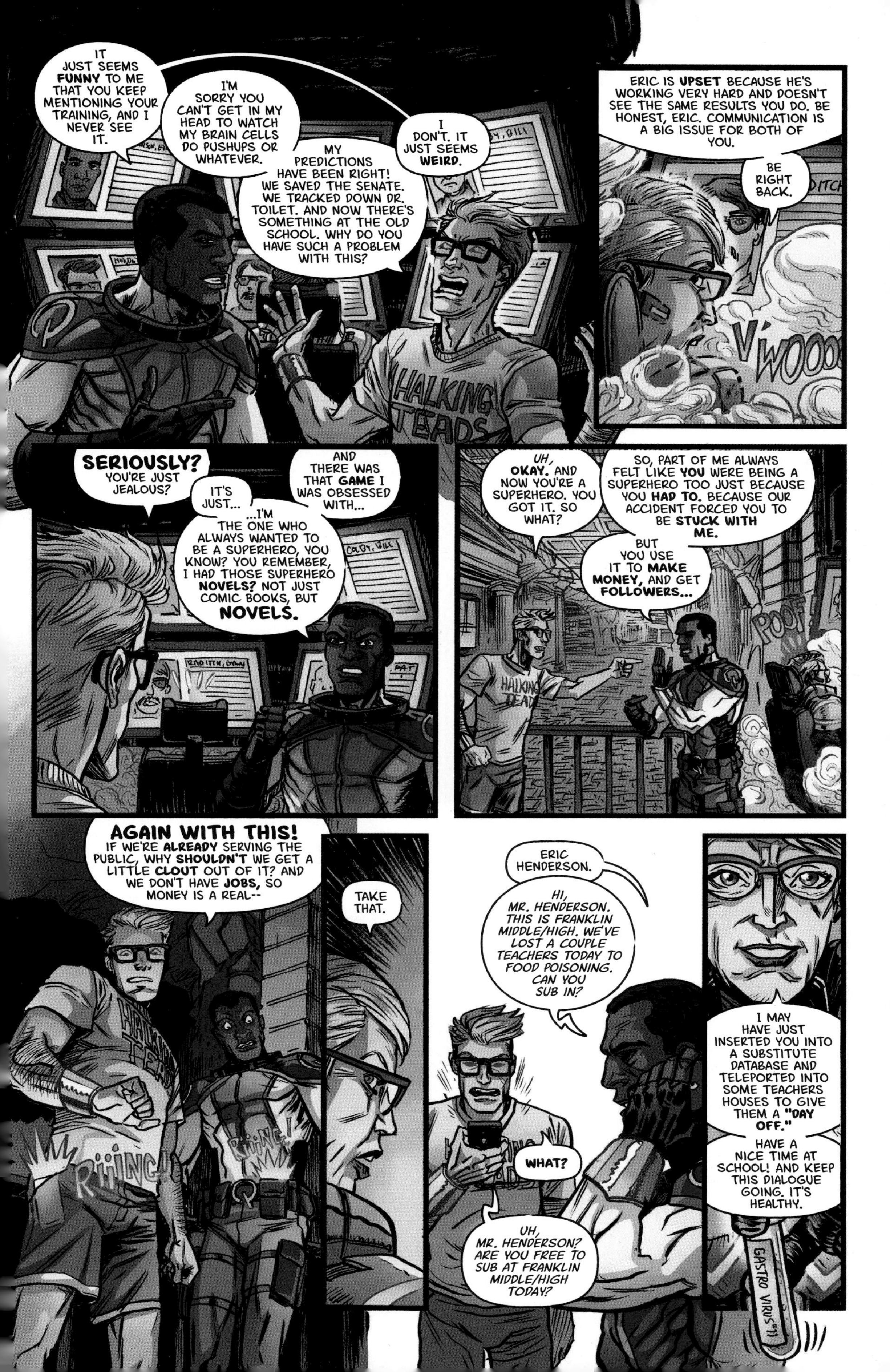
IT JUST SEEMS **FUNNY** TO ME THAT YOU KEEP MENTIONING YOUR TRAINING, AND I NEVER SEE IT.
I'M SORRY YOU CAN'T GET IN MY HEAD TO WATCH MY BRAIN CELLS DO PUSHUPS OR WHATEVER.
I DON'T. IT JUST SEEMS **WEIRD**.
MY PREDICTIONS HAVE BEEN RIGHT! WE SAVED THE SENATE. WE TRACKED DOWN DR. TOILET. AND NOW THERE'S SOMETHING AT THE OLD SCHOOL. WHY DO YOU HAVE SUCH A PROBLEM WITH THIS?
HALKING TEADS
ERIC IS **UPSET** BECAUSE HE'S WORKING VERY HARD AND DOESN'T SEE THE SAME RESULTS YOU DO. BE HONEST, ERIC. COMMUNICATION IS A BIG ISSUE FOR BOTH OF YOU.
BE RIGHT BACK.
VWOOO
SERIOUSLY? YOU'RE JUST JEALOUS?
IT'S JUST...
AND THERE WAS THAT **GAME** I WAS OBSESSED WITH...
...I'M THE ONE WHO ALWAYS WANTED TO BE A SUPERHERO, YOU KNOW? YOU REMEMBER, I HAD THOSE SUPERHERO **NOVELS?** NOT JUST COMIC BOOKS, BUT **NOVELS.**
UH, **OKAY.** AND NOW YOU'RE A SUPERHERO. YOU GOT IT. SO WHAT?
SO, PART OF ME ALWAYS FELT LIKE **YOU** WERE BEING A SUPERHERO TOO JUST BECAUSE YOU **HAD TO.** BECAUSE OUR ACCIDENT FORCED YOU TO BE **STUCK WITH ME.**
BUT YOU USE IT TO **MAKE MONEY,** AND GET **FOLLOWERS...**
POOF!
AGAIN WITH THIS! IF WE'RE **ALREADY** SERVING THE PUBLIC, WHY **SHOULDN'T** WE GET A LITTLE **CLOUT** OUT OF IT? AND WE DON'T HAVE **JOBS,** SO MONEY IS A REAL--
TAKE THAT.
RIIING!
RIIING!
ERIC HENDERSON.
HI, MR. HENDERSON. THIS IS FRANKLIN MIDDLE/HIGH. WE'VE LOST A COUPLE TEACHERS TODAY TO FOOD POISONING. CAN YOU SUB IN?
WHAT?
UH, MR. HENDERSON? ARE YOU FREE TO SUB AT FRANKLIN MIDDLE/HIGH TODAY?
I MAY HAVE JUST INSERTED YOU INTO A SUBSTITUTE DATABASE AND TELEPORTED INTO SOME TEACHERS HOUSES TO GIVE THEM A **"DAY OFF."**
HAVE A NICE TIME AT SCHOOL! AND KEEP THIS DIALOGUE GOING. IT'S HEALTHY.
GASTRO VIRUS

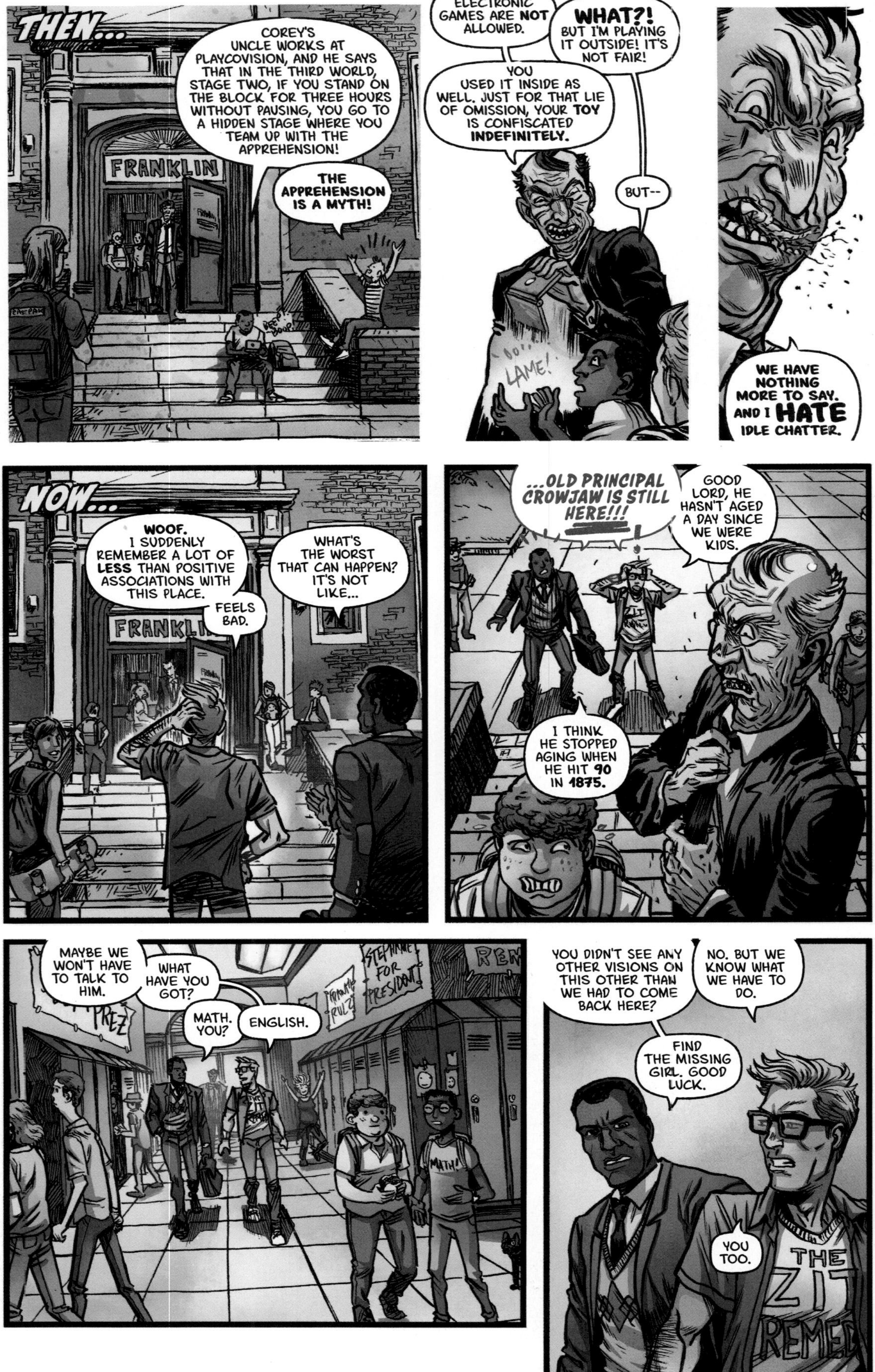

THEN...
COREY'S UNCLE WORKS AT PLAYCOVISION, AND HE SAYS THAT IN THE THIRD WORLD, STAGE TWO, IF YOU STAND ON THE BLOCK FOR THREE HOURS WITHOUT PAUSING, YOU GO TO A HIDDEN STAGE WHERE YOU TEAM UP WITH THE APPREHENSION!
THE APPREHENSION IS A MYTH!
FRANKLIN
BEEP BOOP
ELECTRONIC GAMES ARE NOT ALLOWED.
WHAT?! BUT I'M PLAYING IT OUTSIDE! IT'S NOT FAIR!
YOU USED IT INSIDE AS WELL. JUST FOR THAT LIE OF OMISSION, YOUR TOY IS CONFISCATED INDEFINITELY.
BUT--
OO!
LAME!
WE HAVE NOTHING MORE TO SAY. AND I HATE IDLE CHATTER.
NOW...
WOOF. I SUDDENLY REMEMBER A LOT OF LESS THAN POSITIVE ASSOCIATIONS WITH THIS PLACE.
FEELS BAD.
WHAT'S THE WORST THAT CAN HAPPEN? IT'S NOT LIKE...
FRANKLIN
...OLD PRINCIPAL CROWJAW IS STILL HERE!!!
GOOD LORD, HE HASN'T AGED A DAY SINCE WE WERE KIDS.
I THINK HE STOPPED AGING WHEN HE HIT 90 IN 1875.
MAYBE WE WON'T HAVE TO TALK TO HIM.
WHAT HAVE YOU GOT?
MATH. YOU?
ENGLISH.
STEPHANIE FOR PRESIDENT
PREZ
MATH
YOU DIDN'T SEE ANY OTHER VISIONS ON THIS OTHER THAN WE HAD TO COME BACK HERE?
NO. BUT WE KNOW WHAT WE HAVE TO DO.
FIND THE MISSING GIRL. GOOD LUCK.
YOU TOO.
THE ZIT REMED

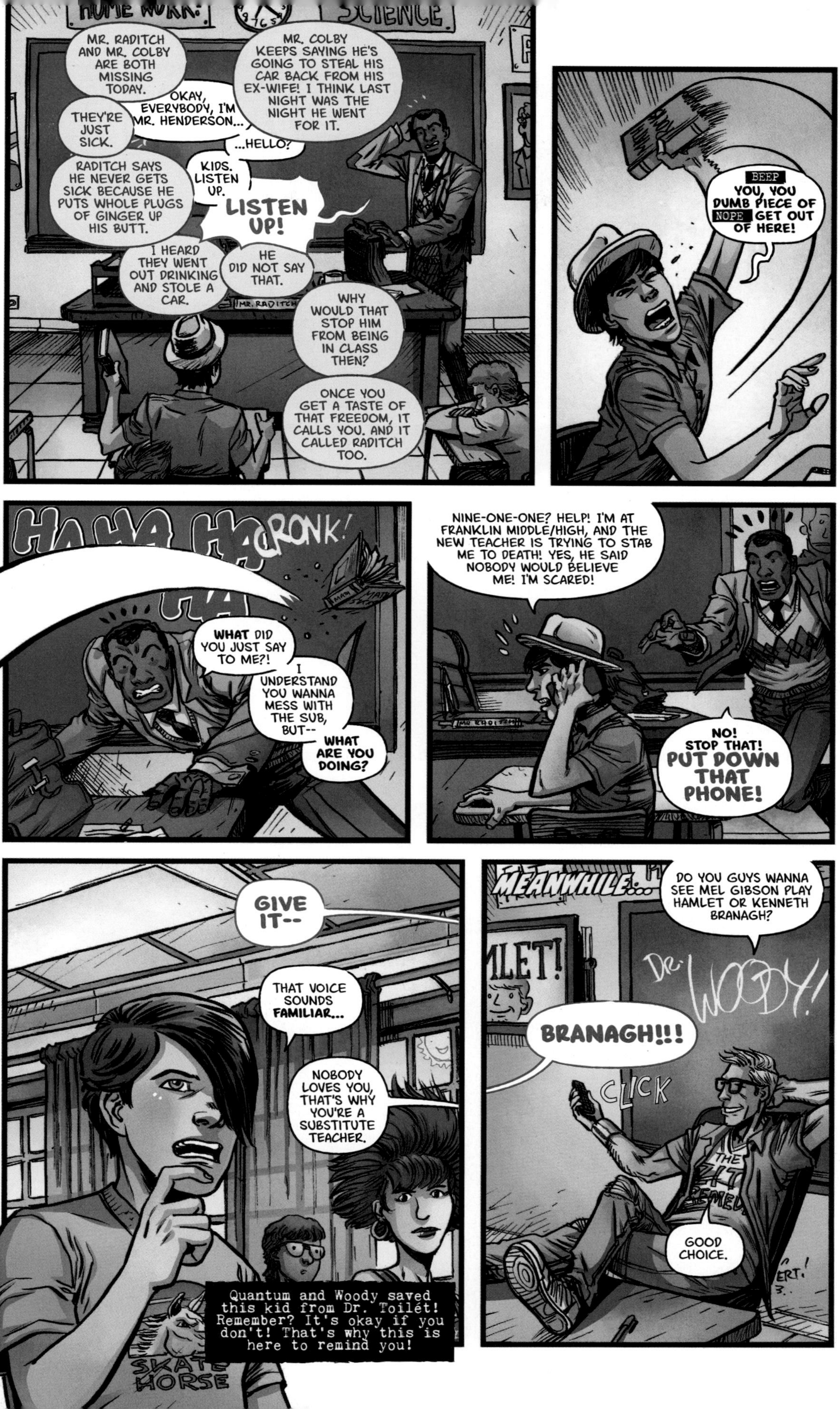
SCIENCE
MR. RADITCH AND MR. COLBY ARE BOTH MISSING TODAY.
MR. COLBY KEEPS SAYING HE'S GOING TO STEAL HIS CAR BACK FROM HIS EX-WIFE! I THINK LAST NIGHT WAS THE NIGHT HE WENT FOR IT.
OKAY, EVERYBODY, I'M MR. HENDERSON...
THEY'RE JUST SICK.
...HELLO?
RADITCH SAYS HE NEVER GETS SICK BECAUSE HE PUTS WHOLE PLUGS OF GINGER UP HIS BUTT.
KIDS. LISTEN UP.
LISTEN UP!
I HEARD THEY WENT OUT DRINKING AND STOLE A CAR.
HE DID NOT SAY THAT.
MR. RADITCH
WHY WOULD THAT STOP HIM FROM BEING IN CLASS THEN?
ONCE YOU GET A TASTE OF THAT FREEDOM, IT CALLS YOU. AND IT CALLED RADITCH TOO.
BEEP YOU, YOU DUMB PIECE OF NOPE GET OUT OF HERE!
HA HA HA HA
CRONK!
WHAT DID YOU JUST SAY TO ME?!
I UNDERSTAND YOU WANNA MESS WITH THE SUB, BUT--
WHAT ARE YOU DOING?
NINE-ONE-ONE? HELP! I'M AT FRANKLIN MIDDLE/HIGH, AND THE NEW TEACHER IS TRYING TO STAB ME TO DEATH! YES, HE SAID NOBODY WOULD BELIEVE ME! I'M SCARED!
MR RADITCH
NO! STOP THAT! PUT DOWN THAT PHONE!
GIVE IT--
THAT VOICE SOUNDS FAMILIAR...
NOBODY LOVES YOU, THAT'S WHY YOU'RE A SUBSTITUTE TEACHER.
SKATE HORSE
Quantum and Woody saved this kid from Dr. Toilét! Remember? It's okay if you don't! That's why this is here to remind you!
MEANWHILE...
DO YOU GUYS WANNA SEE MEL GIBSON PLAY HAMLET OR KENNETH BRANAGH?
MLET!
Dr. WOODY!
BRANAGH!!!
CLICK
GOOD CHOICE.

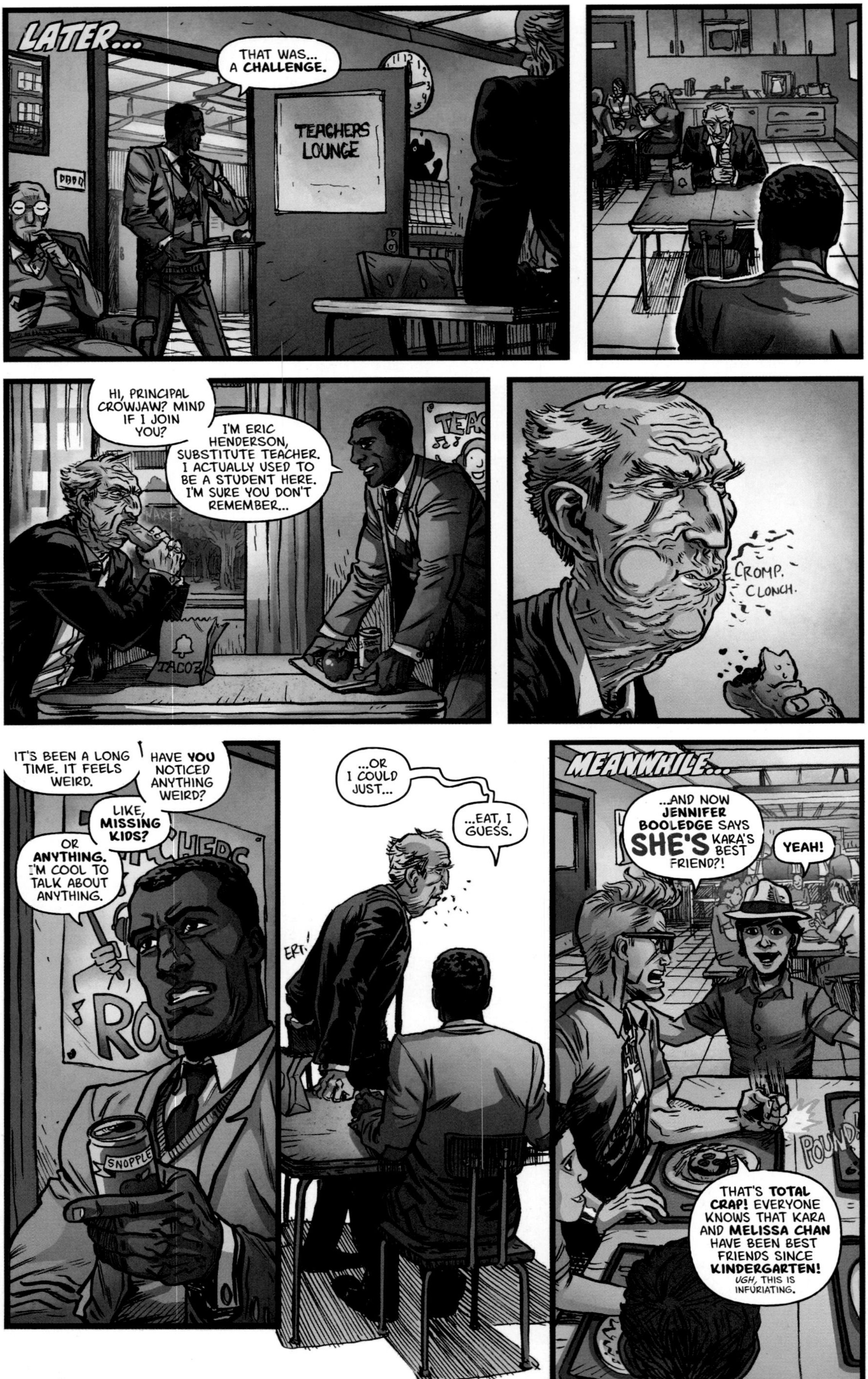
LATER...
THAT WAS... A CHALLENGE.
TEACHERS LOUNGE
HI, PRINCIPAL CROWJAW? MIND IF I JOIN YOU?
I'M ERIC HENDERSON, SUBSTITUTE TEACHER. I ACTUALLY USED TO BE A STUDENT HERE. I'M SURE YOU DON'T REMEMBER...
TACOZ
CROMP. CLONCH.
IT'S BEEN A LONG TIME. IT FEELS WEIRD.
HAVE YOU NOTICED ANYTHING WEIRD?
LIKE, MISSING KIDS?
OR ANYTHING. I'M COOL TO TALK ABOUT ANYTHING.
SNOPPLE
...OR I COULD JUST...
...EAT, I GUESS.
ERT!
MEANWHILE...
...AND NOW JENNIFER BOOLEDGE SAYS SHE'S KARA'S BEST FRIEND?!
YEAH!
POUND!
THAT'S TOTAL CRAP! EVERYONE KNOWS THAT KARA AND MELISSA CHAN HAVE BEEN BEST FRIENDS SINCE KINDERGARTEN! UGH, THIS IS INFURIATING.

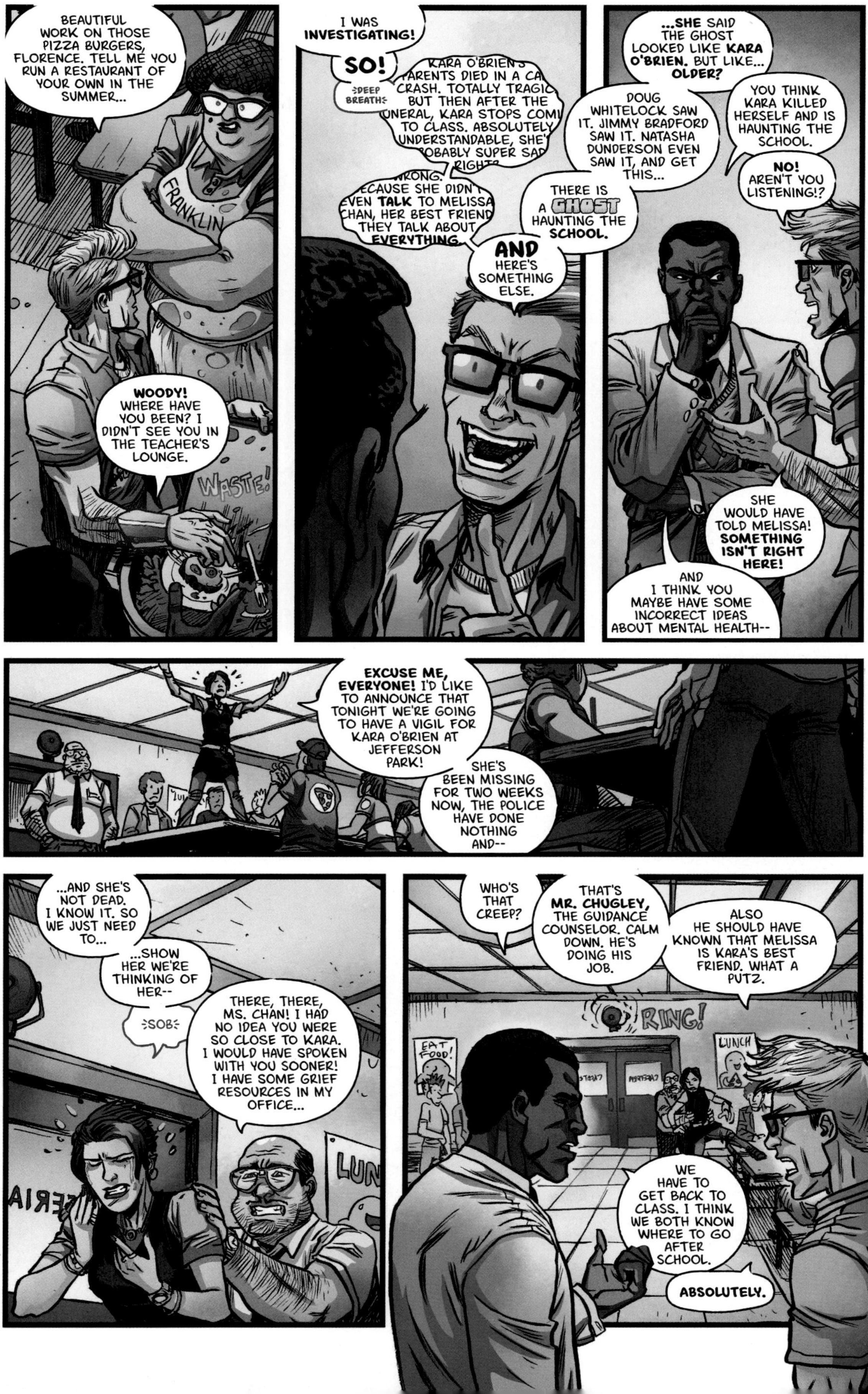

BEAUTIFUL WORK ON THOSE PIZZA BURGERS, FLORENCE. TELL ME YOU RUN A RESTAURANT OF YOUR OWN IN THE SUMMER...
FRANKLIN
WOODY! WHERE HAVE YOU BEEN? I DIDN'T SEE YOU IN THE TEACHER'S LOUNGE.
WASTE!
I WAS INVESTIGATING!
SO!
DEEP BREATH
AND HERE'S SOMETHING ELSE.
...SHE SAID THE GHOST LOOKED LIKE KARA O'BRIEN. BUT LIKE... OLDER?
DOUG WHITELOCK SAW IT. JIMMY BRADFORD SAW IT. NATASHA DUNDERSON EVEN SAW IT, AND GET THIS...
THERE IS A GHOST HAUNTING THE SCHOOL.
YOU THINK KARA KILLED HERSELF AND IS HAUNTING THE SCHOOL.
NO! AREN'T YOU LISTENING!?
SHE WOULD HAVE TOLD MELISSA! SOMETHING ISN'T RIGHT HERE!
AND I THINK YOU MAYBE HAVE SOME INCORRECT IDEAS ABOUT MENTAL HEALTH--
EXCUSE ME, EVERYONE! I'D LIKE TO ANNOUNCE THAT TONIGHT WE'RE GOING TO HAVE A VIGIL FOR KARA O'BRIEN AT JEFFERSON PARK!
SHE'S BEEN MISSING FOR TWO WEEKS NOW, THE POLICE HAVE DONE NOTHING AND--
...AND SHE'S NOT DEAD. I KNOW IT. SO WE JUST NEED TO...
...SHOW HER WE'RE THINKING OF HER--
SOB
THERE, THERE, MS. CHAN! I HAD NO IDEA YOU WERE SO CLOSE TO KARA. I WOULD HAVE SPOKEN WITH YOU SOONER! I HAVE SOME GRIEF RESOURCES IN MY OFFICE...
LUN
WHO'S THAT CREEP?
THAT'S MR. CHUGLEY, THE GUIDANCE COUNSELOR. CALM DOWN. HE'S DOING HIS JOB.
ALSO HE SHOULD HAVE KNOWN THAT MELISSA IS KARA'S BEST FRIEND. WHAT A PUTZ.
RING!
EAT FOOD!
LUNCH
WE HAVE TO GET BACK TO CLASS. I THINK WE BOTH KNOW WHERE TO GO AFTER SCHOOL.
ABSOLUTELY.

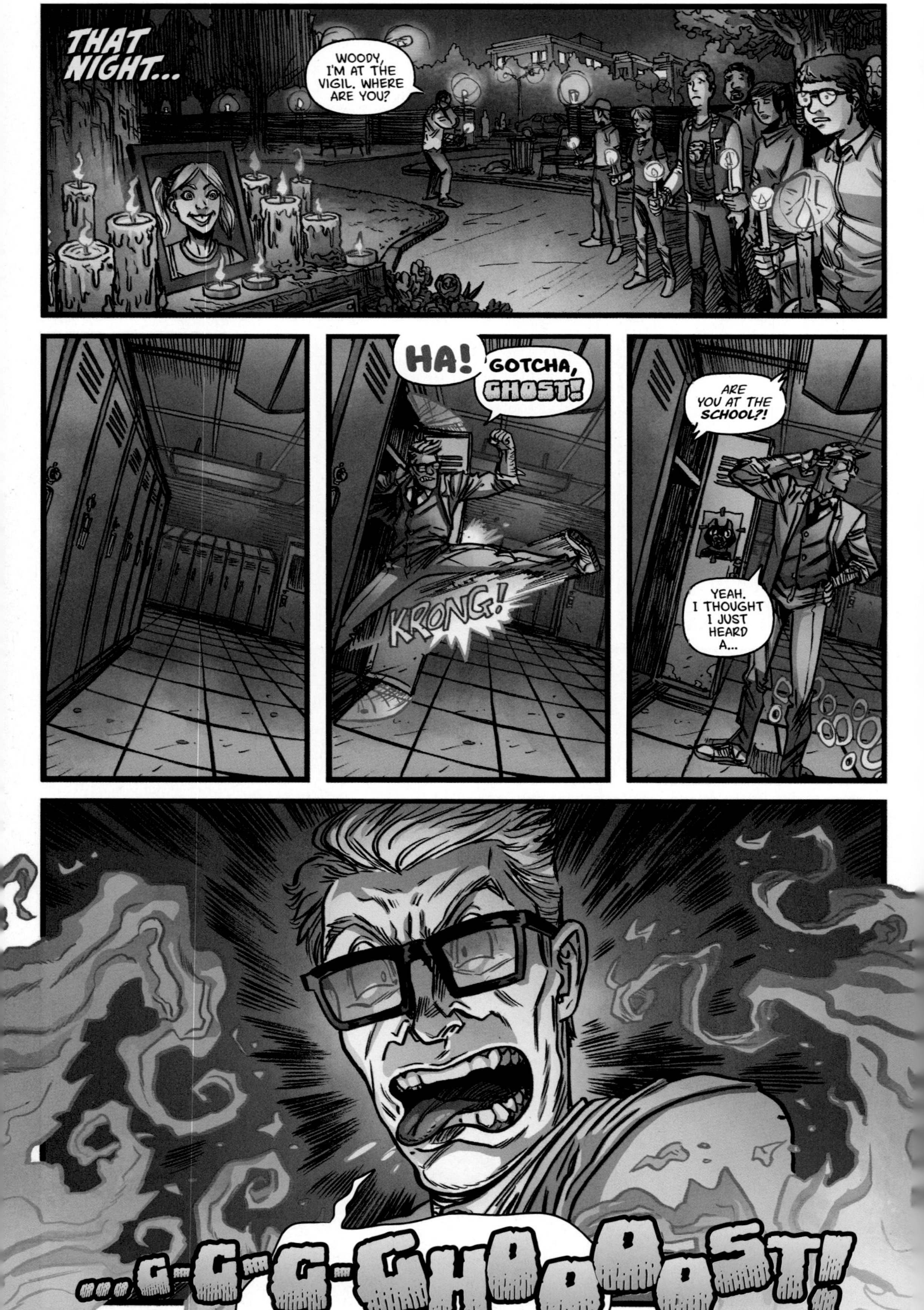
THAT NIGHT...
WOODY, I'M AT THE VIGIL. WHERE ARE YOU?
HA!
GOTCHA, GHOST!
KRONG!
ARE YOU AT THE SCHOOL?!
YEAH. I THOUGHT I JUST HEARD A...
...G-G-G-GHOOOOOST!

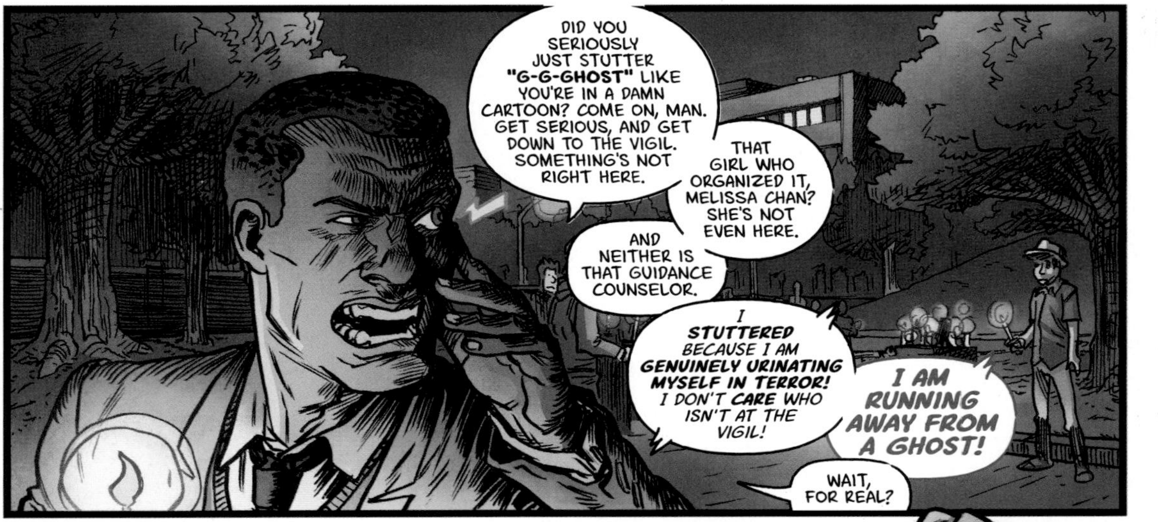
DID YOU SERIOUSLY JUST STUTTER **"G-G-GHOST"** LIKE YOU'RE IN A DAMN CARTOON? COME ON, MAN. GET SERIOUS, AND GET DOWN TO THE VIGIL. SOMETHING'S NOT RIGHT HERE.
THAT GIRL WHO ORGANIZED IT, MELISSA CHAN? SHE'S NOT EVEN HERE.
AND NEITHER IS THAT GUIDANCE COUNSELOR.
I ***STUTTERED*** *BECAUSE I AM* ***GENUINELY URINATING MYSELF IN TERROR!*** *I DON'T* ***CARE*** *WHO ISN'T AT THE VIGIL!*
I AM RUNNING AWAY FROM A GHOST!
WAIT, FOR REAL?

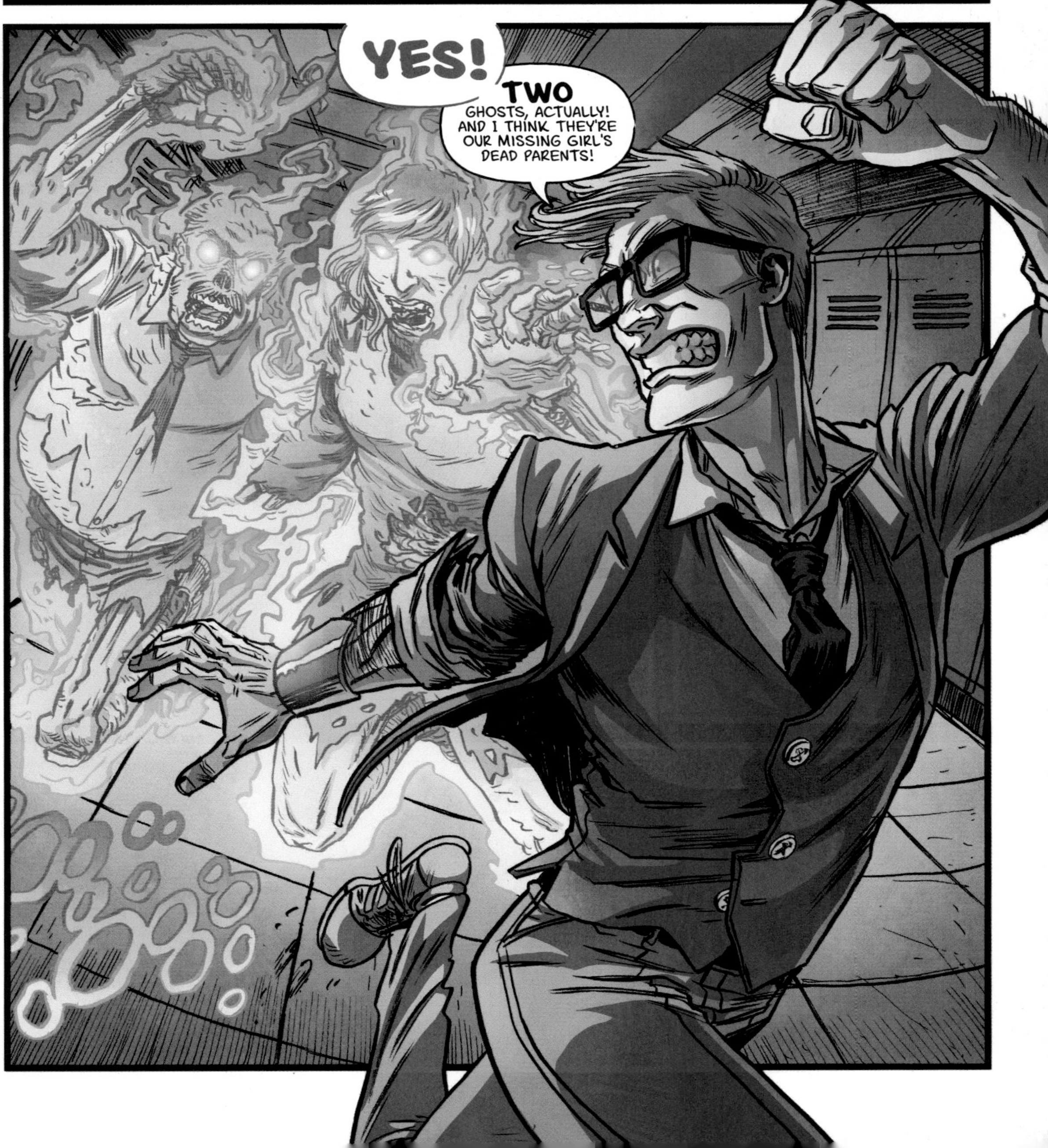
YES!
TWO GHOSTS, ACTUALLY! AND I THINK THEY'RE OUR MISSING GIRL'S DEAD PARENTS!

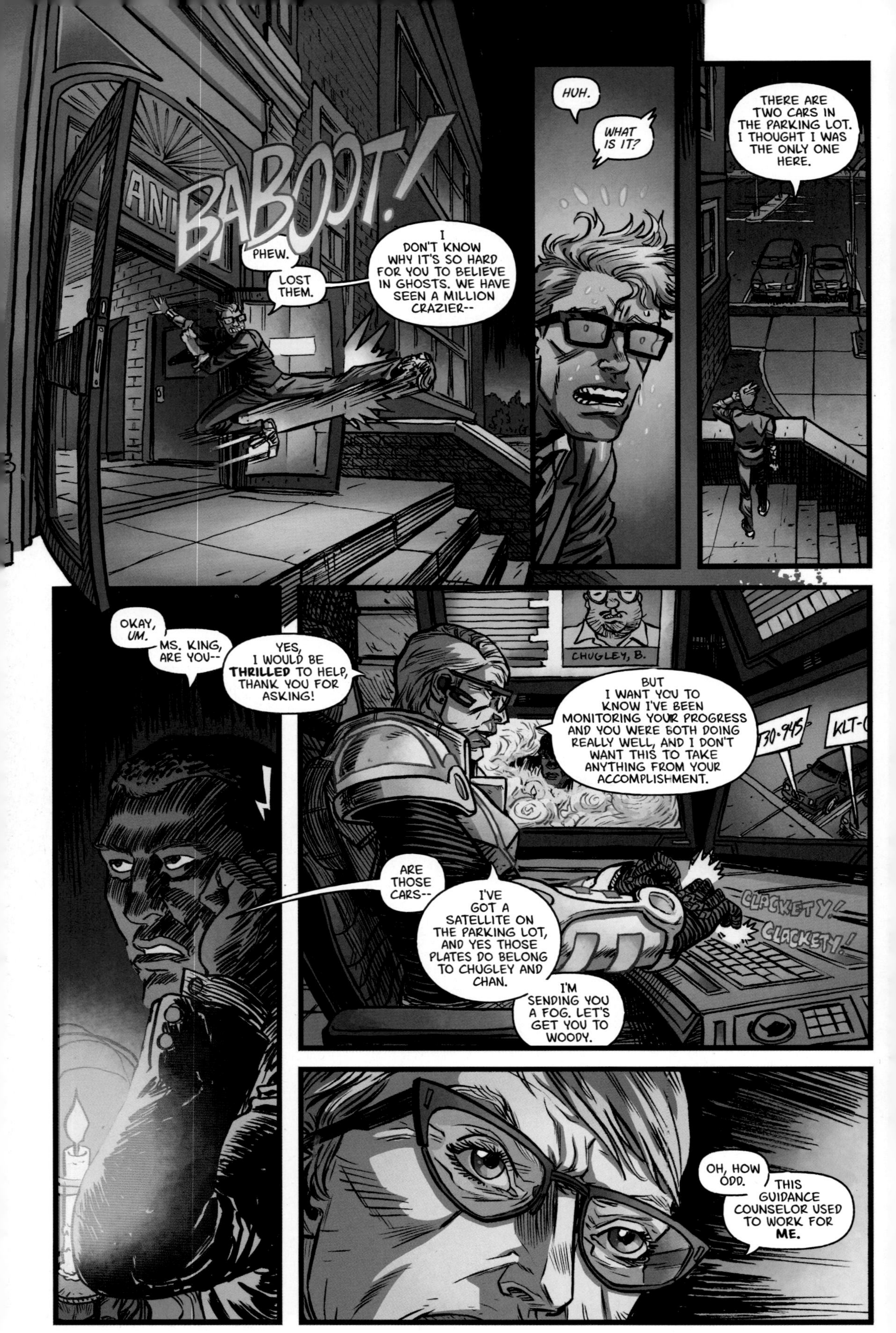
BABOOT!
PHEW.
LOST THEM.
I DON'T KNOW WHY IT'S SO HARD FOR YOU TO BELIEVE IN GHOSTS. WE HAVE SEEN A MILLION CRAZIER--
HUH.
WHAT IS IT?
THERE ARE TWO CARS IN THE PARKING LOT. I THOUGHT I WAS THE ONLY ONE HERE.
OKAY, UM.
MS. KING, ARE YOU--
YES, I WOULD BE THRILLED TO HELP, THANK YOU FOR ASKING!
CHUGLEY, B.
BUT I WANT YOU TO KNOW I'VE BEEN MONITORING YOUR PROGRESS AND YOU WERE BOTH DOING REALLY WELL, AND I DON'T WANT THIS TO TAKE ANYTHING FROM YOUR ACCOMPLISHMENT.
ARE THOSE CARS--
I'VE GOT A SATELLITE ON THE PARKING LOT, AND YES THOSE PLATES DO BELONG TO CHUGLEY AND CHAN.
CLACKETY! CLACKETY!
I'M SENDING YOU A FOG. LET'S GET YOU TO WOODY.
OH, HOW ODD.
THIS GUIDANCE COUNSELOR USED TO WORK FOR ME.

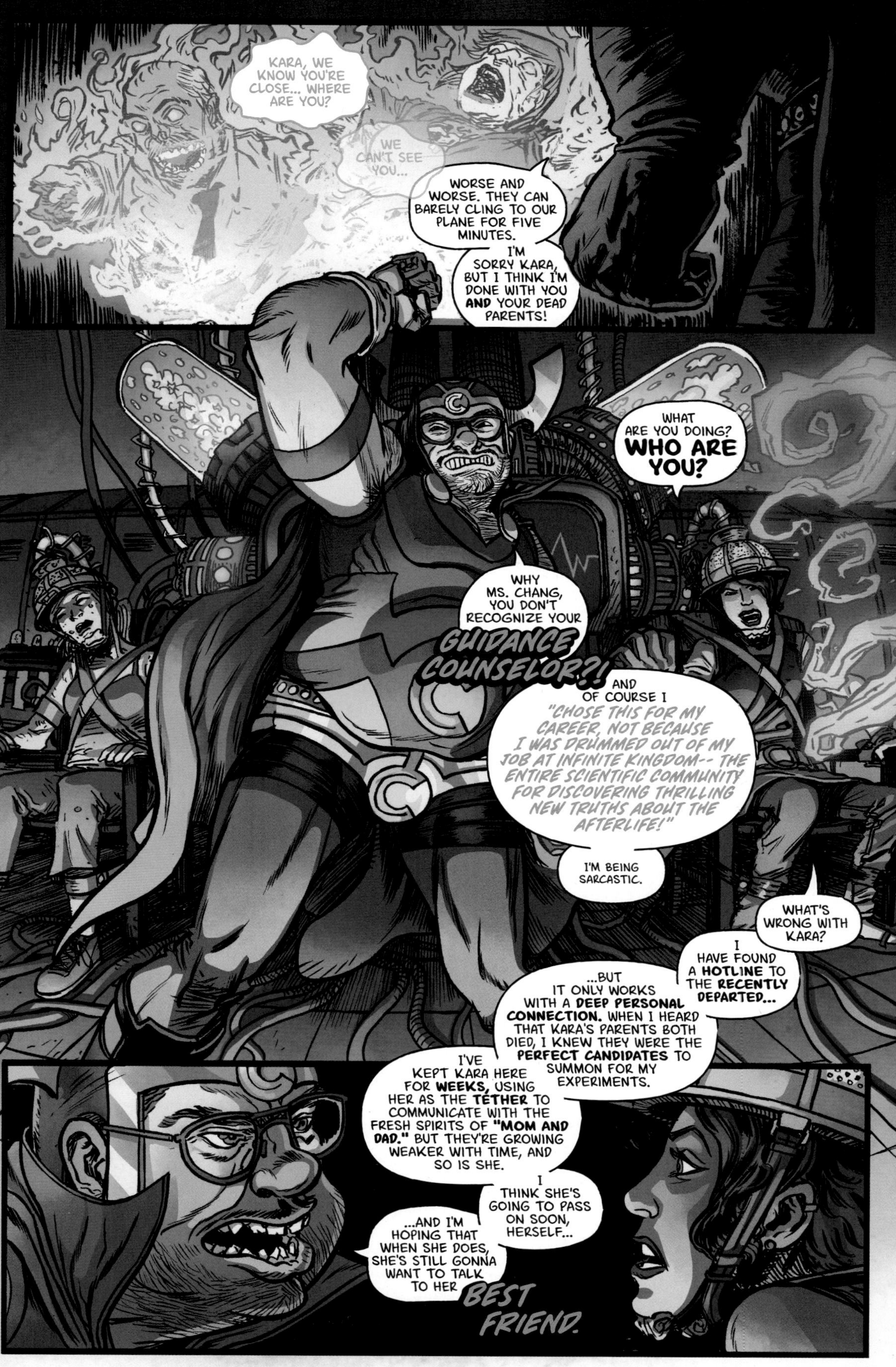
KARA, WE KNOW YOU'RE CLOSE... WHERE ARE YOU?
WE CAN'T SEE YOU...
WORSE AND WORSE. THEY CAN BARELY CLING TO OUR PLANE FOR FIVE MINUTES.
I'M SORRY KARA, BUT I THINK I'M DONE WITH YOU AND YOUR DEAD PARENTS!
WHAT ARE YOU DOING? WHO ARE YOU?
WHY MS. CHANG, YOU DON'T RECOGNIZE YOUR GUIDANCE COUNSELOR?!
AND OF COURSE I "CHOSE THIS FOR MY CAREER, NOT BECAUSE I WAS DRUMMED OUT OF MY JOB AT INFINITE KINGDOM-- THE ENTIRE SCIENTIFIC COMMUNITY FOR DISCOVERING THRILLING NEW TRUTHS ABOUT THE AFTERLIFE!"
I'M BEING SARCASTIC.
WHAT'S WRONG WITH KARA?
I HAVE FOUND A HOTLINE TO THE RECENTLY DEPARTED...
...BUT IT ONLY WORKS WITH A DEEP PERSONAL CONNECTION. WHEN I HEARD THAT KARA'S PARENTS BOTH DIED, I KNEW THEY WERE THE PERFECT CANDIDATES TO SUMMON FOR MY EXPERIMENTS.
I'VE KEPT KARA HERE FOR WEEKS, USING HER AS THE TETHER TO COMMUNICATE WITH THE FRESH SPIRITS OF "MOM AND DAD." BUT THEY'RE GROWING WEAKER WITH TIME, AND SO IS SHE.
I THINK SHE'S GOING TO PASS ON SOON, HERSELF...
...AND I'M HOPING THAT WHEN SHE DOES, SHE'S STILL GONNA WANT TO TALK TO HER BEST FRIEND.

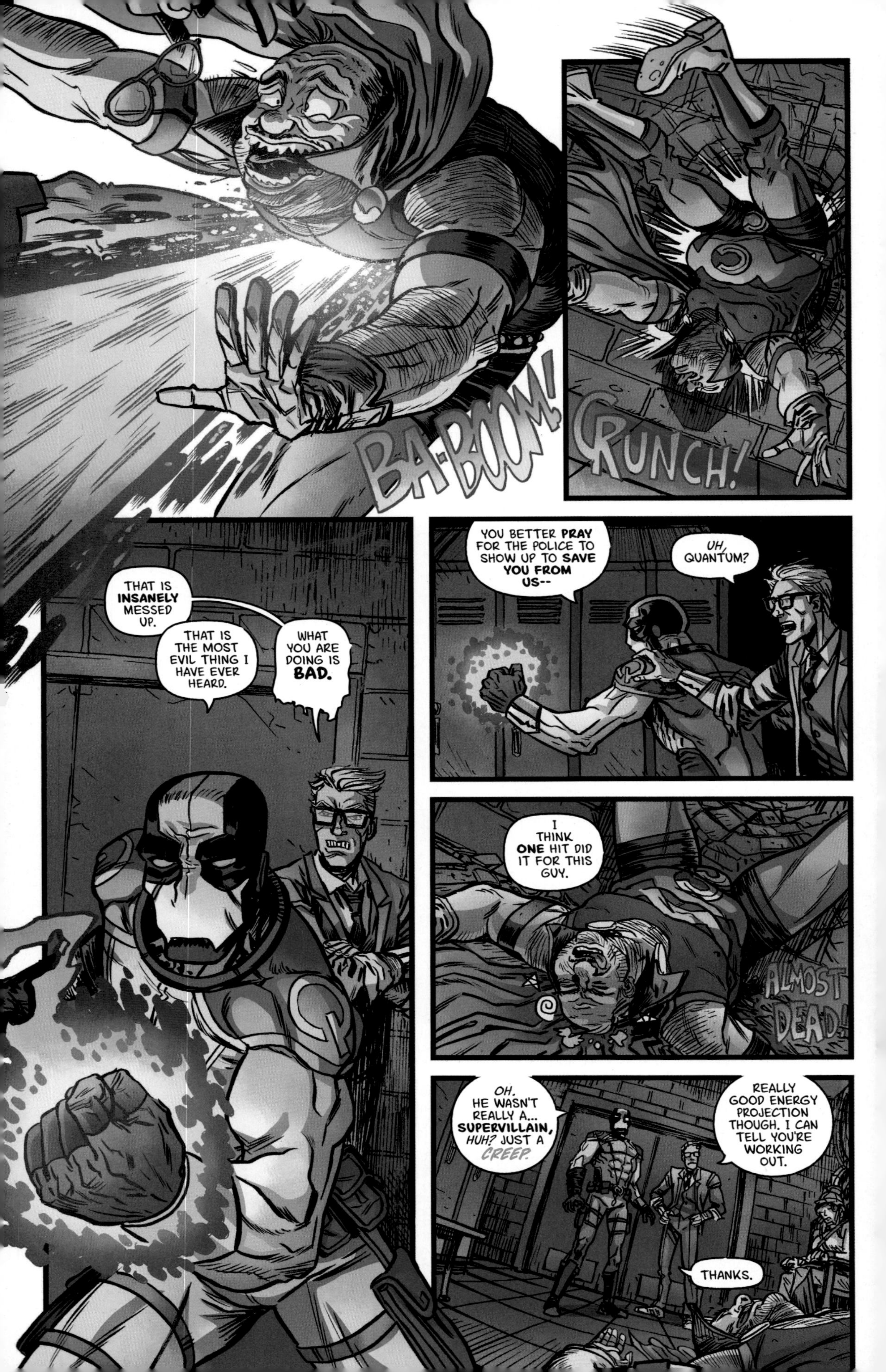
BA-BOOM!
CRUNCH!
THAT IS INSANELY MESSED UP.
THAT IS THE MOST EVIL THING I HAVE EVER HEARD.
WHAT YOU ARE DOING IS BAD.
YOU BETTER PRAY FOR THE POLICE TO SHOW UP TO SAVE YOU FROM US--
UH, QUANTUM?
I THINK ONE HIT DID IT FOR THIS GUY.
ALMOST DEAD!
OH. HE WASN'T REALLY A... SUPERVILLAIN, HUH? JUST A CREEP.
REALLY GOOD ENERGY PROJECTION THOUGH. I CAN TELL YOU'RE WORKING OUT.
THANKS.

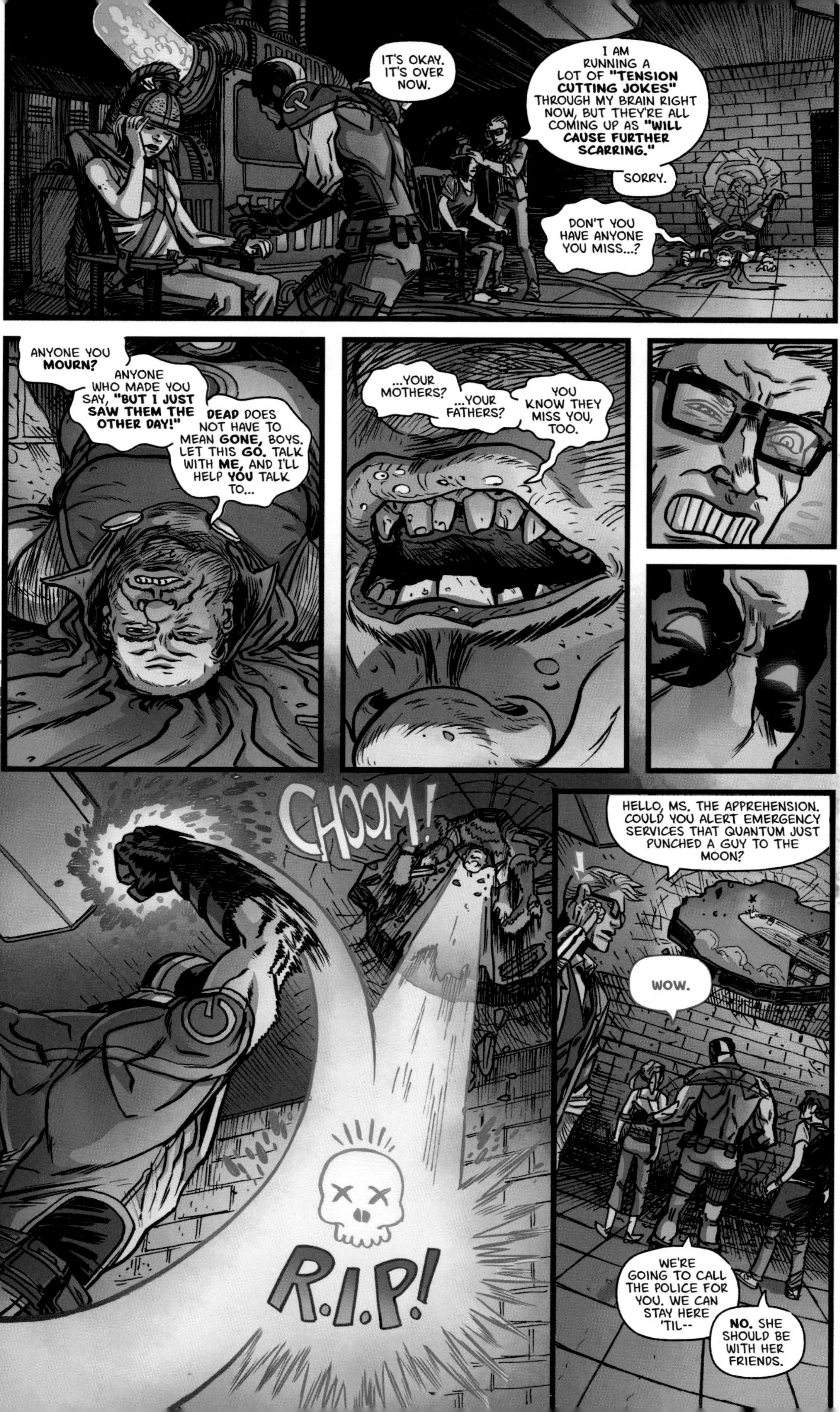
IT'S OKAY. IT'S OVER NOW.
I AM RUNNING A LOT OF "TENSION CUTTING JOKES" THROUGH MY BRAIN RIGHT NOW, BUT THEY'RE ALL COMING UP AS "WILL CAUSE FURTHER SCARRING."
SORRY.
DON'T YOU HAVE ANYONE YOU MISS...?
ANYONE YOU MOURN?
ANYONE WHO MADE YOU SAY, "BUT I JUST SAW THEM THE OTHER DAY!"
DEAD DOES NOT HAVE TO MEAN GONE, BOYS. LET THIS GO. TALK WITH ME, AND I'LL HELP YOU TALK TO...
...YOUR MOTHERS?
...YOUR FATHERS?
YOU KNOW THEY MISS YOU, TOO.
CHOOM!
R.I.P!
HELLO, MS. THE APPREHENSION. COULD YOU ALERT EMERGENCY SERVICES THAT QUANTUM JUST PUNCHED A GUY TO THE MOON?
WOW.
WE'RE GOING TO CALL THE POLICE FOR YOU. WE CAN STAY HERE 'TIL--
NO. SHE SHOULD BE WITH HER FRIENDS.

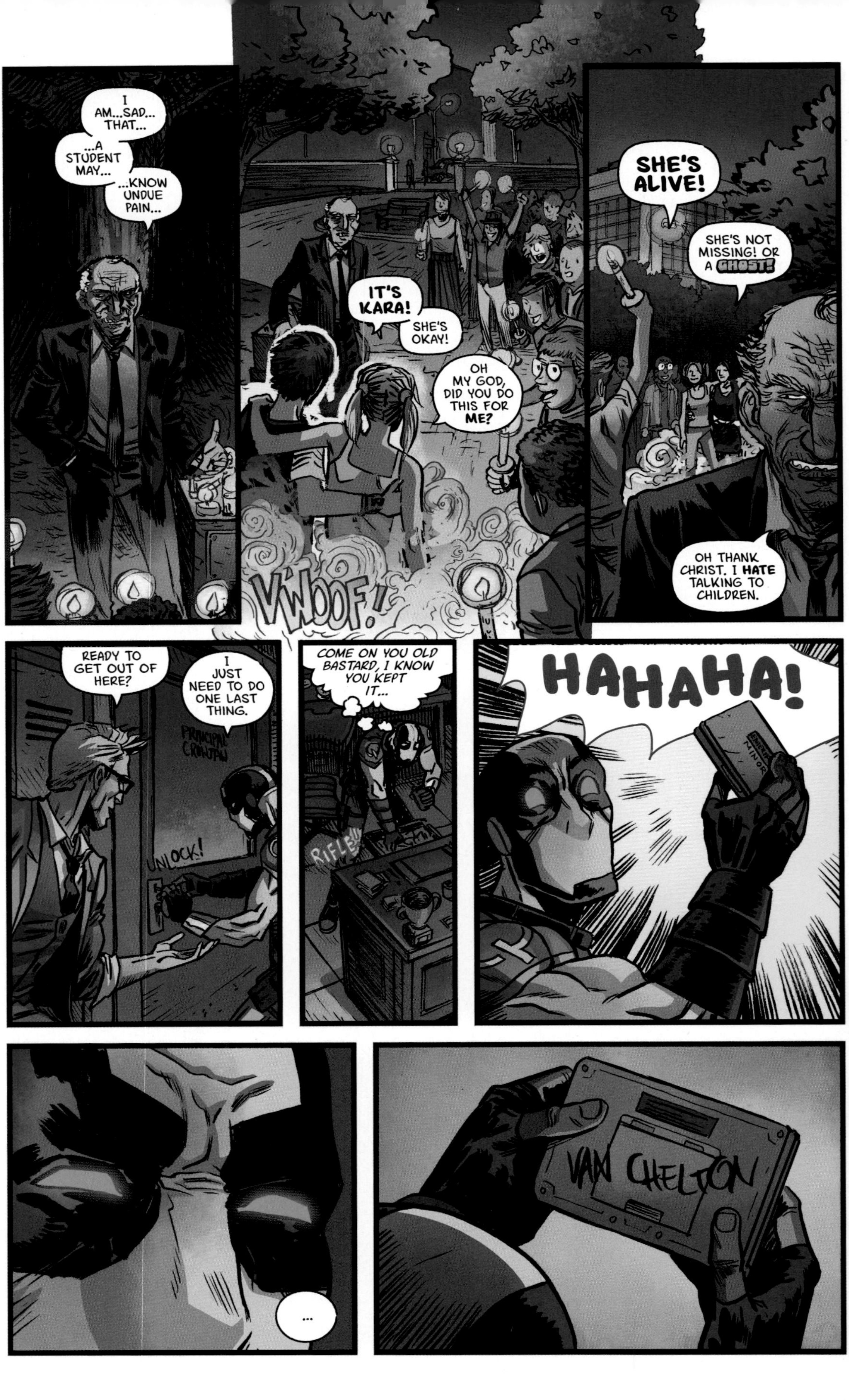
I AM...SAD... THAT...
...A STUDENT MAY...
...KNOW UNDUE PAIN...
IT'S KARA!
SHE'S OKAY!
OH MY GOD, DID YOU DO THIS FOR ME?
VWOOF!
SHE'S ALIVE!
SHE'S NOT MISSING! OR A GHOST!
OH THANK CHRIST. I HATE TALKING TO CHILDREN.
READY TO GET OUT OF HERE?
I JUST NEED TO DO ONE LAST THING.
PRINCIPAL CROWJAW
UNLOCK!
COME ON YOU OLD BASTARD, I KNOW YOU KEPT IT...
RIFLE!
HAHAHA!
...
VAN CHELTON

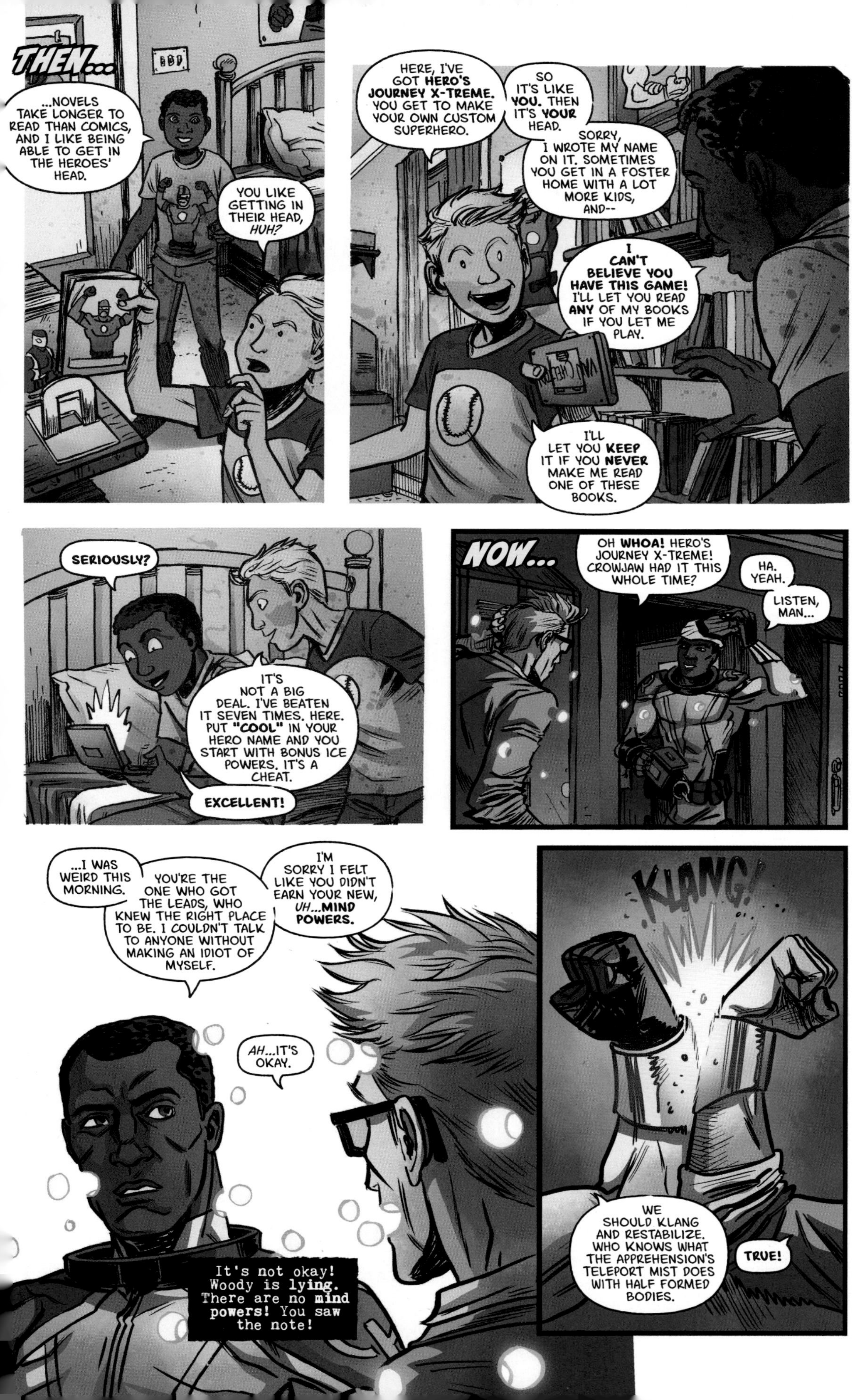
THEN...
...NOVELS TAKE LONGER TO READ THAN COMICS, AND I LIKE BEING ABLE TO GET IN THE HEROES' HEAD.
YOU LIKE GETTING IN THEIR HEAD, HUH?
HERE, I'VE GOT HERO'S JOURNEY X-TREME. YOU GET TO MAKE YOUR OWN CUSTOM SUPERHERO.
SO IT'S LIKE YOU. THEN IT'S YOUR HEAD.
SORRY, I WROTE MY NAME ON IT. SOMETIMES YOU GET IN A FOSTER HOME WITH A LOT MORE KIDS, AND--
I CAN'T BELIEVE YOU HAVE THIS GAME! I'LL LET YOU READ ANY OF MY BOOKS IF YOU LET ME PLAY.
I'LL LET YOU KEEP IT IF YOU NEVER MAKE ME READ ONE OF THESE BOOKS.
SERIOUSLY?
IT'S NOT A BIG DEAL. I'VE BEATEN IT SEVEN TIMES. HERE. PUT "COOL" IN YOUR HERO NAME AND YOU START WITH BONUS ICE POWERS. IT'S A CHEAT.
EXCELLENT!
NOW...
OH WHOA! HERO'S JOURNEY X-TREME! CROWJAW HAD IT THIS WHOLE TIME?
HA. YEAH.
LISTEN, MAN...
...I WAS WEIRD THIS MORNING.
YOU'RE THE ONE WHO GOT THE LEADS, WHO KNEW THE RIGHT PLACE TO BE. I COULDN'T TALK TO ANYONE WITHOUT MAKING AN IDIOT OF MYSELF.
I'M SORRY I FELT LIKE YOU DIDN'T EARN YOUR NEW, UH...MIND POWERS.
AH...IT'S OKAY.
It's not okay! Woody is lying. There are no mind powers! You saw the note!
KLANG!
WE SHOULD KLANG AND RESTABILIZE. WHO KNOWS WHAT THE APPREHENSION'S TELEPORT MIST DOES WITH HALF FORMED BODIES.
TRUE!

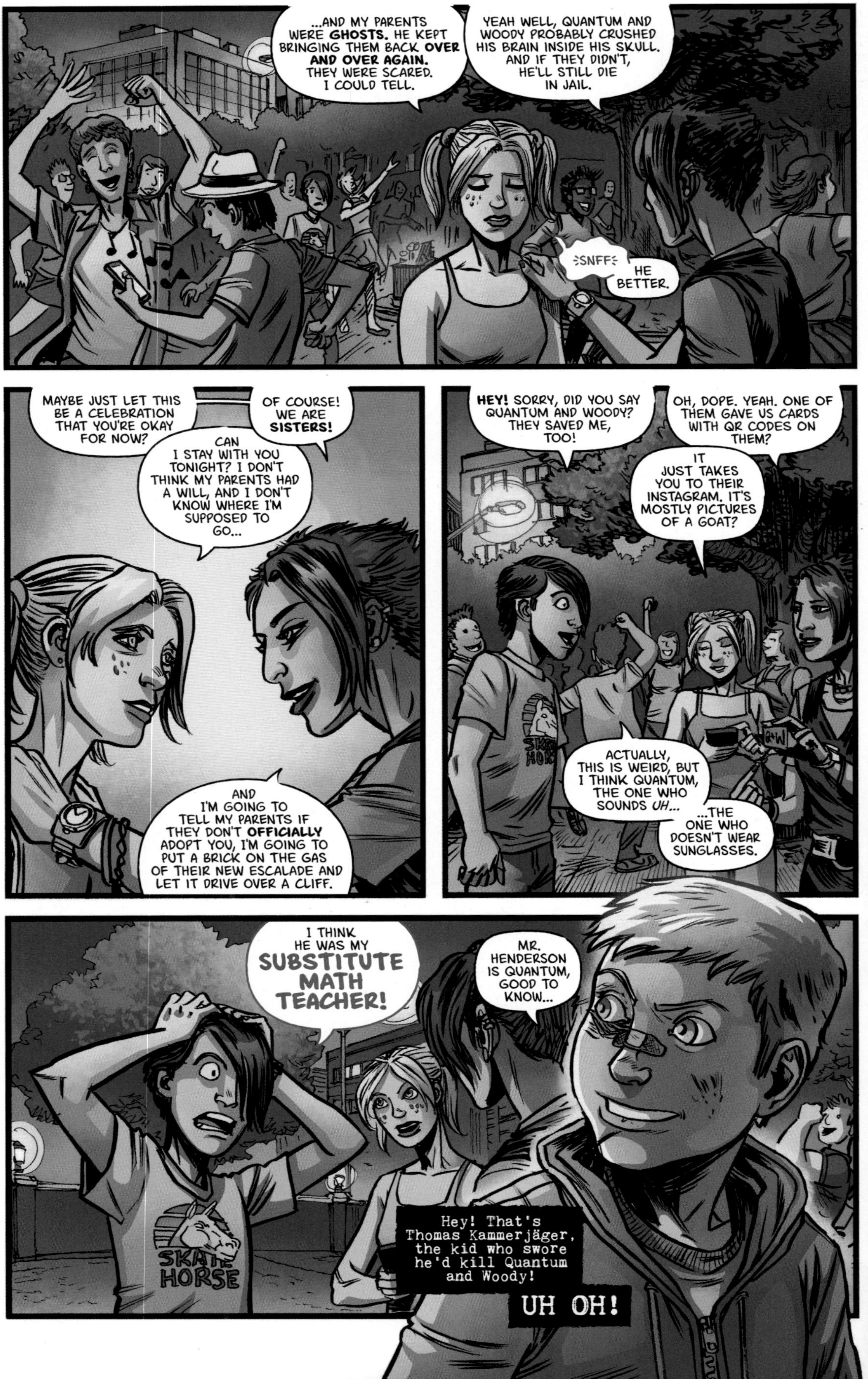
...AND MY PARENTS WERE GHOSTS. HE KEPT BRINGING THEM BACK OVER AND OVER AGAIN. THEY WERE SCARED. I COULD TELL.
YEAH WELL, QUANTUM AND WOODY PROBABLY CRUSHED HIS BRAIN INSIDE HIS SKULL. AND IF THEY DIDN'T, HE'LL STILL DIE IN JAIL.
SNFF
HE BETTER.
MAYBE JUST LET THIS BE A CELEBRATION THAT YOU'RE OKAY FOR NOW?
CAN I STAY WITH YOU TONIGHT? I DON'T THINK MY PARENTS HAD A WILL, AND I DON'T KNOW WHERE I'M SUPPOSED TO GO...
OF COURSE! WE ARE SISTERS!
AND I'M GOING TO TELL MY PARENTS IF THEY DON'T OFFICIALLY ADOPT YOU, I'M GOING TO PUT A BRICK ON THE GAS OF THEIR NEW ESCALADE AND LET IT DRIVE OVER A CLIFF.
HEY! SORRY, DID YOU SAY QUANTUM AND WOODY? THEY SAVED ME, TOO!
OH, DOPE. YEAH. ONE OF THEM GAVE US CARDS WITH QR CODES ON THEM?
IT JUST TAKES YOU TO THEIR INSTAGRAM. IT'S MOSTLY PICTURES OF A GOAT?
ACTUALLY, THIS IS WEIRD, BUT I THINK QUANTUM, THE ONE WHO SOUNDS UH...
...THE ONE WHO DOESN'T WEAR SUNGLASSES.
I THINK HE WAS MY SUBSTITUTE MATH TEACHER!
MR. HENDERSON IS QUANTUM, GOOD TO KNOW...
SKATE HORSE
Hey! That's Thomas Kammerjäger, the kid who swore he'd kill Quantum and Woody!
UH OH!

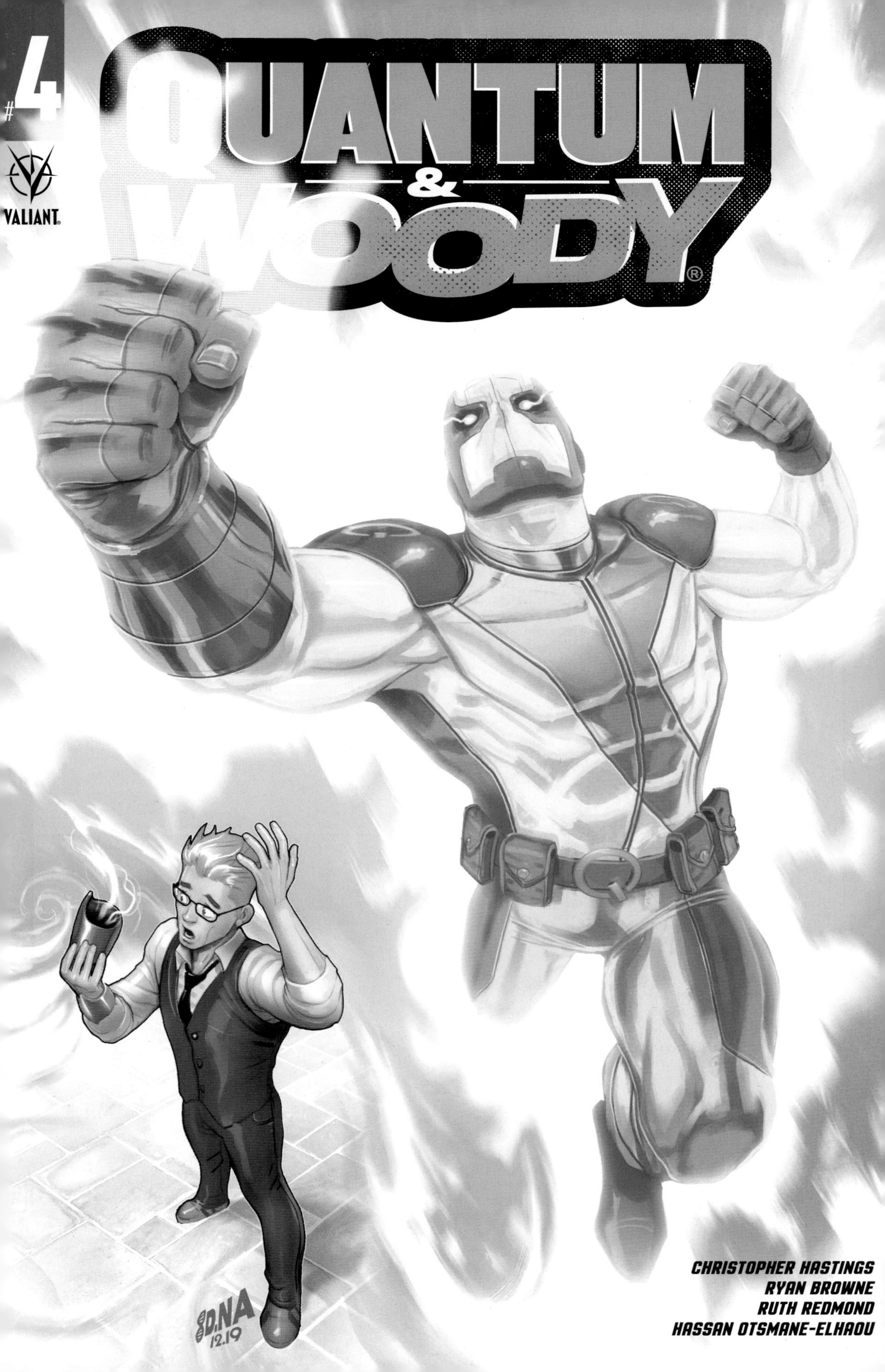
#4
VALIANT
QUANTUM & WOODY
CHRISTOPHER HASTINGS
RYAN BROWNE
RUTH REDMOND
HASSAN OTSMANE-ELHAOU

VOICE IT

Search

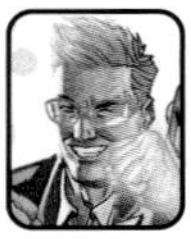

White_Chocolate
189k Cheers

v/DListDisasters Posted by OhThatTyler 9 hours ago

60.2k

SPOTTED: Quantum & Woody at a local middle school

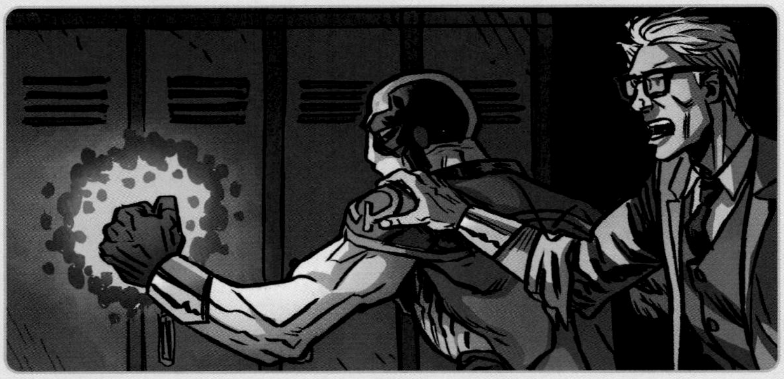

427 comments Share Hide

"Say Something!"

B U I

VOICE IT

OhThatTyler - 55.3k cheers - 9 hours ago
They saved some kidz. Mayb they r OK after all...
Reply Report

scoopsdad - 54.7k cheers - 9 hours ago
My niece goes to that school. Said these two idiots were posing as substitute teachers earlier that day.
Reply Report

OhThatTyler - 52k cheers - 9 hours ago
Id believe it. Theez 2 r the worst at covering their tracks.
Reply Report

scoopsdad - 49.1k cheers - 8 hours ago
It's like they're not even trying.
Reply Report

White_Chocolate - 50.7k cheers - 6 hours ago
CALL ME AN IDIOT AGAIN I DARE YOU
Reply Report

scoopsdad - 53.1k cheers - 6 hours ago
Case in point.
Reply Report

Black Mamba - 20.8k cheers - 5 hours ago
It's almost like using your real name and not covering your face was a bad idea.
Reply Report

White_Chocolate - 19.4k cheers - 4 hours ago
pfft. you were just looking for an excuse to call yourself quantum, eric. we've got a dope underground hideout now - i aint scrrrd.
Reply Report

Black Mamba - 15.2k cheers - 2 hours ago
I'd really love to go for a two-hour training session without you exposing us to more security risks.
Reply Report

horses_on_ice - 43.1k cheers - 2 hours ago
I go to that school, too, and they were def there as subs. Anyone here know anything about geolocating IP addresses?
Reply Report

KammerScout - 10.9k cheers - 1 hour ago
DMed!
Reply Report

v/DListDisasters

844 ONLINE | 193k MEMBERS

The "Who's Who" of internet fame -- A place to follow celebrities even TNZ thinks aren't worth their time! Find your cult following here!

SUBSCRIBE

CREDITS

Writer...**Christopher Hastings**
Artist...**Ryan Browne**
Colorist...**Ruth Redmond**
Letterer...**Hassan Otsmane-Elhaou**
Cover Artist...**David Nakayama**
Assistant Editor...**Drew Baumgartner**
Senior Editor...**Heather Antos**

TRENDING COMMUNITIES

v/ValiantComicFans
167k members
JOIN

v/legionofthunder
33k members
JOIN

v/MythosOrMadScience
22k members
JOIN

v/deadsidedeadbeats
4k members
JOIN

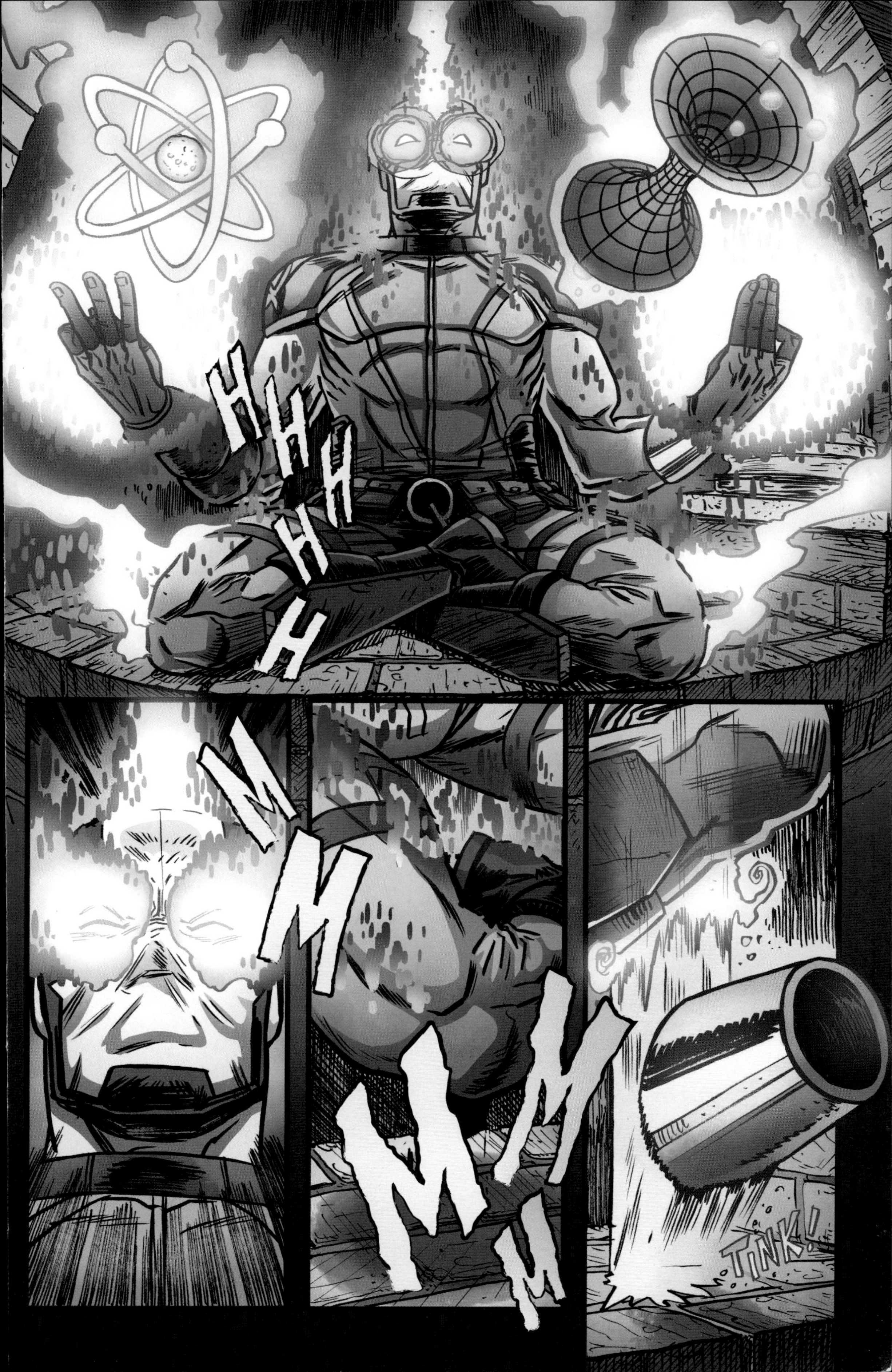
HHHHH
MMMMMM
TINK!

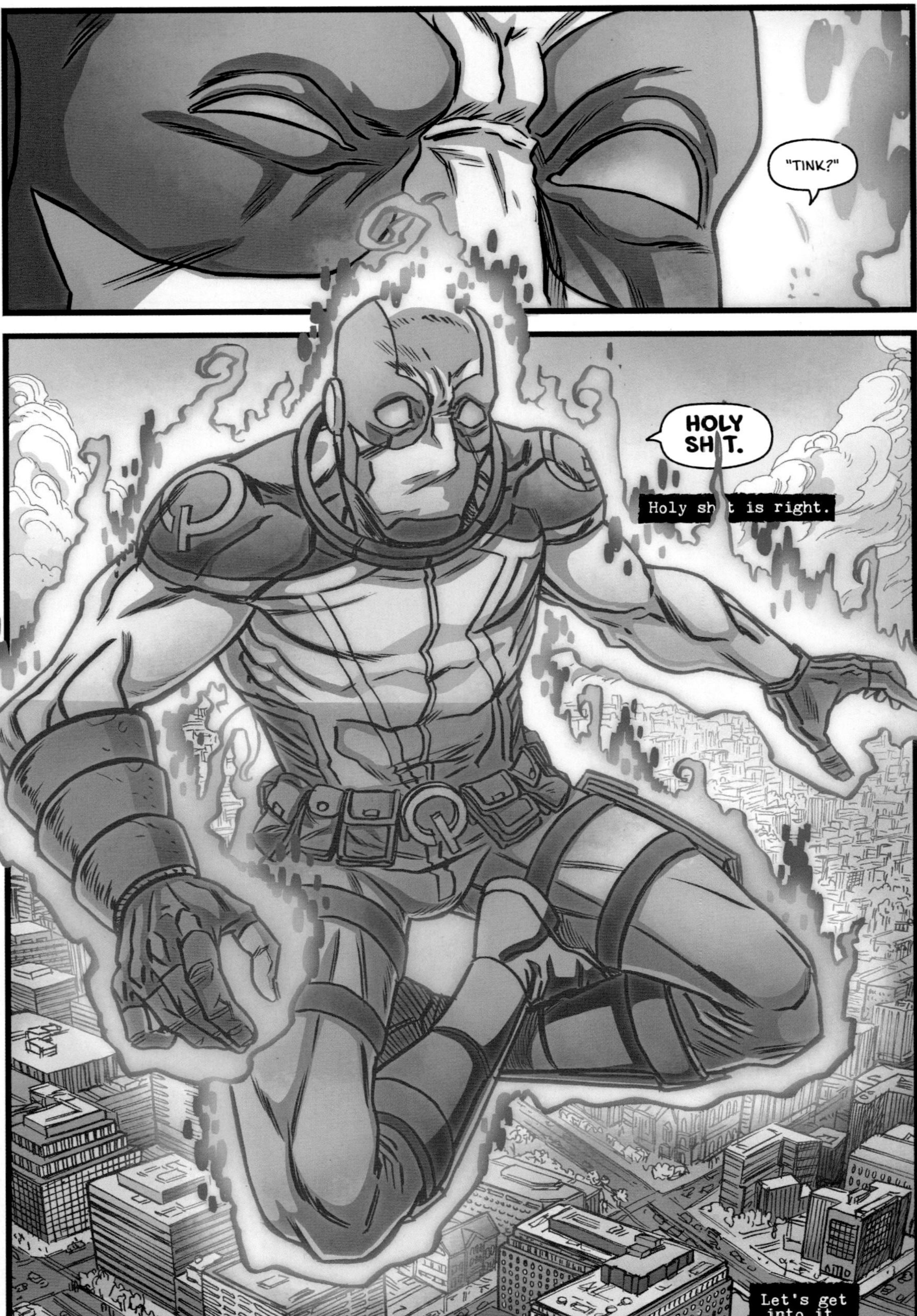
"TINK?"
HOLY SH T.
Holy sh t is right.
Let's get into it...

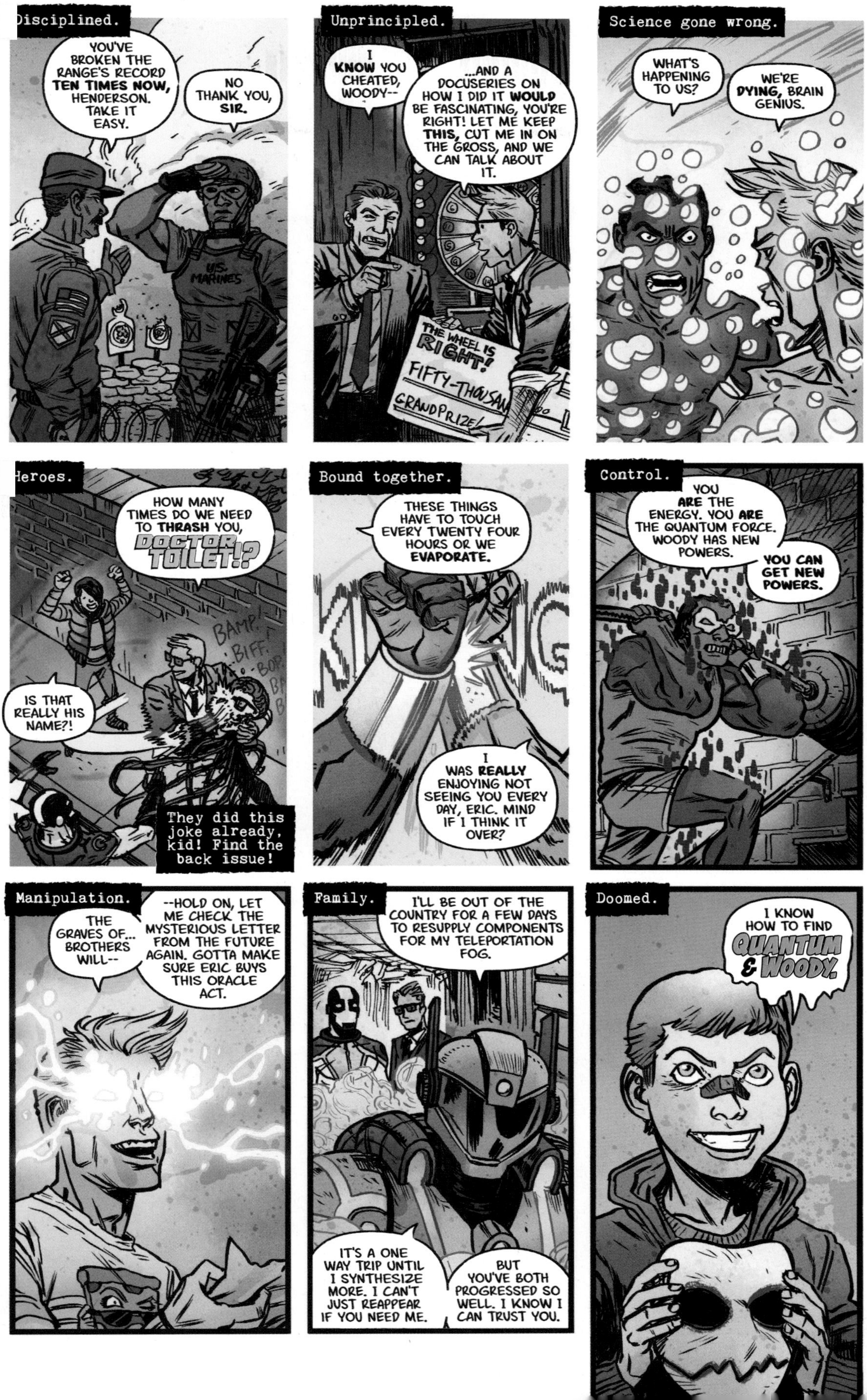

Disciplined.
YOU'VE BROKEN THE RANGE'S RECORD TEN TIMES NOW, HENDERSON. TAKE IT EASY.
NO THANK YOU, SIR.
U.S. MARINES
Unprincipled.
I KNOW YOU CHEATED, WOODY--
...AND A DOCUSERIES ON HOW I DID IT WOULD BE FASCINATING, YOU'RE RIGHT! LET ME KEEP THIS, CUT ME IN ON THE GROSS, AND WE CAN TALK ABOUT IT.
THE WHEEL IS RIGHT!
FIFTY-THOUSAN
GRANDPRIZE!
Science gone wrong.
WHAT'S HAPPENING TO US?
WE'RE DYING, BRAIN GENIUS.
Heroes.
HOW MANY TIMES DO WE NEED TO THRASH YOU, DOCTOR TOILET!?
BAMP! BIFF! BOP!
IS THAT REALLY HIS NAME?!
They did this joke already, kid! Find the back issue!
Bound together.
THESE THINGS HAVE TO TOUCH EVERY TWENTY FOUR HOURS OR WE EVAPORATE.
I WAS REALLY ENJOYING NOT SEEING YOU EVERY DAY, ERIC. MIND IF I THINK IT OVER?
Control.
YOU ARE THE ENERGY. YOU ARE THE QUANTUM FORCE. WOODY HAS NEW POWERS.
YOU CAN GET NEW POWERS.
Manipulation.
THE GRAVES OF... BROTHERS WILL--
--HOLD ON, LET ME CHECK THE MYSTERIOUS LETTER FROM THE FUTURE AGAIN. GOTTA MAKE SURE ERIC BUYS THIS ORACLE ACT.
Family.
I'LL BE OUT OF THE COUNTRY FOR A FEW DAYS TO RESUPPLY COMPONENTS FOR MY TELEPORTATION FOG.
IT'S A ONE WAY TRIP UNTIL I SYNTHESIZE MORE. I CAN'T JUST REAPPEAR IF YOU NEED ME.
BUT YOU'VE BOTH PROGRESSED SO WELL. I KNOW I CAN TRUST YOU.
Doomed.
I KNOW HOW TO FIND QUANTUM & WOODY.

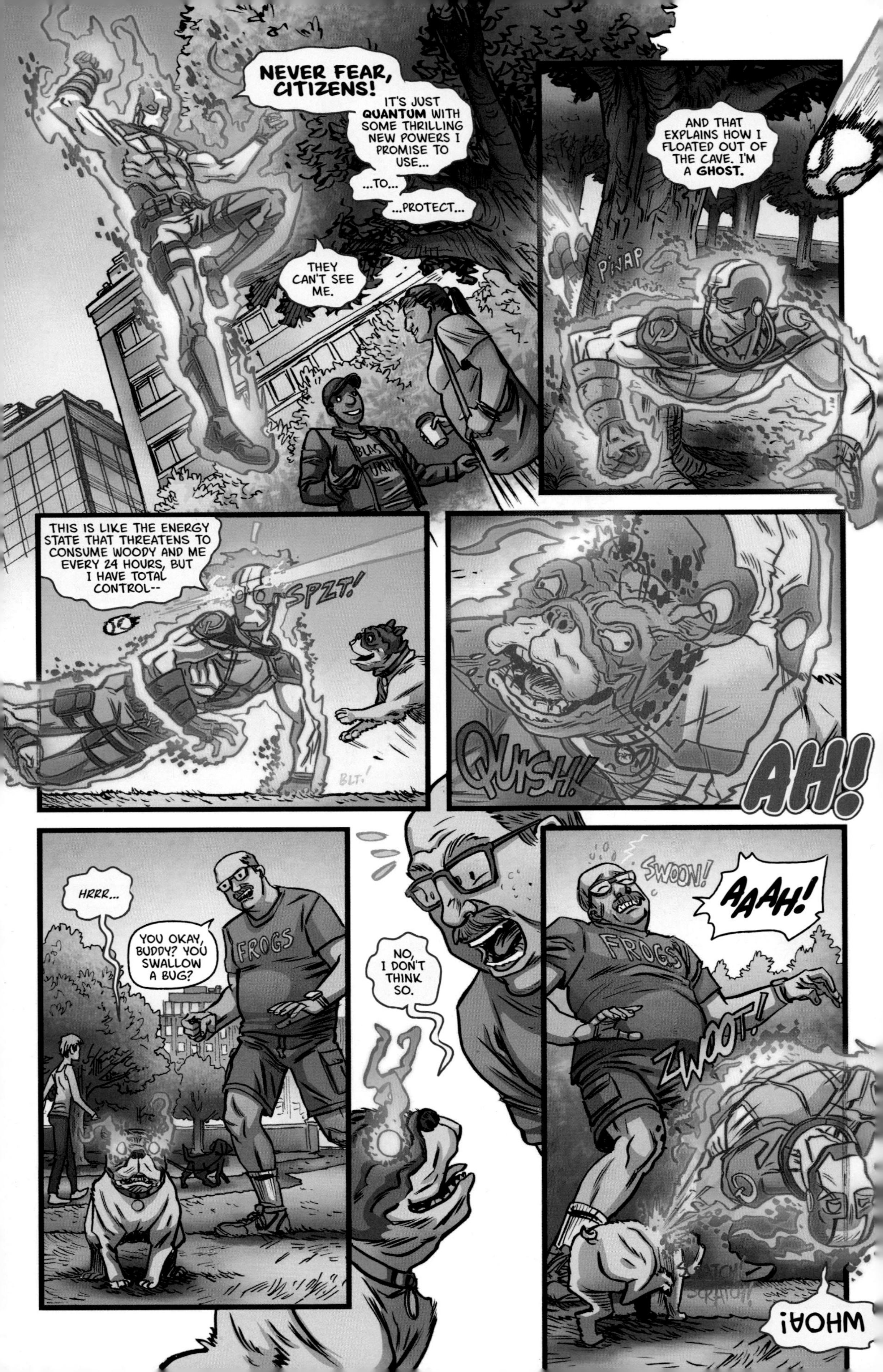
NEVER FEAR, CITIZENS!
IT'S JUST QUANTUM WITH SOME THRILLING NEW POWERS I PROMISE TO USE...
...TO...
...PROTECT...
THEY CAN'T SEE ME.
AND THAT EXPLAINS HOW I FLOATED OUT OF THE CAVE. I'M A GHOST.
PWAP
THIS IS LIKE THE ENERGY STATE THAT THREATENS TO CONSUME WOODY AND ME EVERY 24 HOURS, BUT I HAVE TOTAL CONTROL--
!
SPZT!
BLT!
QUISH!
AH!
HRRR...
YOU OKAY, BUDDY? YOU SWALLOW A BUG?
FROGS
NO, I DON'T THINK SO.
SWOON!
AAAH!
ZWOOT!
SCRATCH!
SCRATCH!
WHOA!

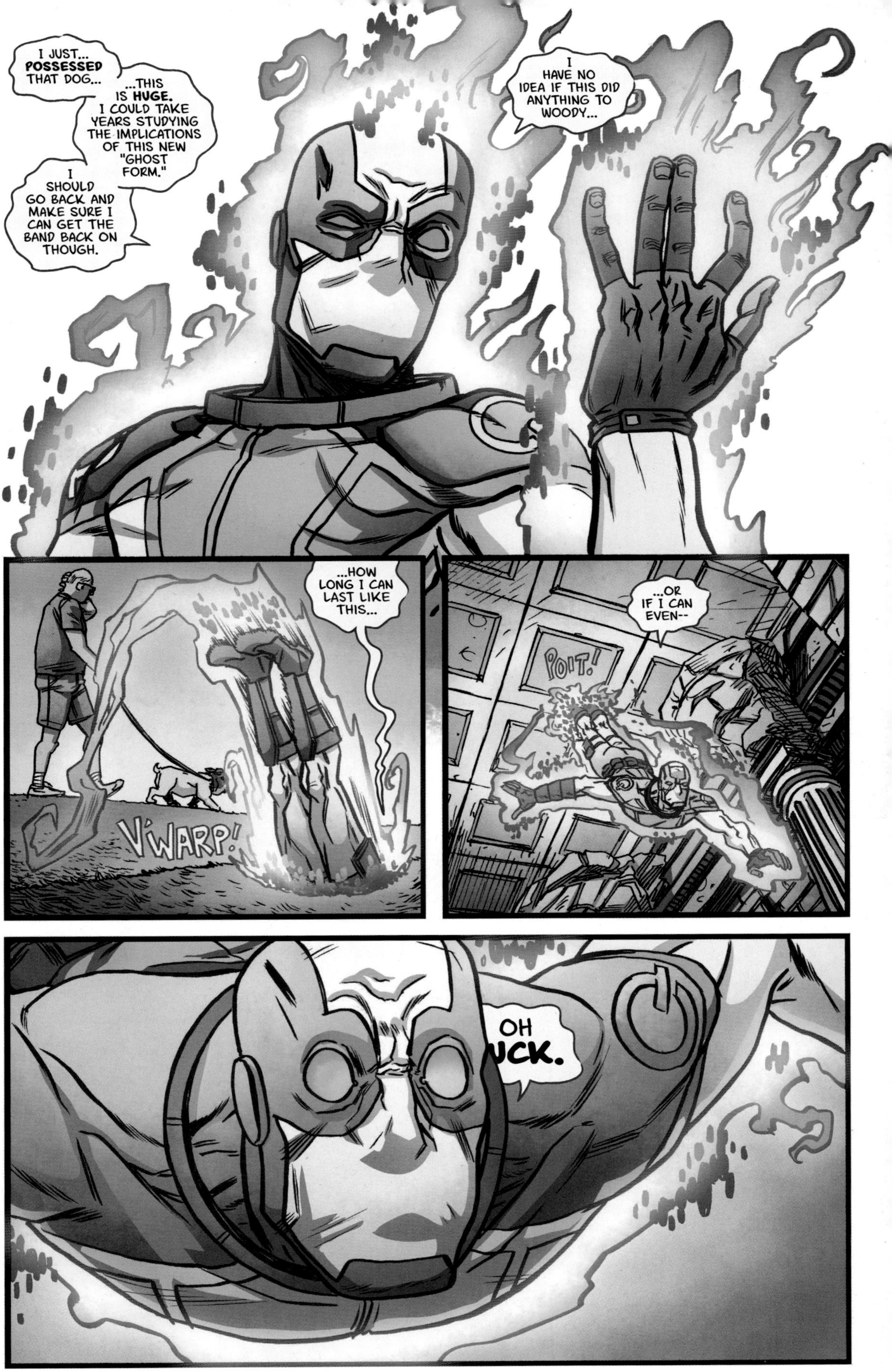
I JUST... POSSESSED THAT DOG...
...THIS IS HUGE. I COULD TAKE YEARS STUDYING THE IMPLICATIONS OF THIS NEW "GHOST FORM."
I SHOULD GO BACK AND MAKE SURE I CAN GET THE BAND BACK ON THOUGH.
I HAVE NO IDEA IF THIS DID ANYTHING TO WOODY...
...HOW LONG I CAN LAST LIKE THIS...
V'WARP!
...OR IF I CAN EVEN--
POIT!
OH
UCK.

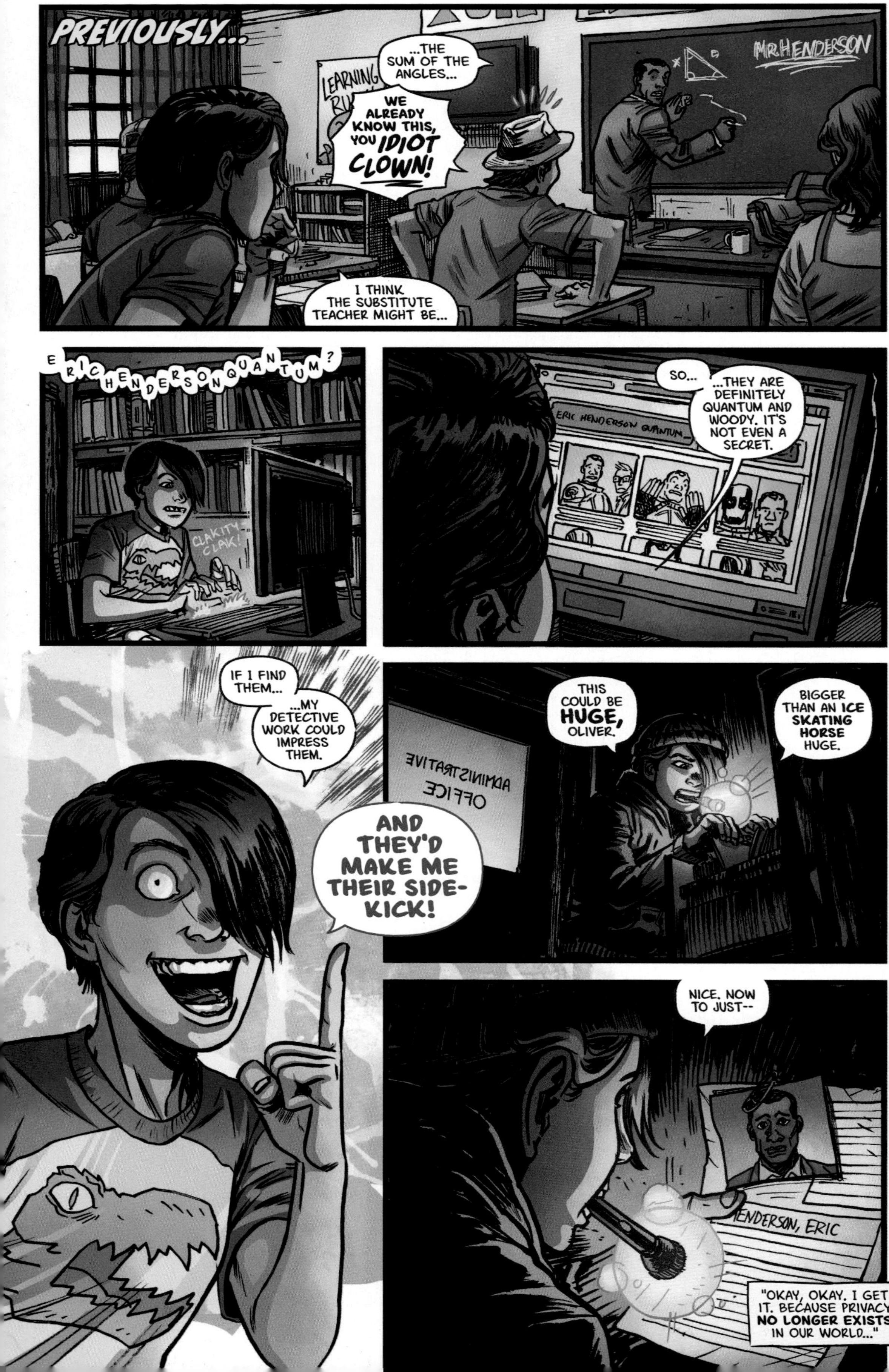
PREVIOUSLY...
...THE SUM OF THE ANGLES...
WE ALREADY KNOW THIS, YOU IDIOT CLOWN!
MR HENDERSON
I THINK THE SUBSTITUTE TEACHER MIGHT BE...
ERIC HENDERSON QUANTUM?
CLAKITY-CLAK!
SO...
...THEY ARE DEFINITELY QUANTUM AND WOODY. IT'S NOT EVEN A SECRET.
ERIC HENDERSON QUANTUM
IF I FIND THEM...
...MY DETECTIVE WORK COULD IMPRESS THEM.
AND THEY'D MAKE ME THEIR SIDE-KICK!
ADMINISTRATIVE OFFICE
THIS COULD BE HUGE, OLIVER.
BIGGER THAN AN ICE SKATING HORSE HUGE.
NICE. NOW TO JUST--
HENDERSON, ERIC
"OKAY, OKAY. I GET IT. BECAUSE PRIVACY NO LONGER EXISTS IN OUR WORLD..."

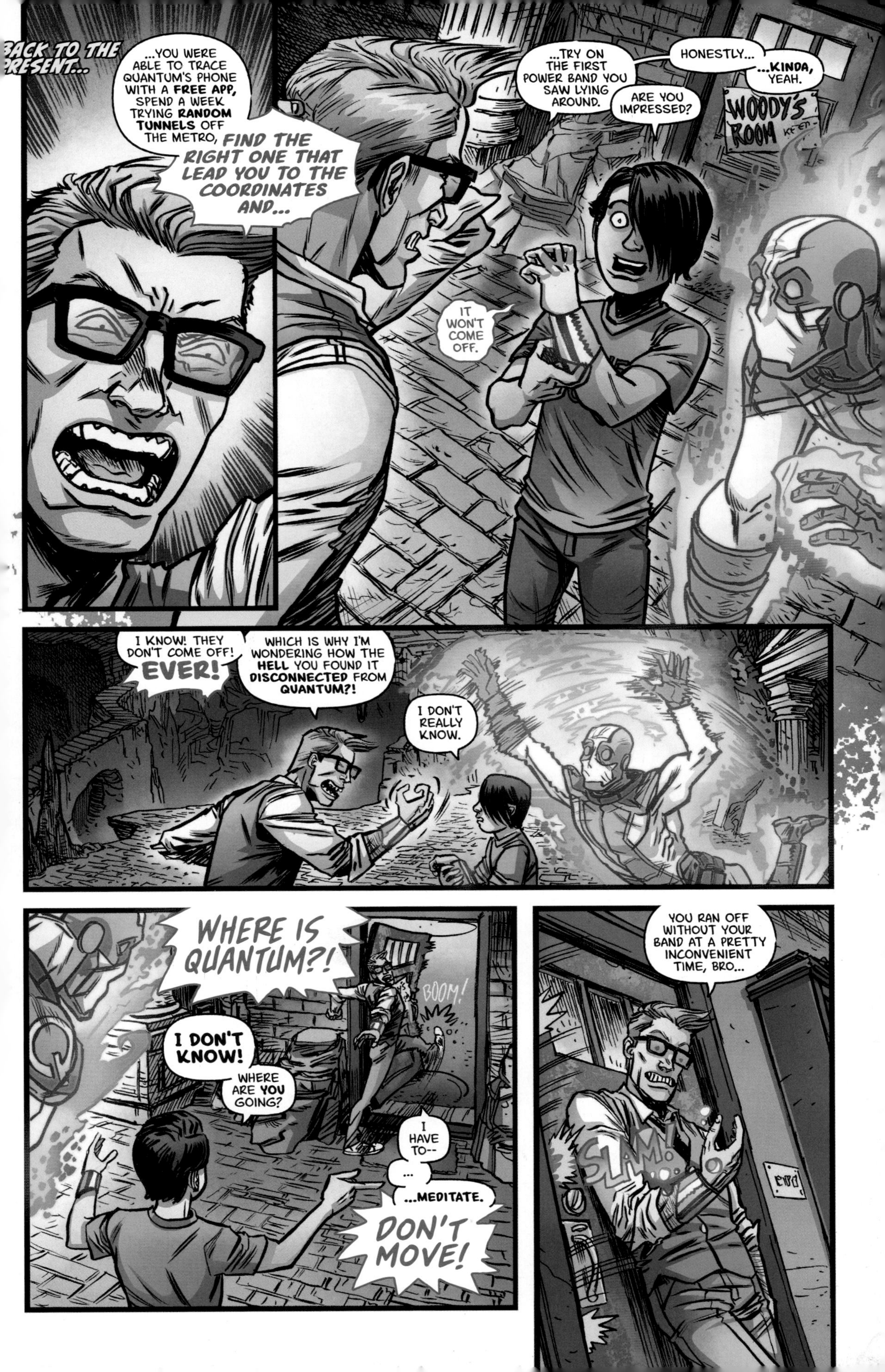
BACK TO THE PRESENT...
...YOU WERE ABLE TO TRACE QUANTUM'S PHONE WITH A FREE APP, SPEND A WEEK TRYING RANDOM TUNNELS OFF THE METRO, FIND THE RIGHT ONE THAT LEAD YOU TO THE COORDINATES AND...
...TRY ON THE FIRST POWER BAND YOU SAW LYING AROUND.
ARE YOU IMPRESSED?
HONESTLY...
...KINDA, YEAH.
WOODY'S ROOM
IT WON'T COME OFF.
I KNOW! THEY DON'T COME OFF! EVER!
WHICH IS WHY I'M WONDERING HOW THE HELL YOU FOUND IT DISCONNECTED FROM QUANTUM?!
I DON'T REALLY KNOW.
WHERE IS QUANTUM?!
I DON'T KNOW!
WHERE ARE YOU GOING?
BOOM!
I HAVE TO--
...
...MEDITATE.
DON'T MOVE!
YOU RAN OFF WITHOUT YOUR BAND AT A PRETTY INCONVENIENT TIME, BRO...
SLAM!

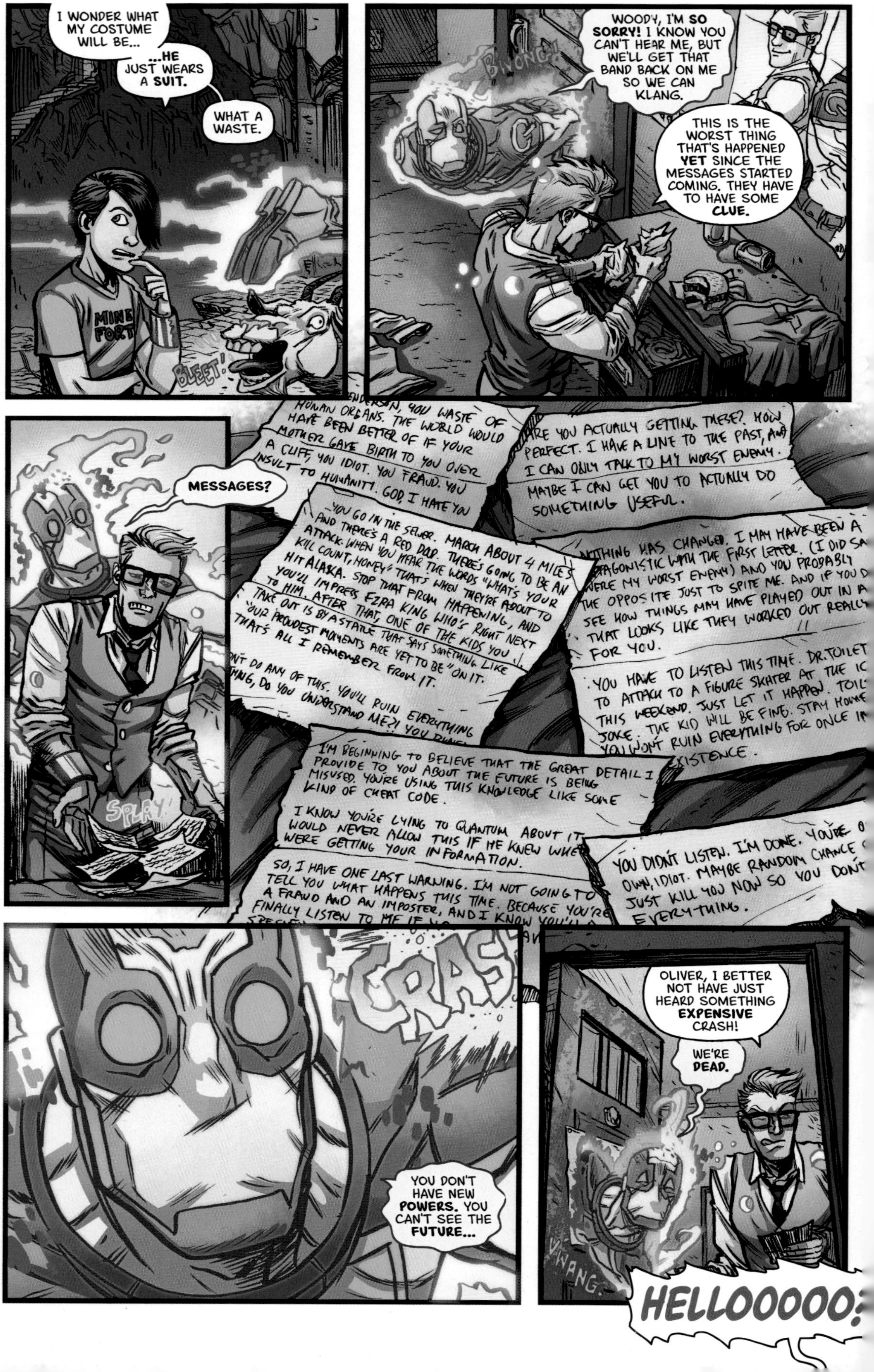

I WONDER WHAT MY COSTUME WILL BE...
...HE JUST WEARS A **SUIT.**
WHAT A WASTE.
BLEET!
BWONG!
WOODY, I'M **SO SORRY!** I KNOW YOU CAN'T HEAR ME, BUT WE'LL GET THAT BAND BACK ON ME SO WE CAN KLANG.
THIS IS THE WORST THING THAT'S HAPPENED **YET** SINCE THE MESSAGES STARTED COMING. THEY HAVE TO HAVE SOME **CLUE.**
MESSAGES?
SPLAY
HUMAN ORGANS. THE WORLD WOULD HAVE BEEN BETTER OF IF YOUR MOTHER GAVE BIRTH TO YOU OVER A CLIFF, YOU IDIOT. YOU FRAUD. YOU INSULT TO HUMANITY. GOD, I HATE YOU
ARE YOU ACTUALLY GETTING THESE? HOW PERFECT. I HAVE A LINE TO THE PAST, AND I CAN ONLY TALK TO MY WORST ENEMY. MAYBE I CAN GET YOU TO ACTUALLY DO SOMETHING USEFUL.
...YOU GO IN THE SEWER. MARCH ABOUT 4 MILES AND THERE'S A RED DOOR. THERE'S GOING TO BE AN ATTACK. WHEN YOU HEAR THE WORDS "WHAT'S YOUR KILL COUNT, HONEY," THAT'S WHEN THEY'RE ABOUT TO HIT ALASKA. STOP THAT FROM HAPPENING, AND YOU'LL IMPRESS EZRA KING WHO'S RIGHT NEXT TO HIM. AFTER THAT, ONE OF THE KIDS YOU TAKE OUT IS BY A STATUE THAT SAYS SOMETHING LIKE "OUR PROUDEST MOMENTS ARE YET TO BE" ON IT. THAT'S ALL I REMEMBER FROM IT.
NOTHING HAS CHANGED. I MAY HAVE BEEN A ...AGONISTIC WITH THE FIRST LETTER (I DID SA... WERE MY WORST ENEMY) AND YOU PROBABLY ...THE OPPOSITE JUST TO SPITE ME. AND IF YOU D... SEE HOW THINGS MAY HAVE PLAYED OUT IN A... THAT LOOKS LIKE THEY WORKED OUT REALLY ... FOR YOU.
...DON'T DO ANY OF THIS. YOU'LL RUIN EVERYTHING ...THING, DO YOU UNDERSTAND ME?! YOU...
YOU HAVE TO LISTEN THIS TIME. DR. TOILET... TO ATTACK TO A FIGURE SKATER AT THE IC... THIS WEEKEND. JUST LET IT HAPPEN. TOIL... JOKE. THE KID WILL BE FINE. STAY HOME... YOU WON'T RUIN EVERYTHING FOR ONCE IN ... EXISTENCE.
I'M BEGINNING TO BELIEVE THAT THE GREAT DETAIL I PROVIDE TO YOU ABOUT THE FUTURE IS BEING MISUSED. YOU'RE USING THIS KNOWLEDGE LIKE SOME KIND OF CHEAT CODE.
I KNOW YOU'RE LYING TO QUANTUM ABOUT IT... WOULD NEVER ALLOW THIS IF HE KNEW WHE... WERE GETTING YOUR INFORMATION.
SO, I HAVE ONE LAST WARNING. I'M NOT GOING TO TELL YOU WHAT HAPPENS THIS TIME. BECAUSE YOU'RE A FRAUD AND AN IMPOSTER, AND I KNOW YOU'LL FINALLY LISTEN TO ME IF...
YOU DIDN'T LISTEN. I'M DONE. YOU'RE ... OWN, IDIOT. MAYBE RANDOM CHANCE ... JUST KILL YOU NOW SO YOU DON'T ... EVERYTHING.
CRASH
YOU DON'T HAVE NEW **POWERS.** YOU CAN'T SEE THE **FUTURE...**
OLIVER, I BETTER NOT HAVE JUST HEARD SOMETHING **EXPENSIVE** CRASH!
WE'RE **DEAD.**
VWANG
HELLOOOOO?

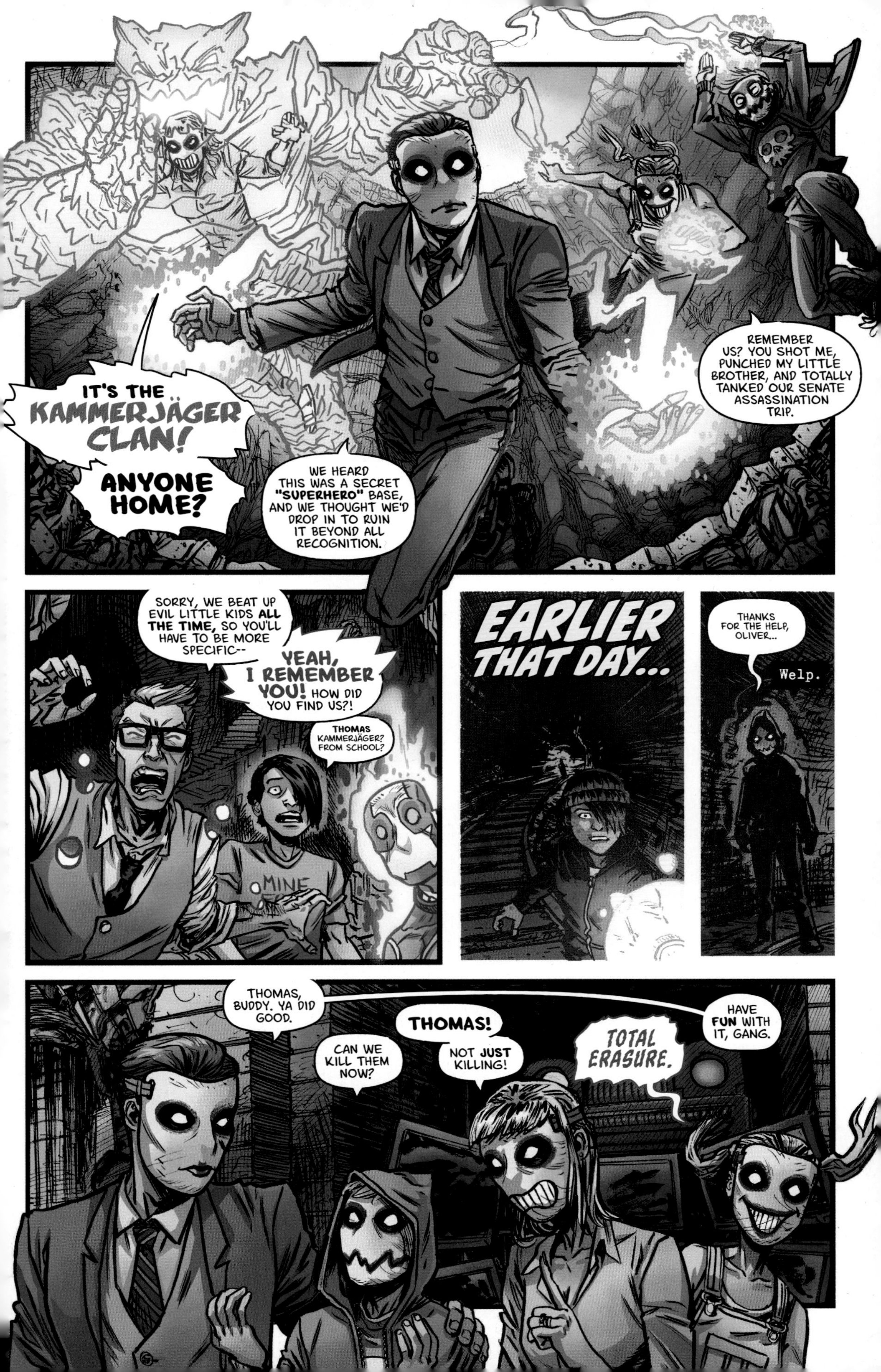

IT'S THE KAMMERJÄGER CLAN!
ANYONE HOME?
WE HEARD THIS WAS A SECRET "SUPERHERO" BASE, AND WE THOUGHT WE'D DROP IN TO RUIN IT BEYOND ALL RECOGNITION.
REMEMBER US? YOU SHOT ME, PUNCHED MY LITTLE BROTHER, AND TOTALLY TANKED OUR SENATE ASSASSINATION TRIP.
SORRY, WE BEAT UP EVIL LITTLE KIDS ALL THE TIME, SO YOU'LL HAVE TO BE MORE SPECIFIC--
YEAH, I REMEMBER YOU! HOW DID YOU FIND US?!
THOMAS KAMMERJÄGER? FROM SCHOOL?
EARLIER THAT DAY...
THANKS FOR THE HELP, OLIVER...
Welp.
THOMAS, BUDDY. YA DID GOOD.
CAN WE KILL THEM NOW?
THOMAS!
NOT JUST KILLING!
TOTAL ERASURE.
HAVE FUN WITH IT, GANG.

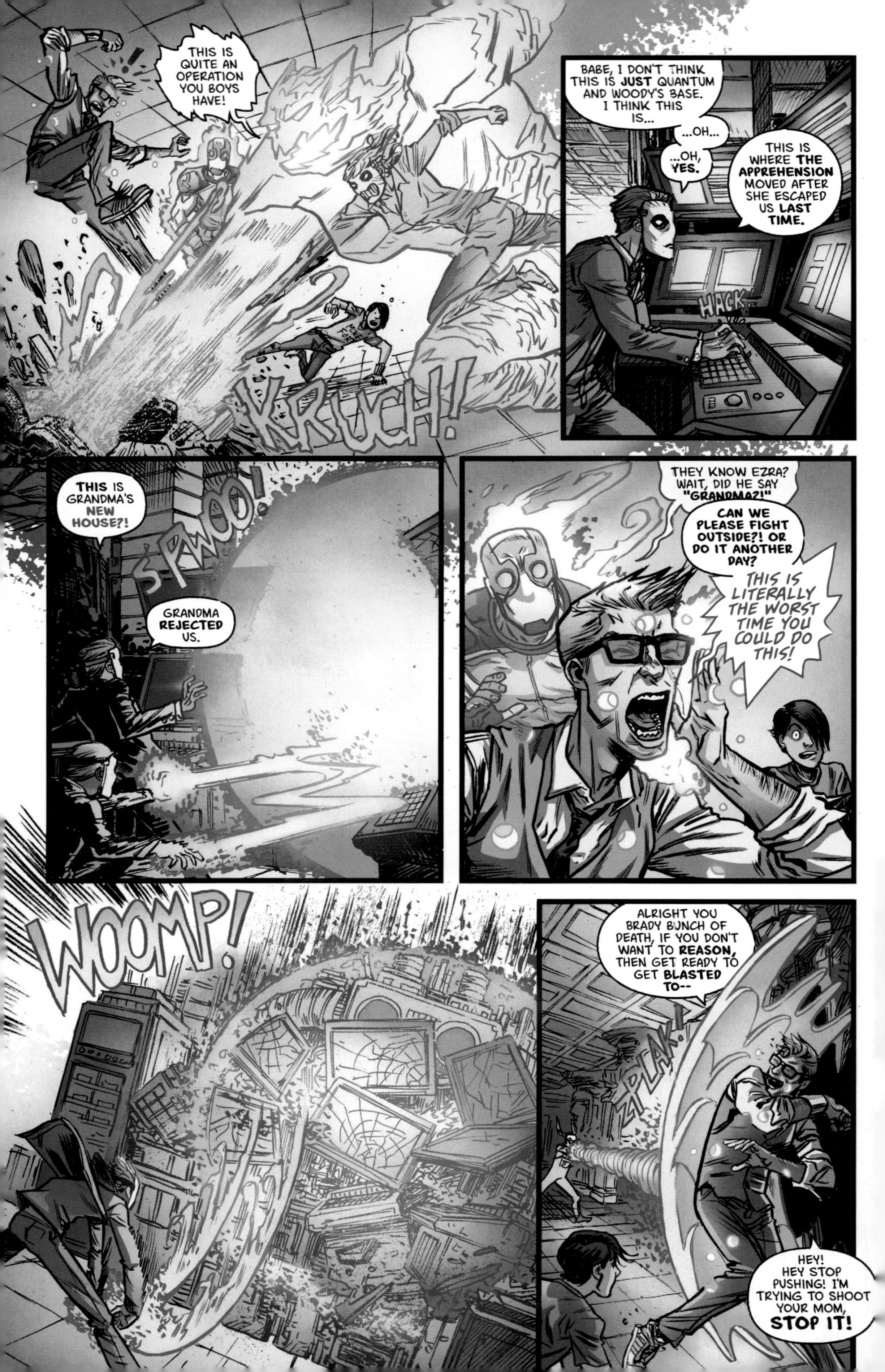
THIS IS QUITE AN OPERATION YOU BOYS HAVE!
KRUCH!
BABE, I DON'T THINK THIS IS JUST QUANTUM AND WOODY'S BASE. I THINK THIS IS...
...OH...
...OH, YES.
THIS IS WHERE THE APPREHENSION MOVED AFTER SHE ESCAPED US LAST TIME.
HACK
THIS IS GRANDMA'S NEW HOUSE?!
SPWOO!
GRANDMA REJECTED US.
THEY KNOW EZRA? WAIT, DID HE SAY "GRANDMA?!"
CAN WE PLEASE FIGHT OUTSIDE?! OR DO IT ANOTHER DAY?
THIS IS LITERALLY THE WORST TIME YOU COULD DO THIS!
WOOMP!
ALRIGHT YOU BRADY BUNCH OF DEATH, IF YOU DON'T WANT TO REASON, THEN GET READY TO GET BLASTED TO--
ZPLAK!
HEY! HEY STOP PUSHING! I'M TRYING TO SHOOT YOUR MOM, STOP IT!

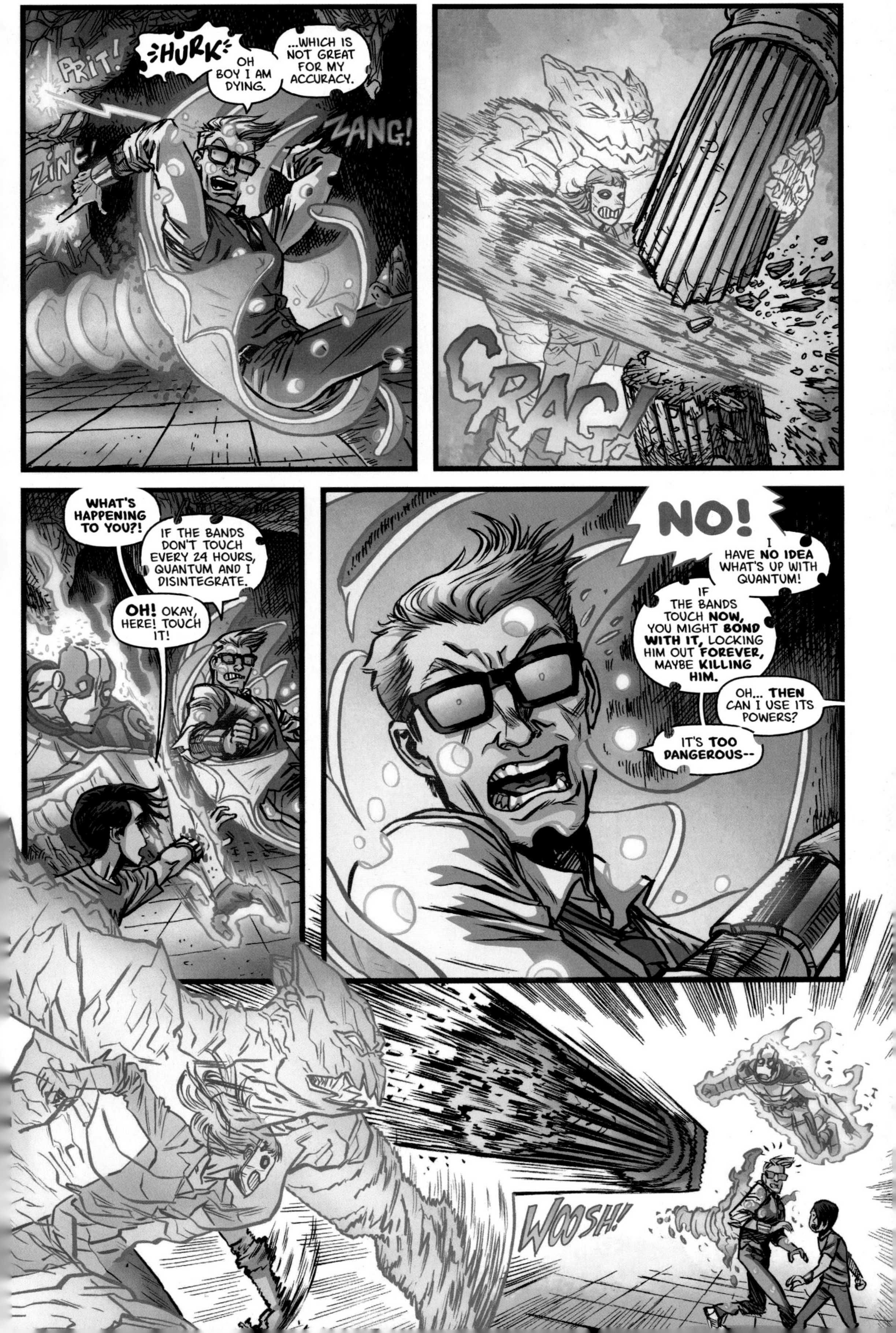
PRIT!
HURK
OH BOY I AM DYING.
...WHICH IS NOT GREAT FOR MY ACCURACY.
ZING!
ZANG!
CRACK!
WHAT'S HAPPENING TO YOU?!
IF THE BANDS DON'T TOUCH EVERY 24 HOURS, QUANTUM AND I DISINTEGRATE.
OH! OKAY, HERE! TOUCH IT!
NO!
I HAVE NO IDEA WHAT'S UP WITH QUANTUM!
IF THE BANDS TOUCH NOW, YOU MIGHT BOND WITH IT, LOCKING HIM OUT FOREVER, MAYBE KILLING HIM.
OH... THEN CAN I USE ITS POWERS?
IT'S TOO DANGEROUS--
WOOSH!

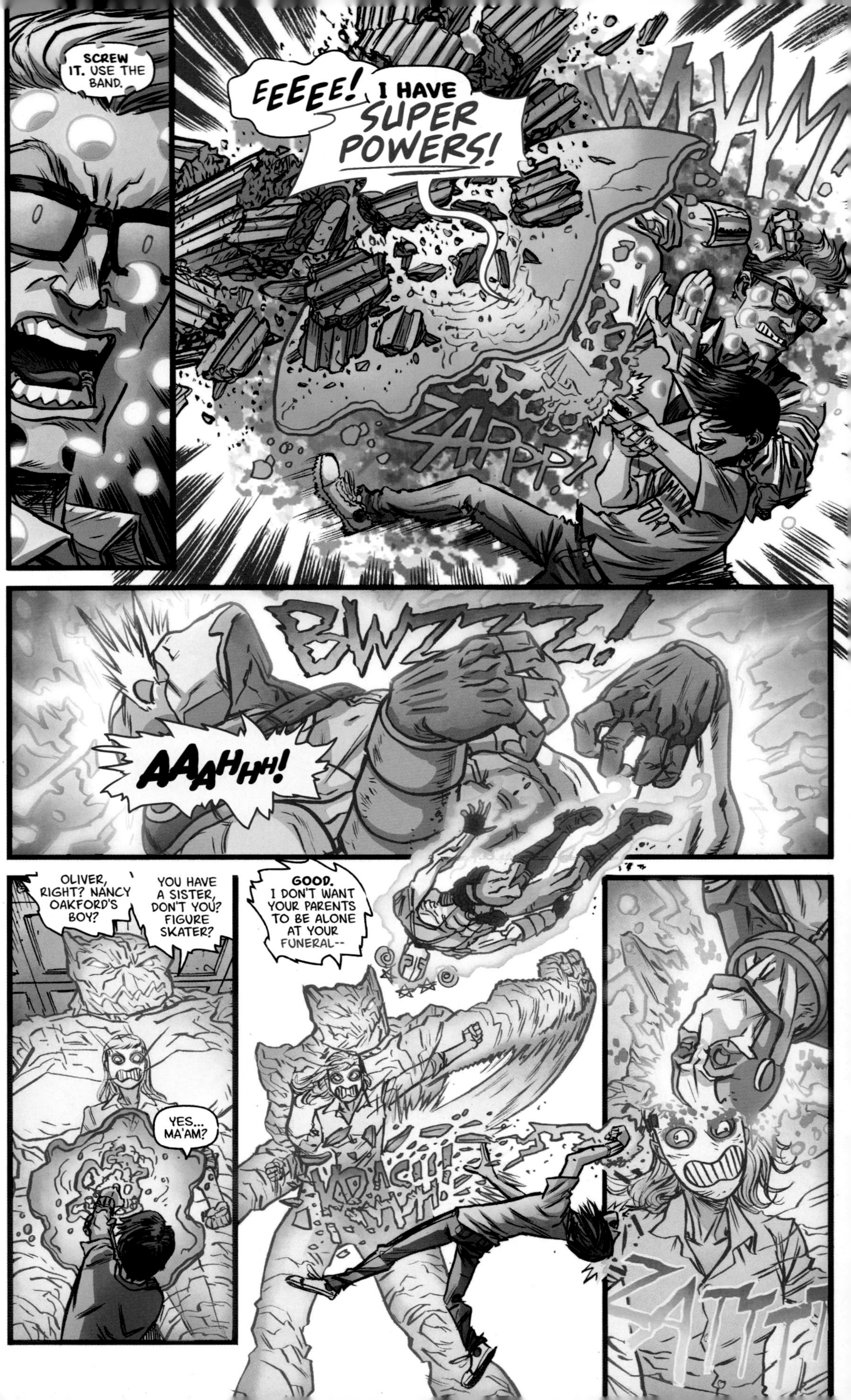
SCREW IT. USE THE BAND.
EEEEE! I HAVE SUPER POWERS!
WHAM!
ZAPP!
BWZZZZ!
AAAHHH!
OLIVER, RIGHT? NANCY OAKFORD'S BOY?
YES... MA'AM?
YOU HAVE A SISTER, DON'T YOU? FIGURE SKATER?
GOOD. I DON'T WANT YOUR PARENTS TO BE ALONE AT YOUR FUNERAL--

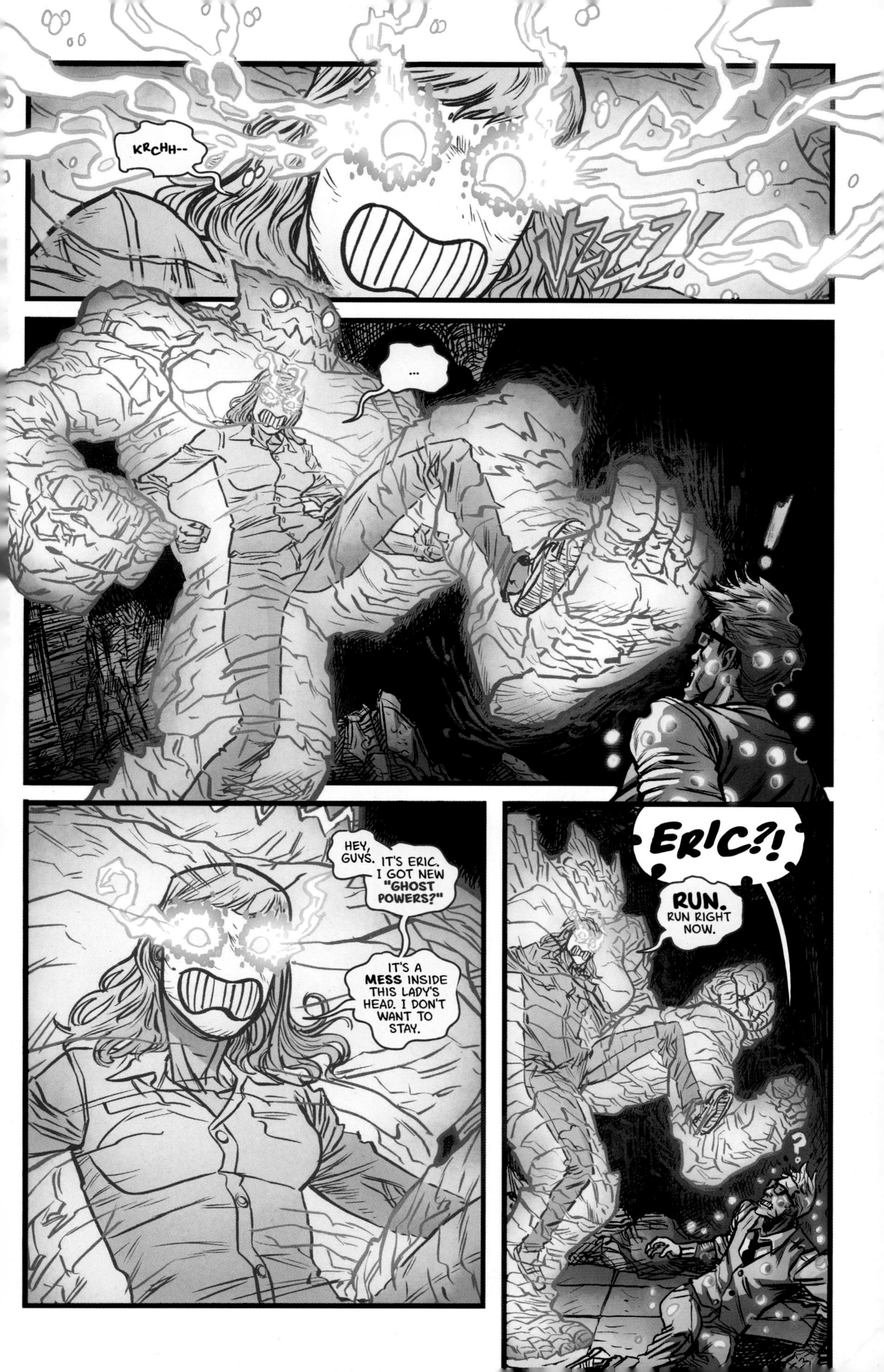
KRCHH--
VZZZ!
...
!
HEY, GUYS. IT'S ERIC. I GOT NEW "GHOST POWERS?"
IT'S A MESS INSIDE THIS LADY'S HEAD. I DON'T WANT TO STAY.
ERIC?!
RUN. RUN RIGHT NOW.
?

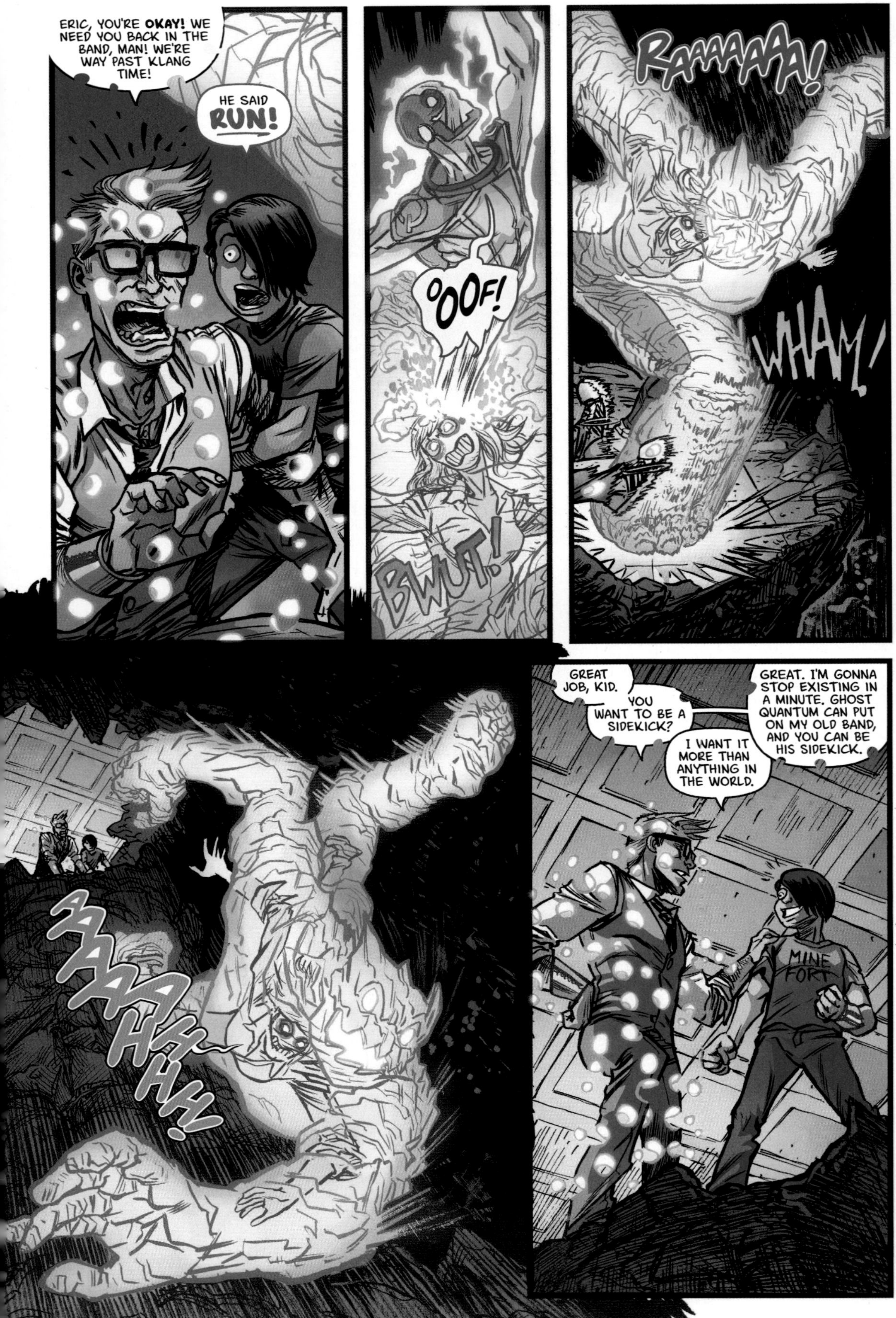
ERIC, YOU'RE OKAY! WE NEED YOU BACK IN THE BAND, MAN! WE'RE WAY PAST KLANG TIME!
HE SAID RUN!
OOF!
BWUT!
RAAAAAAA!
WHAM!
AAAAHHHHH!
GREAT JOB, KID.
YOU WANT TO BE A SIDEKICK?
I WANT IT MORE THAN ANYTHING IN THE WORLD.
GREAT. I'M GONNA STOP EXISTING IN A MINUTE. GHOST QUANTUM CAN PUT ON MY OLD BAND, AND YOU CAN BE HIS SIDEKICK.
MINE FORT

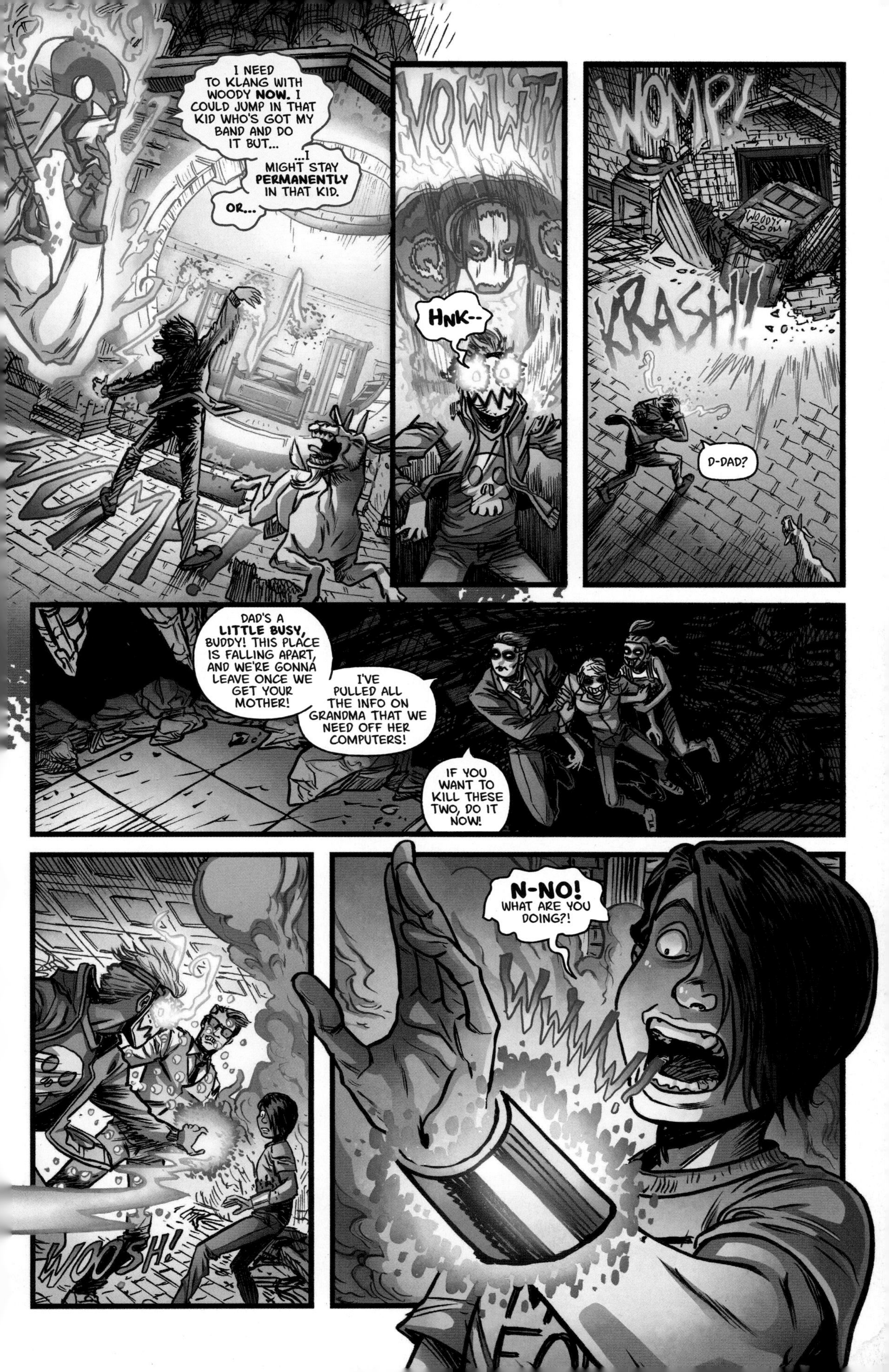
I NEED TO KLANG WITH WOODY NOW. I COULD JUMP IN THAT KID WHO'S GOT MY BAND AND DO IT BUT...
...I MIGHT STAY PERMANENTLY IN THAT KID.
OR...
WOMP!
VOWWH!
HNK--
WOMP!
WOODY'S ROOM
KRASH!!
D-DAD?
DAD'S A LITTLE BUSY, BUDDY! THIS PLACE IS FALLING APART, AND WE'RE GONNA LEAVE ONCE WE GET YOUR MOTHER!
I'VE PULLED ALL THE INFO ON GRANDMA THAT WE NEED OFF HER COMPUTERS!
IF YOU WANT TO KILL THESE TWO, DO IT NOW!
WOOSH!
N-NO! WHAT ARE YOU DOING?!

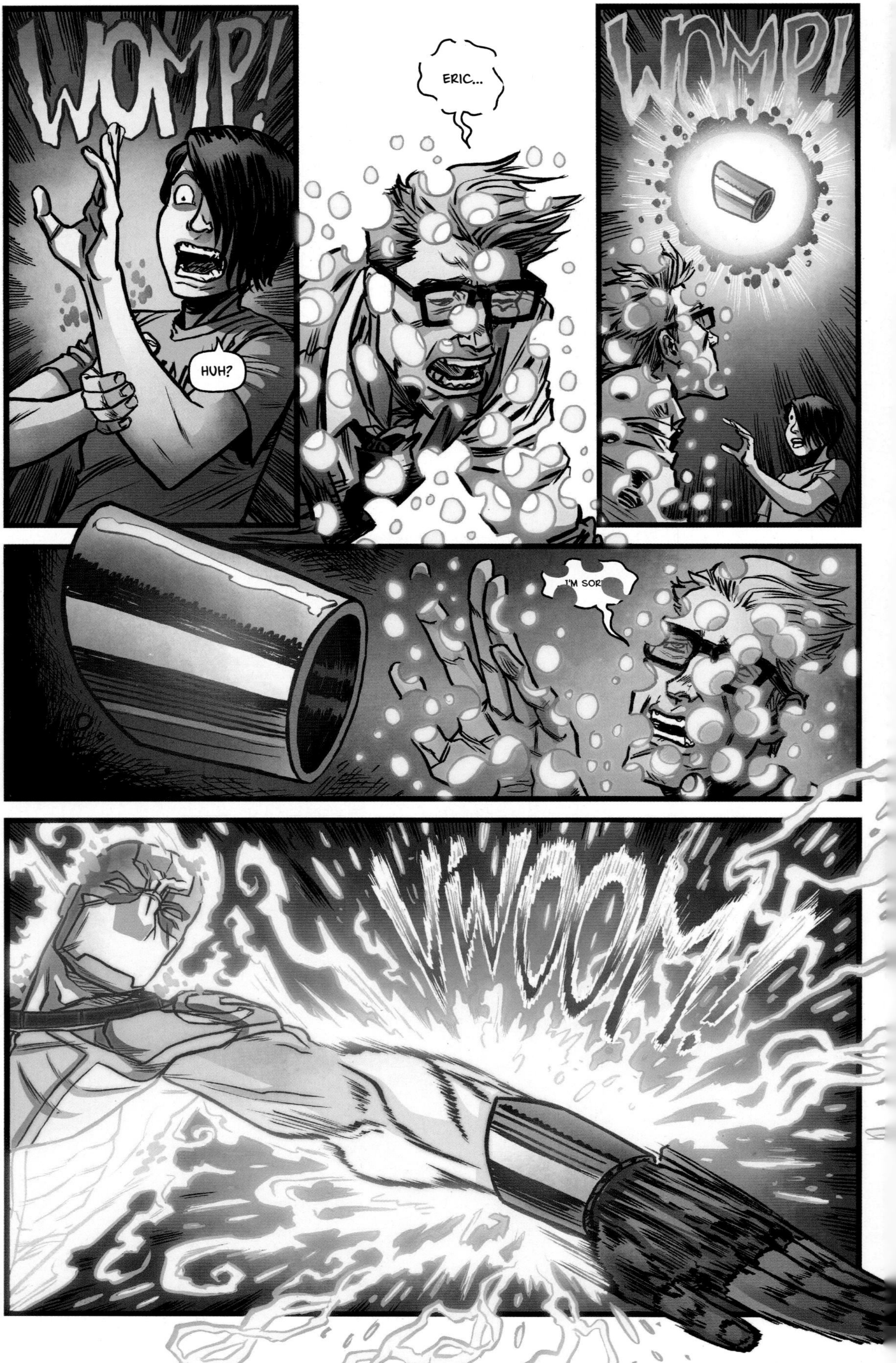
WOMP!
HUH?
ERIC...
WOMP!
I'M SOR
WHOOM!

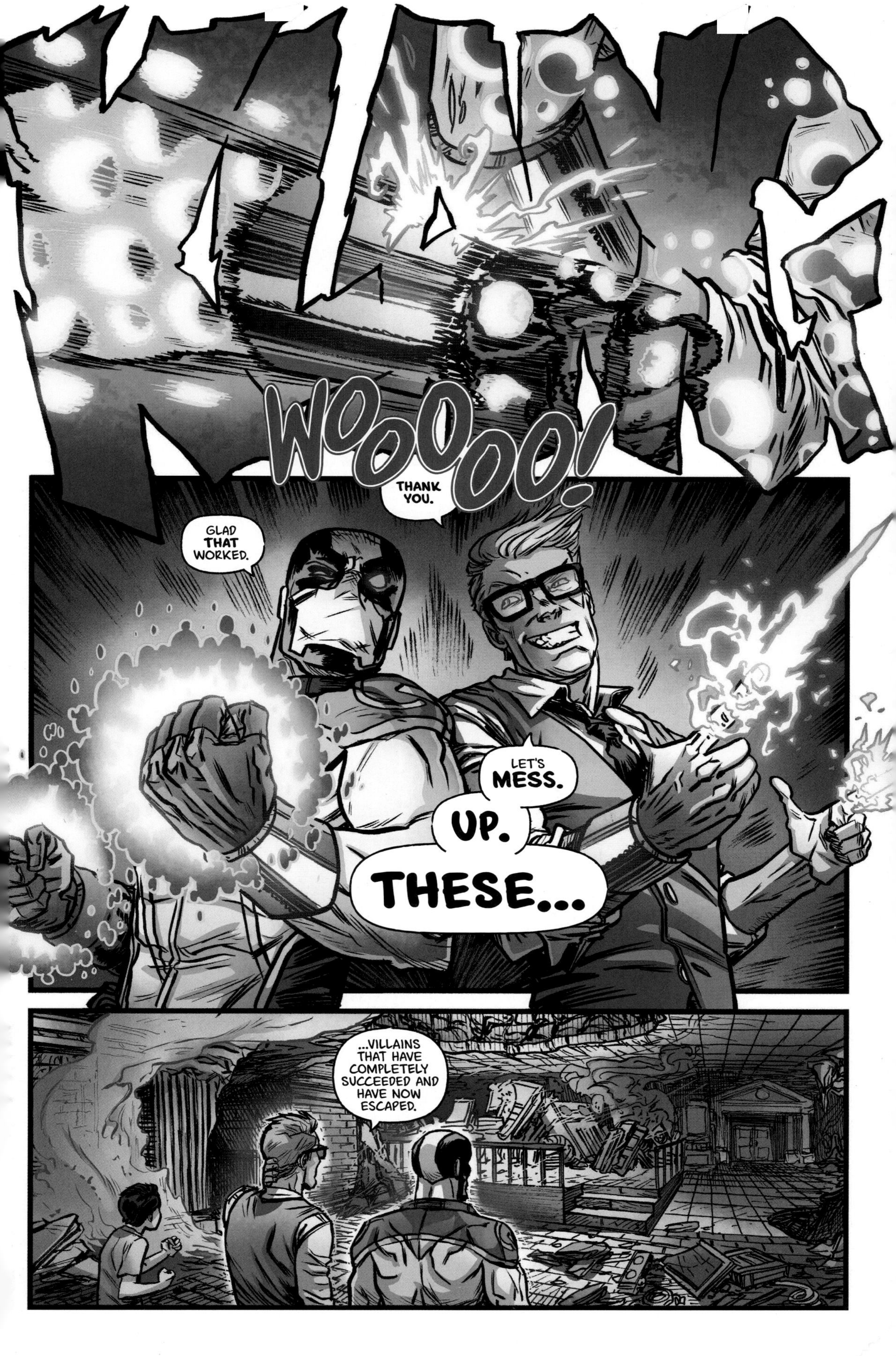
WOOOOO!
THANK YOU.
GLAD THAT WORKED.
LET'S MESS.
UP.
THESE...
...VILLAINS THAT HAVE COMPLETELY SUCCEEDED AND HAVE NOW ESCAPED.

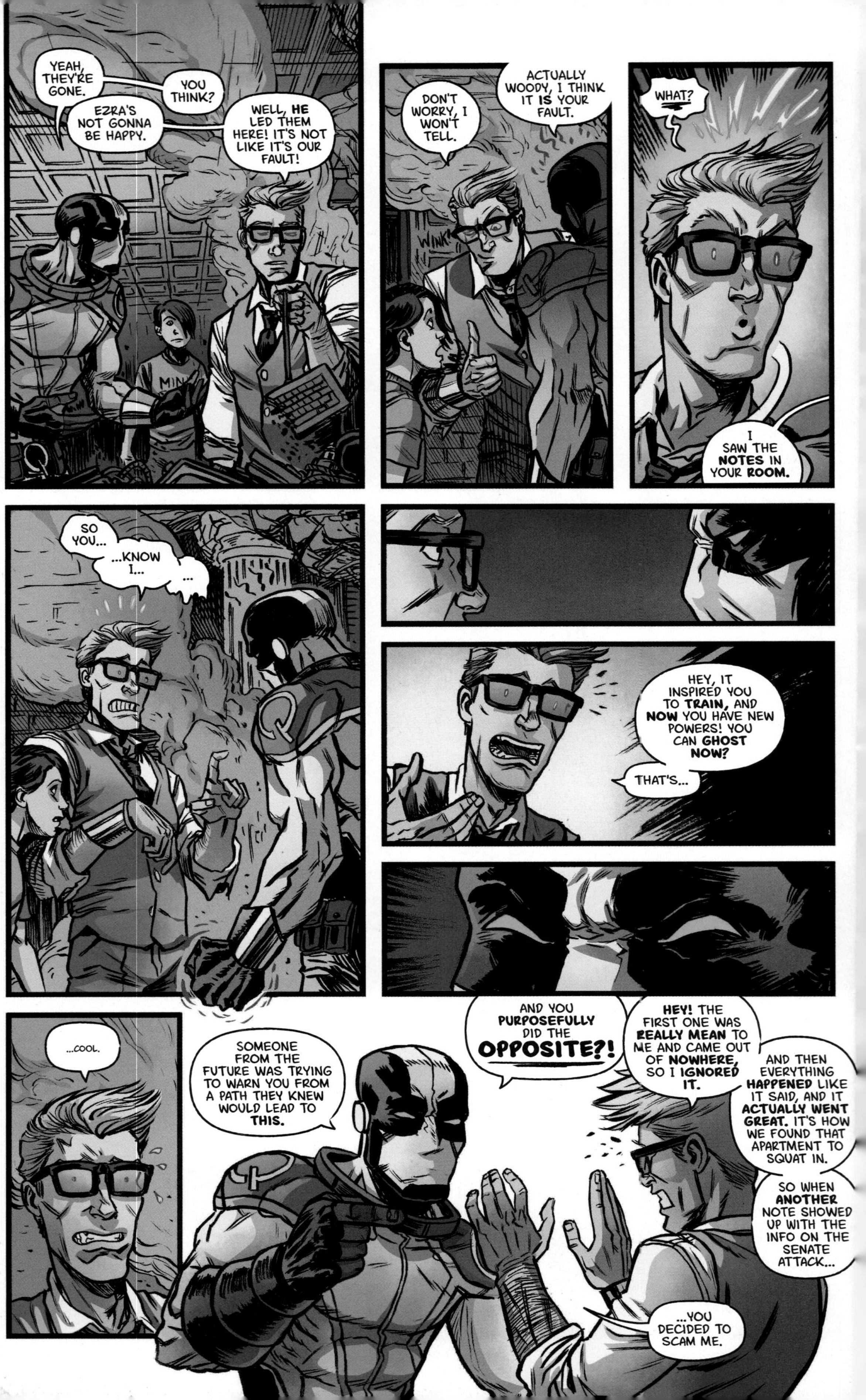
YEAH, THEY'RE GONE.
YOU THINK?
EZRA'S NOT GONNA BE HAPPY.
WELL, HE LED THEM HERE! IT'S NOT LIKE IT'S OUR FAULT!
DON'T WORRY, I WON'T TELL.
ACTUALLY WOODY, I THINK IT IS YOUR FAULT.
WINK
WHAT?
I SAW THE NOTES IN YOUR ROOM.
SO YOU...
...KNOW I...
...
HEY, IT INSPIRED YOU TO TRAIN, AND NOW YOU HAVE NEW POWERS! YOU CAN GHOST NOW?
THAT'S...
...COOL.
SOMEONE FROM THE FUTURE WAS TRYING TO WARN YOU FROM A PATH THEY KNEW WOULD LEAD TO THIS.
AND YOU PURPOSEFULLY DID THE OPPOSITE?!
HEY! THE FIRST ONE WAS REALLY MEAN TO ME AND CAME OUT OF NOWHERE, SO I IGNORED IT.
AND THEN EVERYTHING HAPPENED LIKE IT SAID, AND IT ACTUALLY WENT GREAT. IT'S HOW WE FOUND THAT APARTMENT TO SQUAT IN.
SO WHEN ANOTHER NOTE SHOWED UP WITH THE INFO ON THE SENATE ATTACK...
...YOU DECIDED TO SCAM ME.

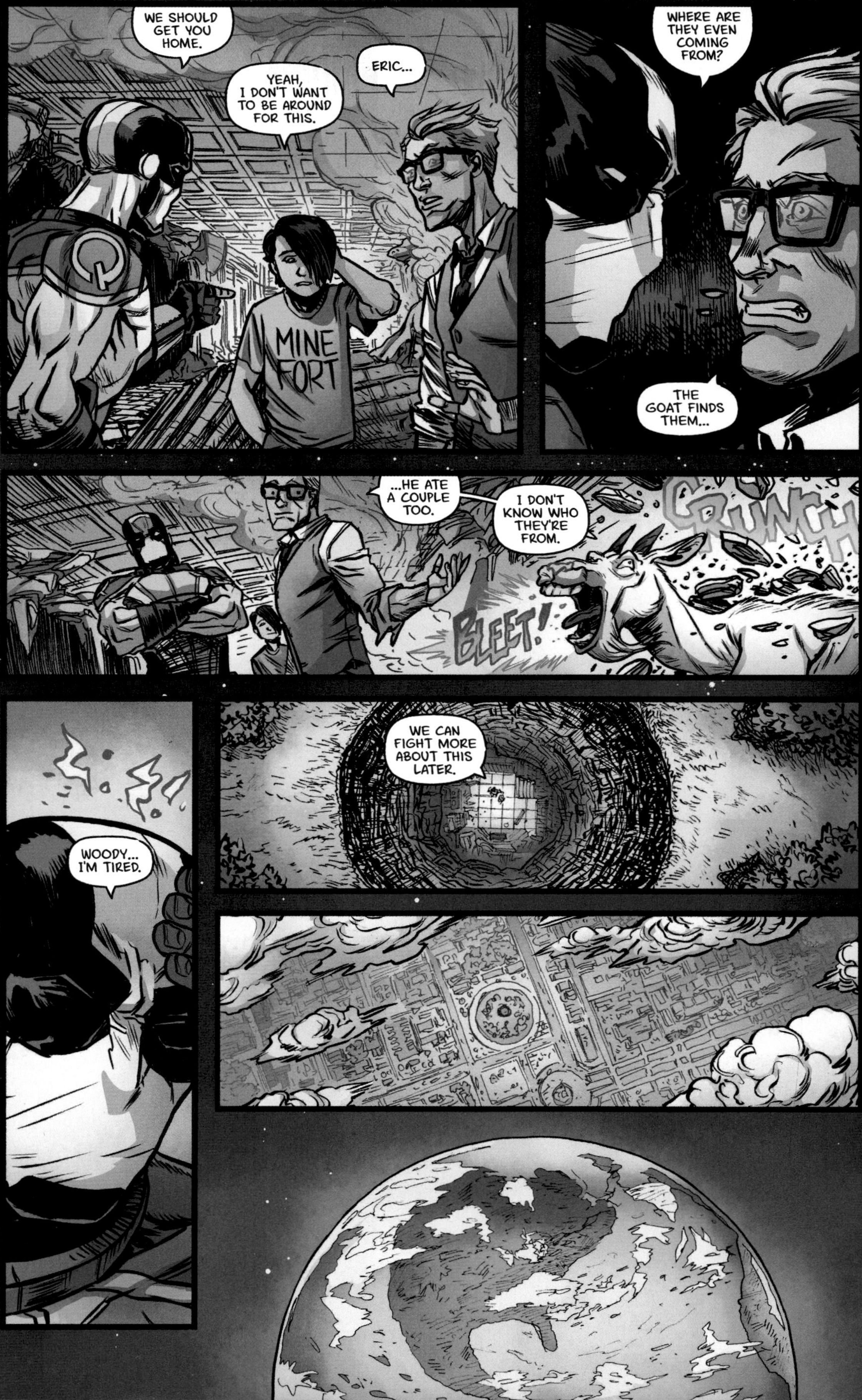
WE SHOULD GET YOU HOME.
YEAH, I DON'T WANT TO BE AROUND FOR THIS.
ERIC...
MINE FORT
WHERE ARE THEY EVEN COMING FROM?
THE GOAT FINDS THEM...
...HE ATE A COUPLE TOO.
I DON'T KNOW WHO THEY'RE FROM.
CRUNCH
BLEET!
WOODY... I'M TIRED.
WE CAN FIGHT MORE ABOUT THIS LATER.

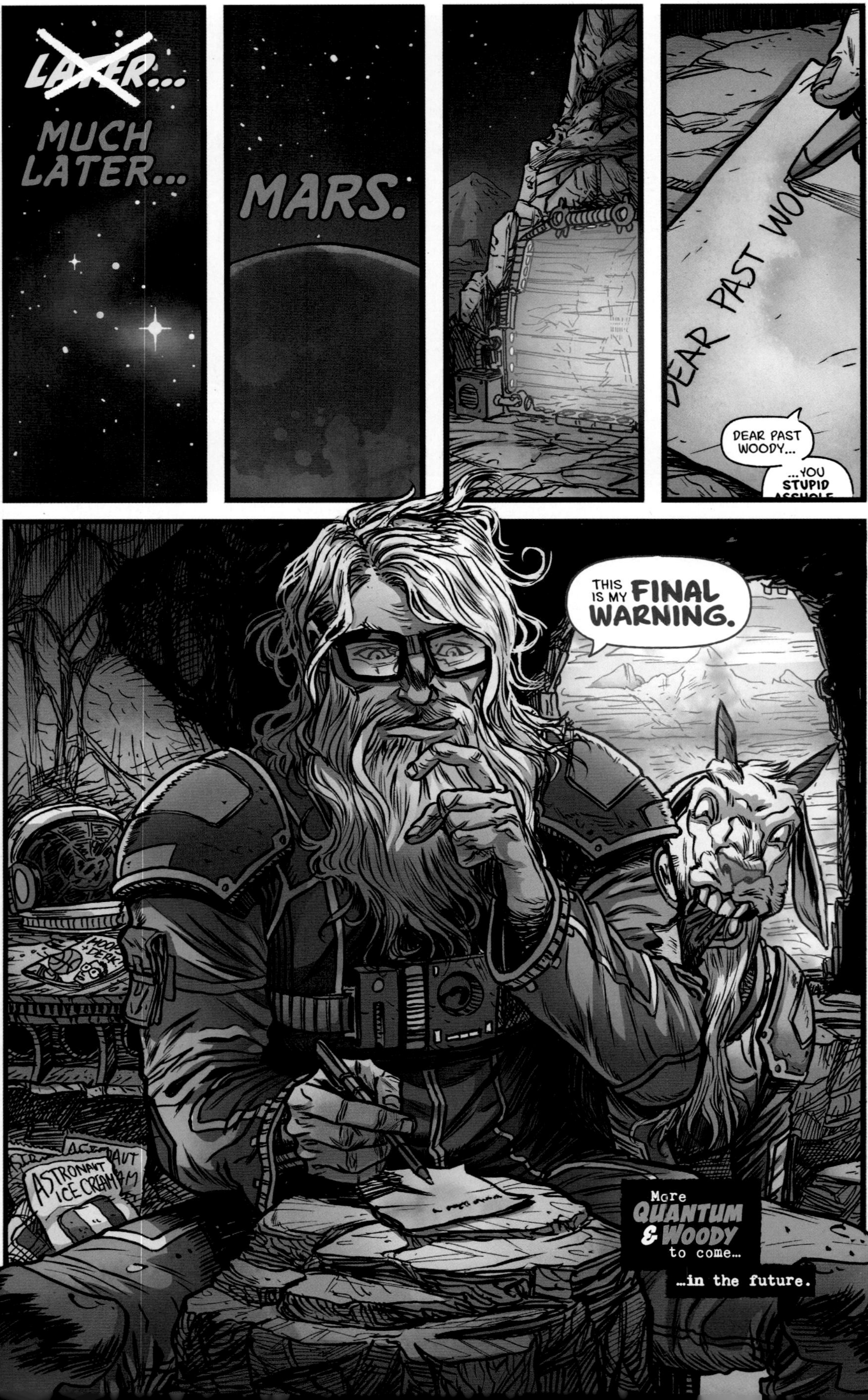

LATER...
MUCH LATER...
MARS.
DEAR PAST WO
DEAR PAST WOODY...
...YOU STUPID
THIS IS MY FINAL WARNING.
ASTRONAUT ICE CREAM
More QUANTUM & WOODY to come...
...in the future.

GALLERY

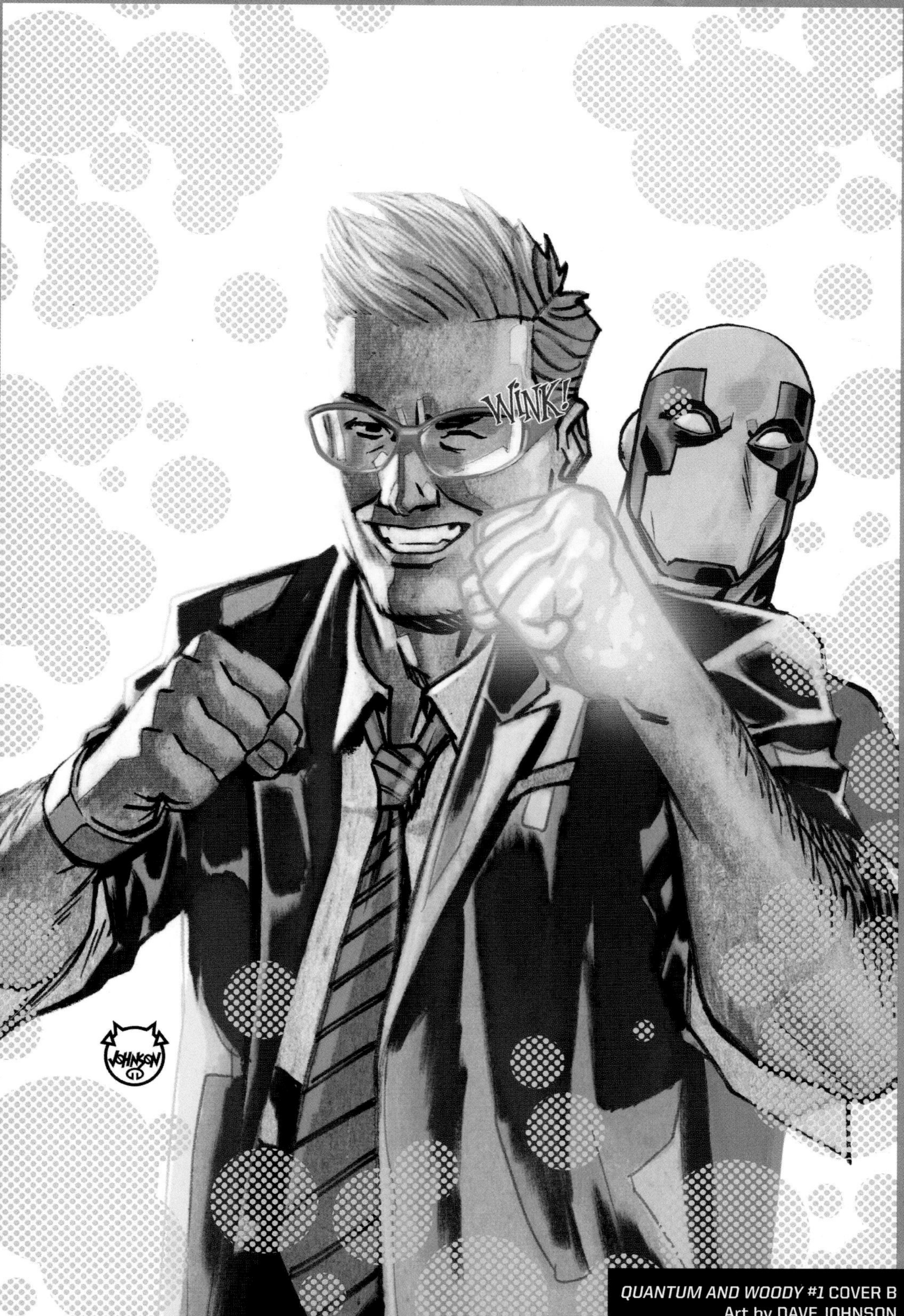
WINK!
JOHNSON

QUANTUM AND WOODY #1 COVER B
Art by DAVE JOHNSON

____
Plural fan group nickname like "Trekkies" or "Whovians" or "Catholics"

Thank you so much for spending your hard earned or stolen money on this first issue of ______________
random scientific term

& ______________. My name is ______________ and I am the ______________
first name that can also be a sexual euphemism — any name on the cover — job title

on this comic.

I have been a ______ of this ______ since ______ and it has been a ______ ______ to get to ______
noun — noun — noun — adjective — mood or feeling — verb

this newest version for 2020. When I first got the job, I had just found out I had ______________ and only
debilitating fictional illness

had seven ______________ to live, and even less to ______. So I ______________ began to brainstorm as much
plural unit of time — verb — adverb ending in 'ly'

as I possibly could about what I wanted to see in my dream version of Quantum and Woody before I died. I discovered

that despite the ______ of ______ stories from previous runs on the characters, there was so much more
unit of time — adjective

I wanted to explore! Super villains who are also just a ______ ______. Super villains who are also ______.
adjective — noun — noun

A new ______. New ______. And since Quantum and Woody have already had at least ______ perfectly
noun — plural noun — any number

good origin stories, I was ready to lay down as many new paths building outward into the future for them, instead of

trying to rewrite the past like you might expect in a ______. But I've done my best to keep to the core of what we love
noun

about Quantum and Woody. They are ______ superheroes that wind up in ______ adventures, but they're also
adjective — adjective

just two ______ trying to figure out their relationship in a ______ world, and you can't help but ______ with them.
plural noun — adjective — verb

Now that I have ______________ this issue, and the other exciting tales that will come after it, I'm ______________
past tense verb — adverb ending in 'y'

to say that my illness is completely cured. In fact, every doctor I've talked to has insisted I never even had it in the

first place. ______________, I guess that's just the magic of comics. These doctors, my spouse, our ______________,
Exclamation — profession

and every single ______________ working at Valiant have advised me not to go on to claim that simply reading this
profession 2

comic might also cure ______________. So I won't do that. But I will write "Wink", like I'm winking at
another fictional disease

you as I write this. And you'll know what that means.

wink

Thanks again for ______________, and I hope you actually wrote the words in this letter, ruining what was
verb ending in "ing"

once a priceless collector's item.

Chris Hastings

Chris Hastings

Originally published in *QUANTUM AND WOODY #1 PRE-ORDER EDITION*

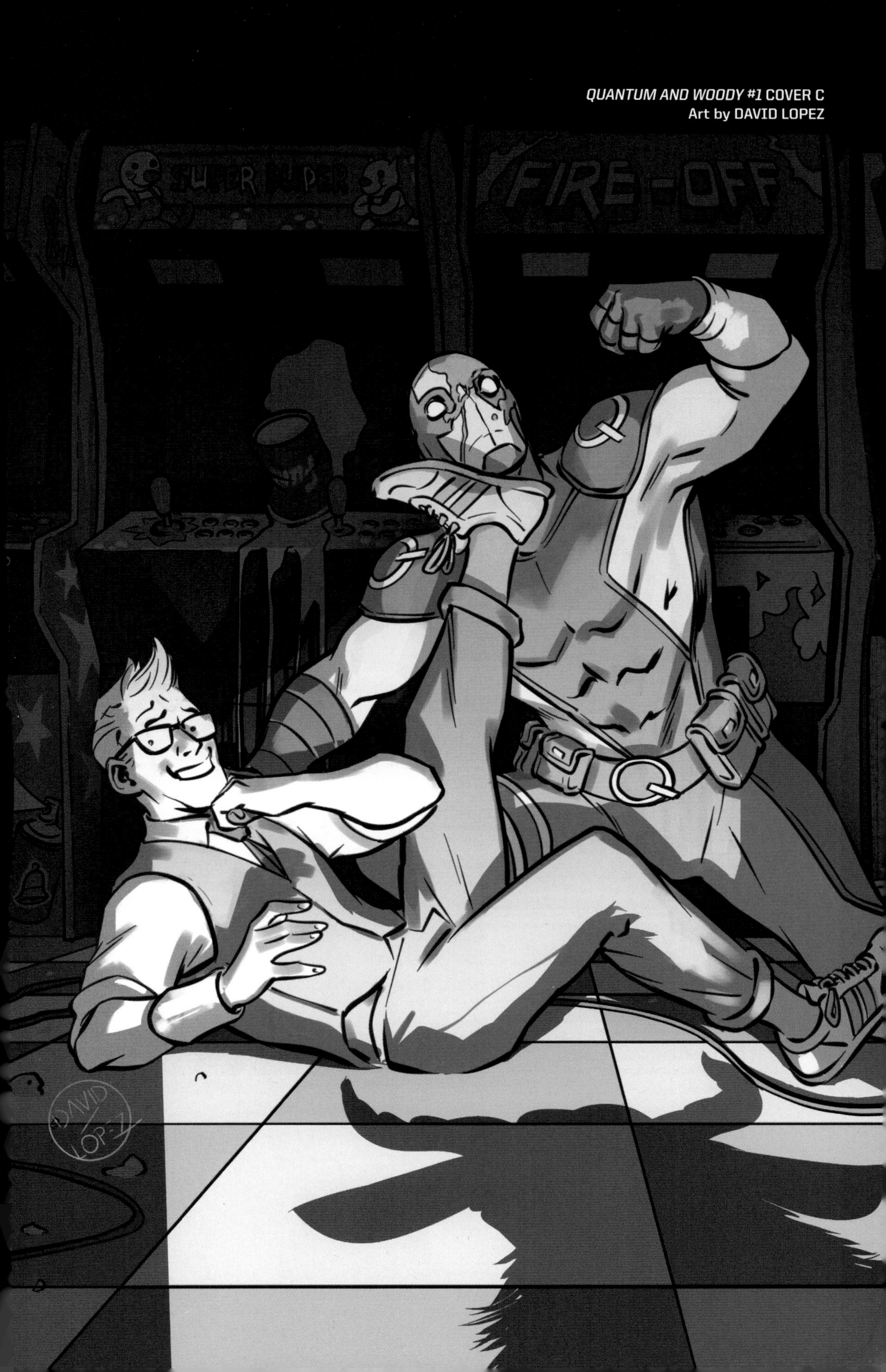
SUPER DUPER
FIRE-OFF

QUANTUM AND WOODY #1 COVER C
Art by DAVID LOPEZ

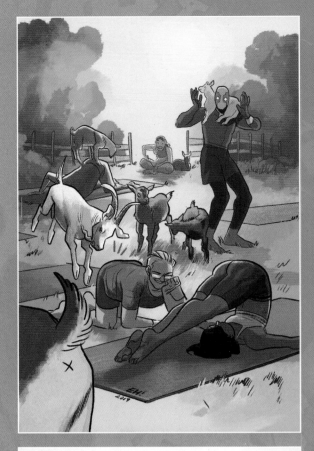

QUANTUM AND WOODY #1 COVER D
Art by ERICA HENDERSON

QUANTUM AND WOODY #2 COVER C
Art by REILLY BROWN with JIM CHARALAMPIDIS

QUANTUM AND WOODY #2 COVER B
Art by JOE QUINONES

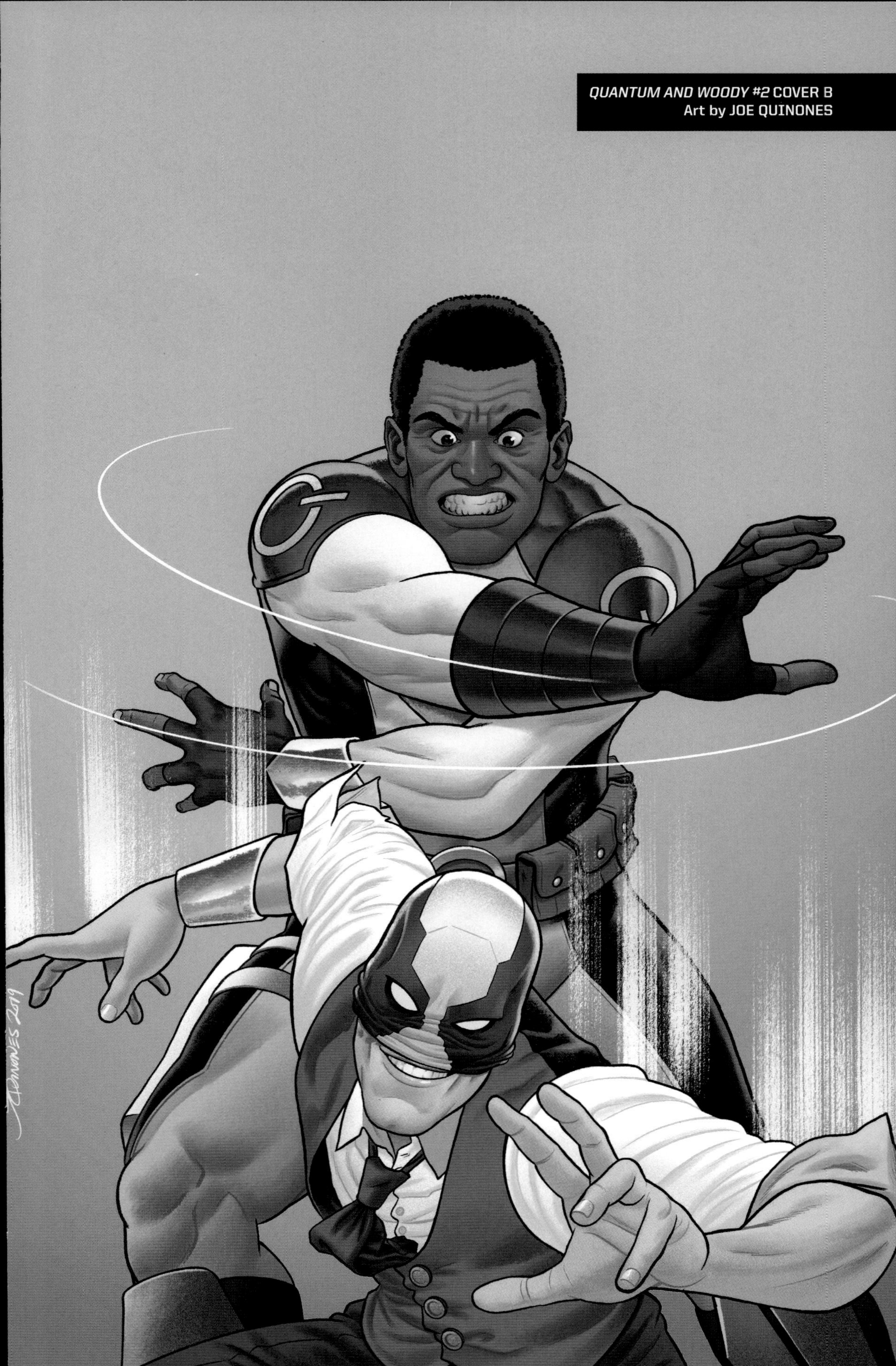

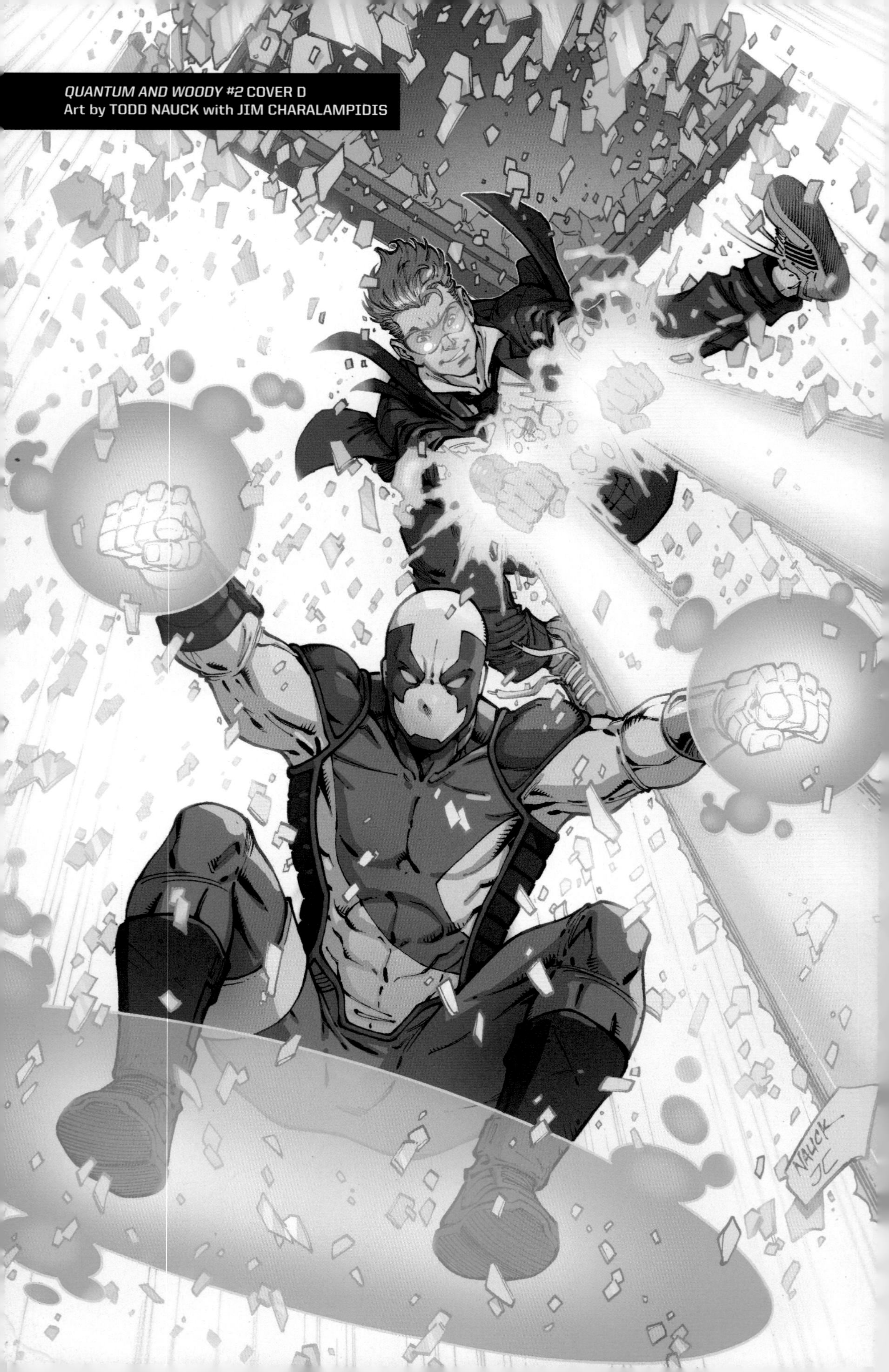
NAUCK
JC

QUANTUM AND WOODY #2 COVER D
Art by TODD NAUCK with JIM CHARALAMPIDIS

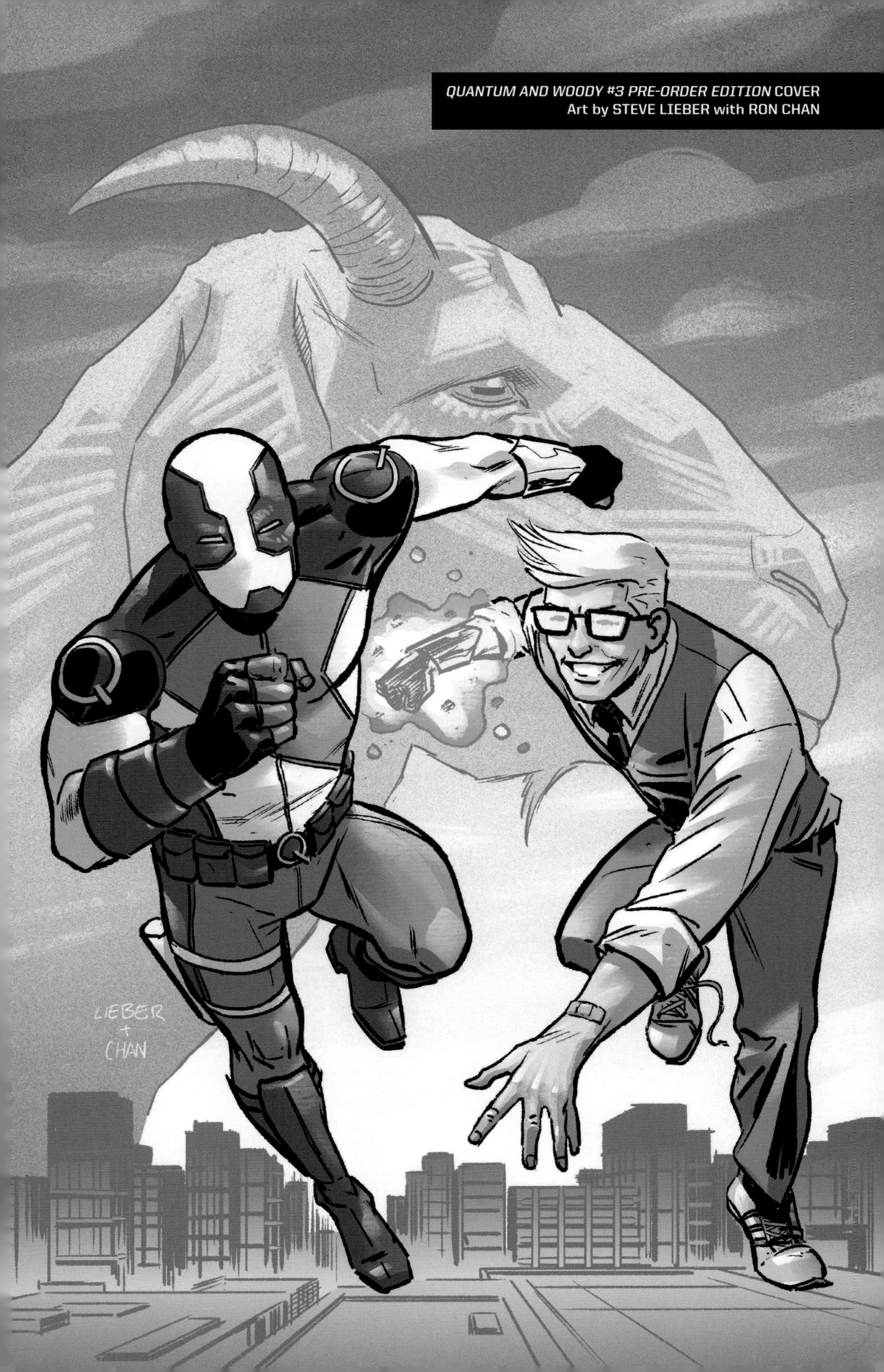
LIEBER
+
CHAN

QUANTUM AND WOODY #3 PRE-ORDER EDITION COVER
Art by STEVE LIEBER with RON CHAN

QUANTUM AND WOODY #3 COVER B
Art by CASPAR WIJNGAARD

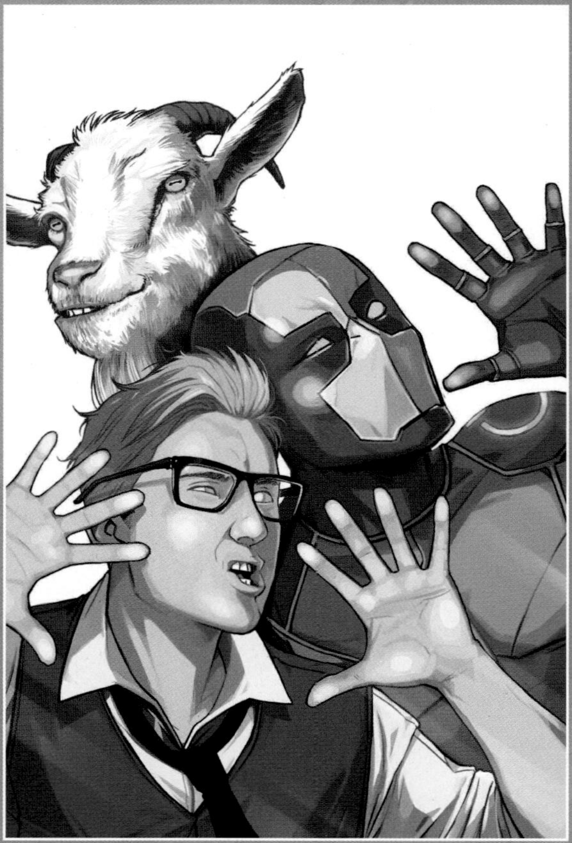

QUANTUM AND WOODY #4
PRE-ORDER EDITION COVER
Art by GURIHIRU

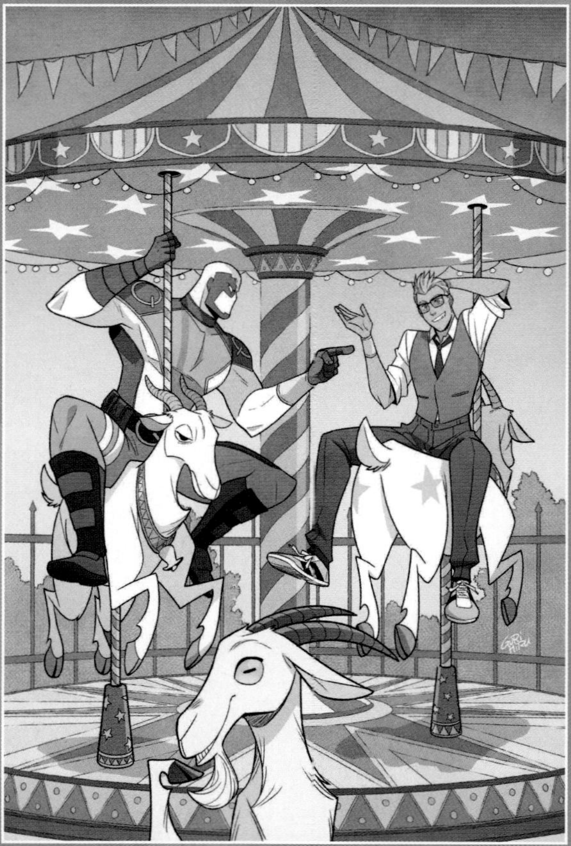

QUANTUM AND WOODY #4 COVER C
Art by RAMON ROSANAS

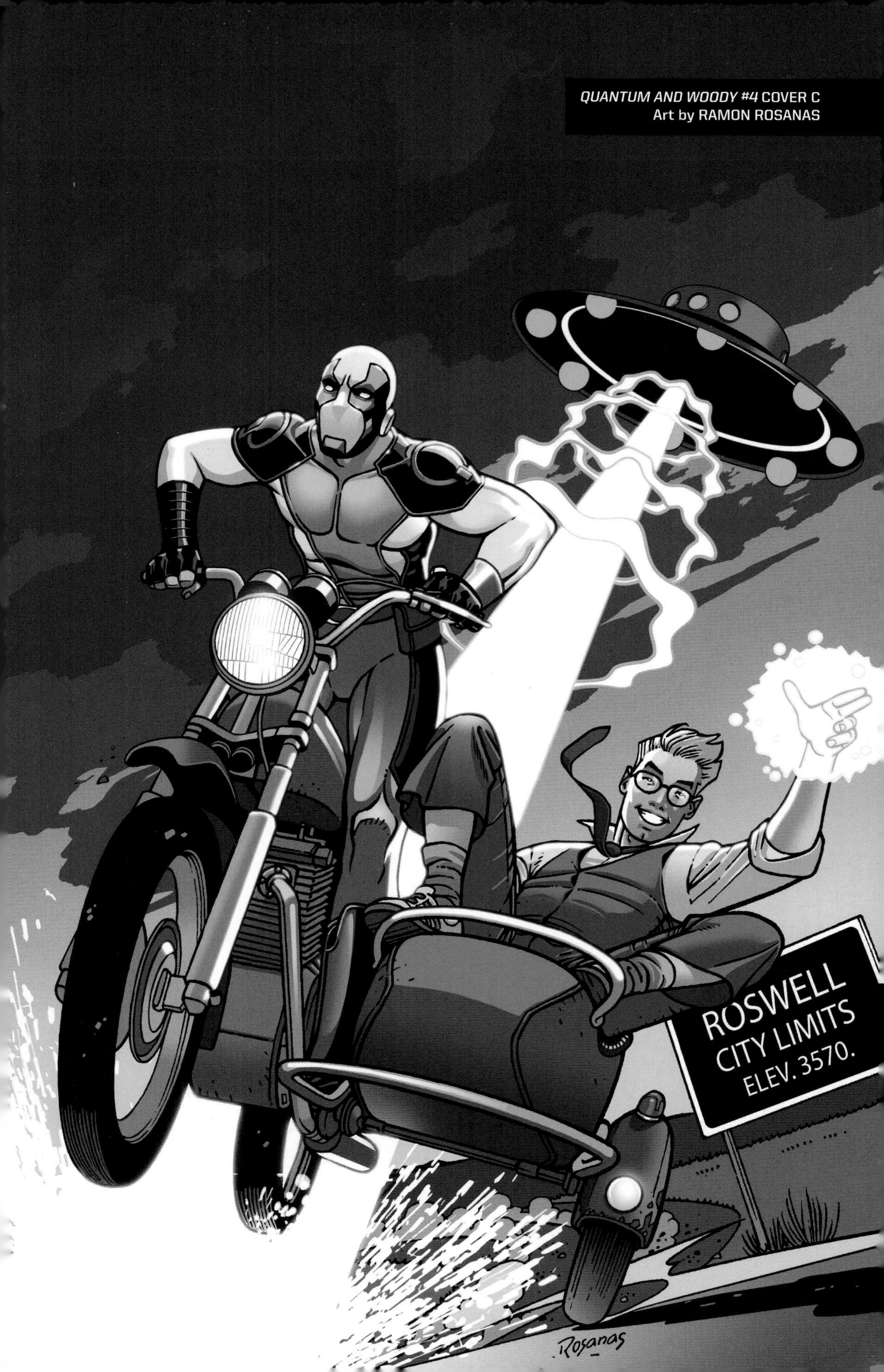
ROSWELL
CITY LIMITS
ELEV. 3570.
ROSANAS

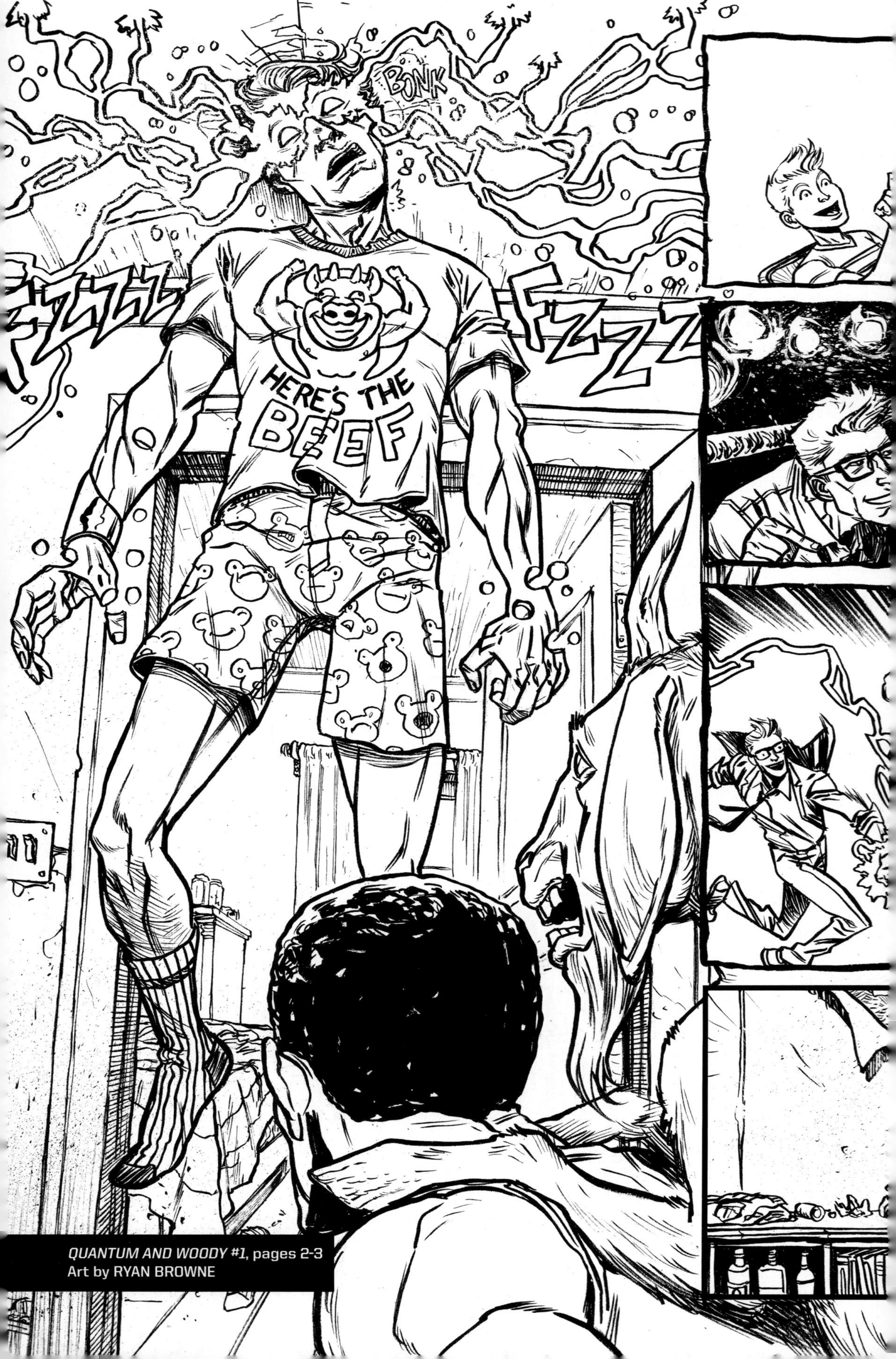
BONK
FZZZZ
HERE'S THE BEEF
FZZZ

QUANTUM AND WOODY #1, pages 2-3
Art by RYAN BROWNE

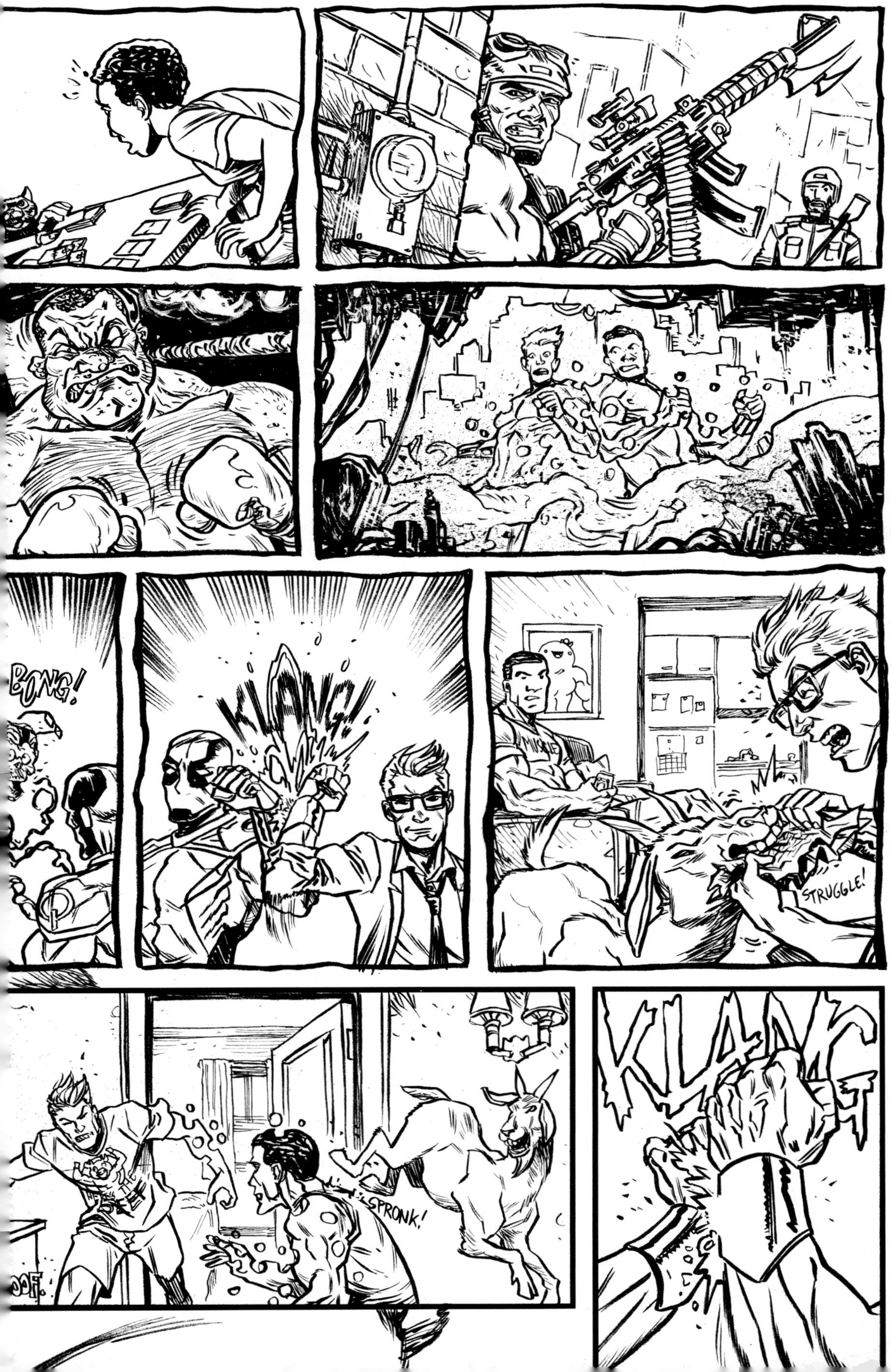
BONG!
KLANG!
STRUGGLE!
SPRONK!
KLANG

QUANTUM AND WOODY #2,
pages 18, 19, and (facing) 20
Art by RYAN BROWNE

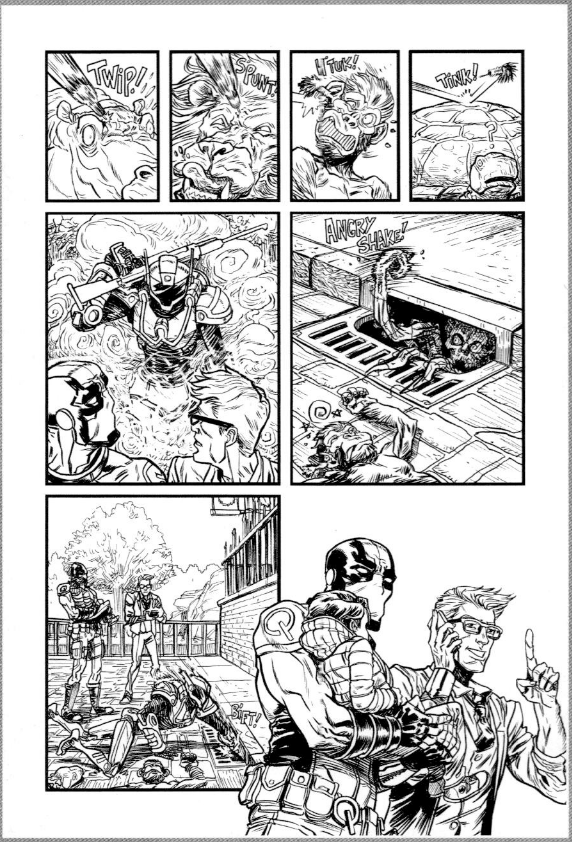
TWIP!
SPUNT!
H'TUK!
TINK!
?
ANGRY SHAKE!
BIFT!

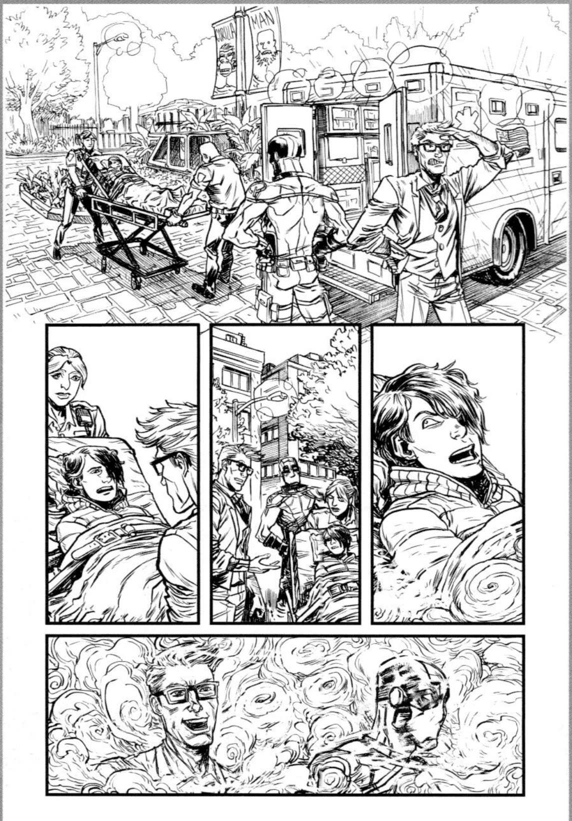
MAN

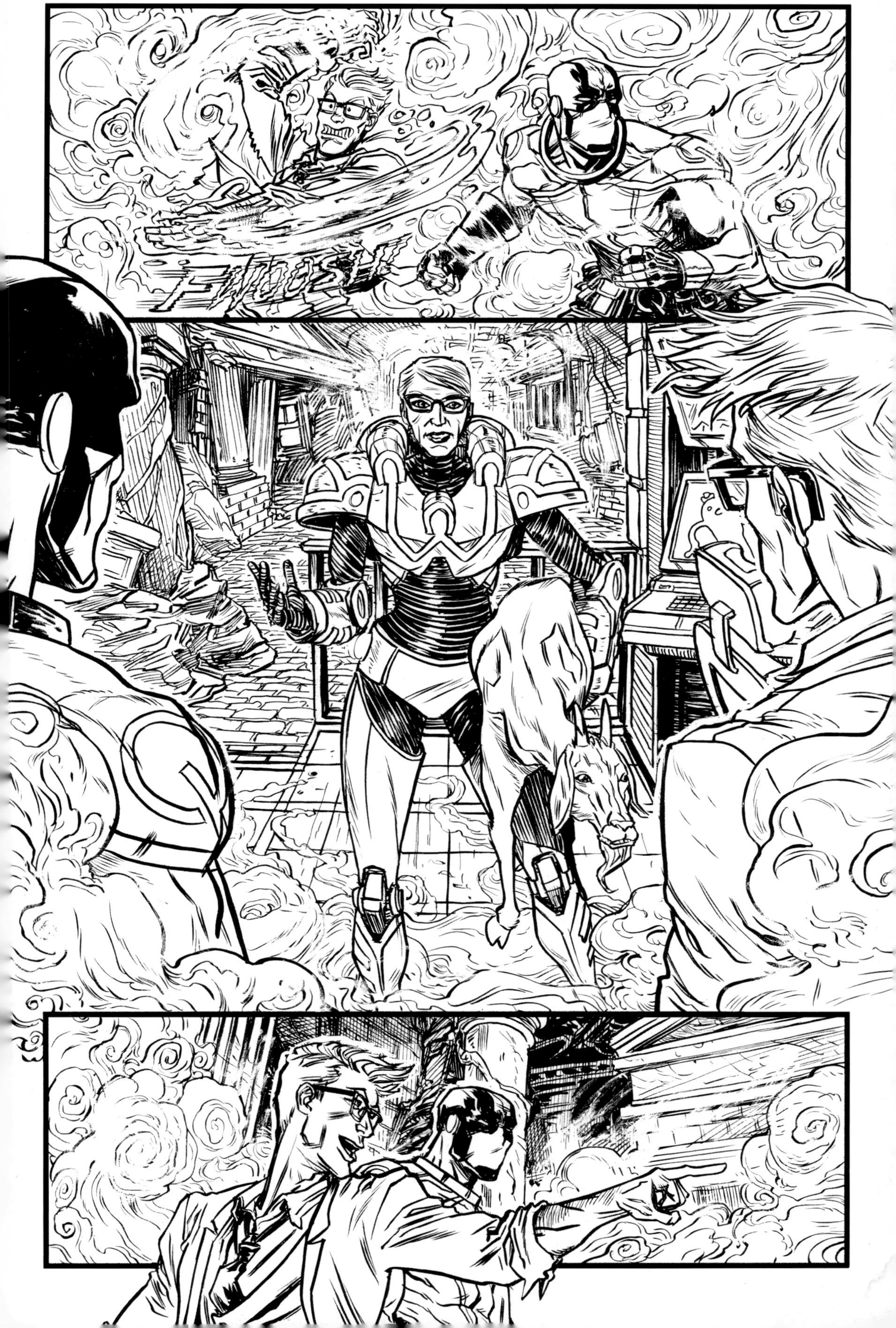
FWOOSH

QUANTUM AND WOODY #3,
pages 11, 12, and (facing) 13
Art by RYAN BROWNE

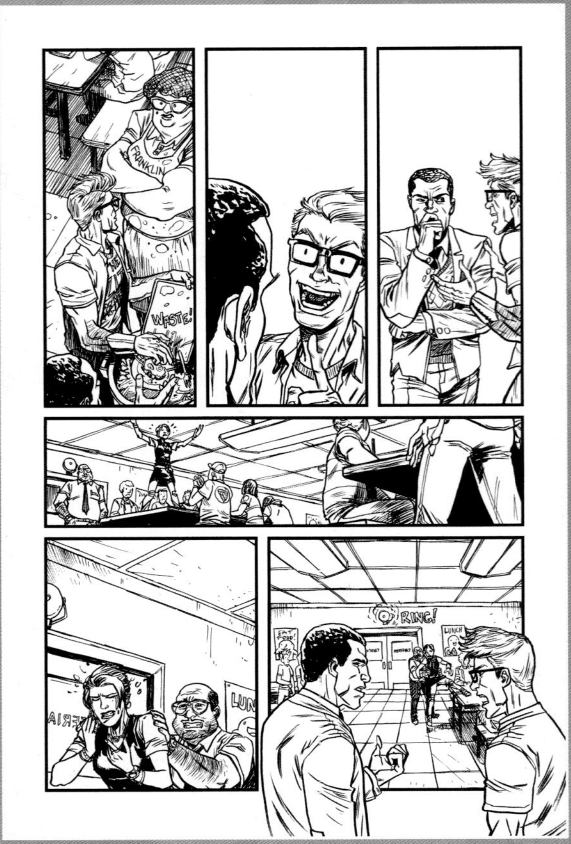
WASTE!
RING!

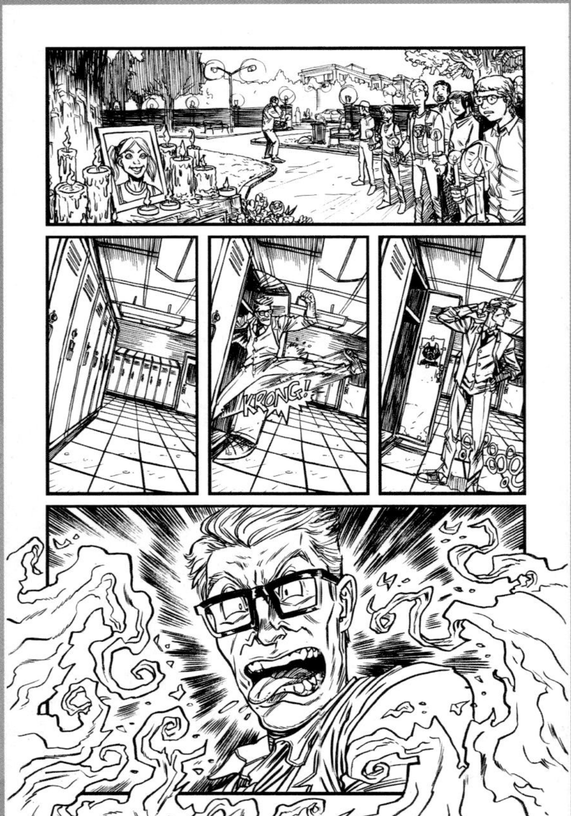
KRONG!

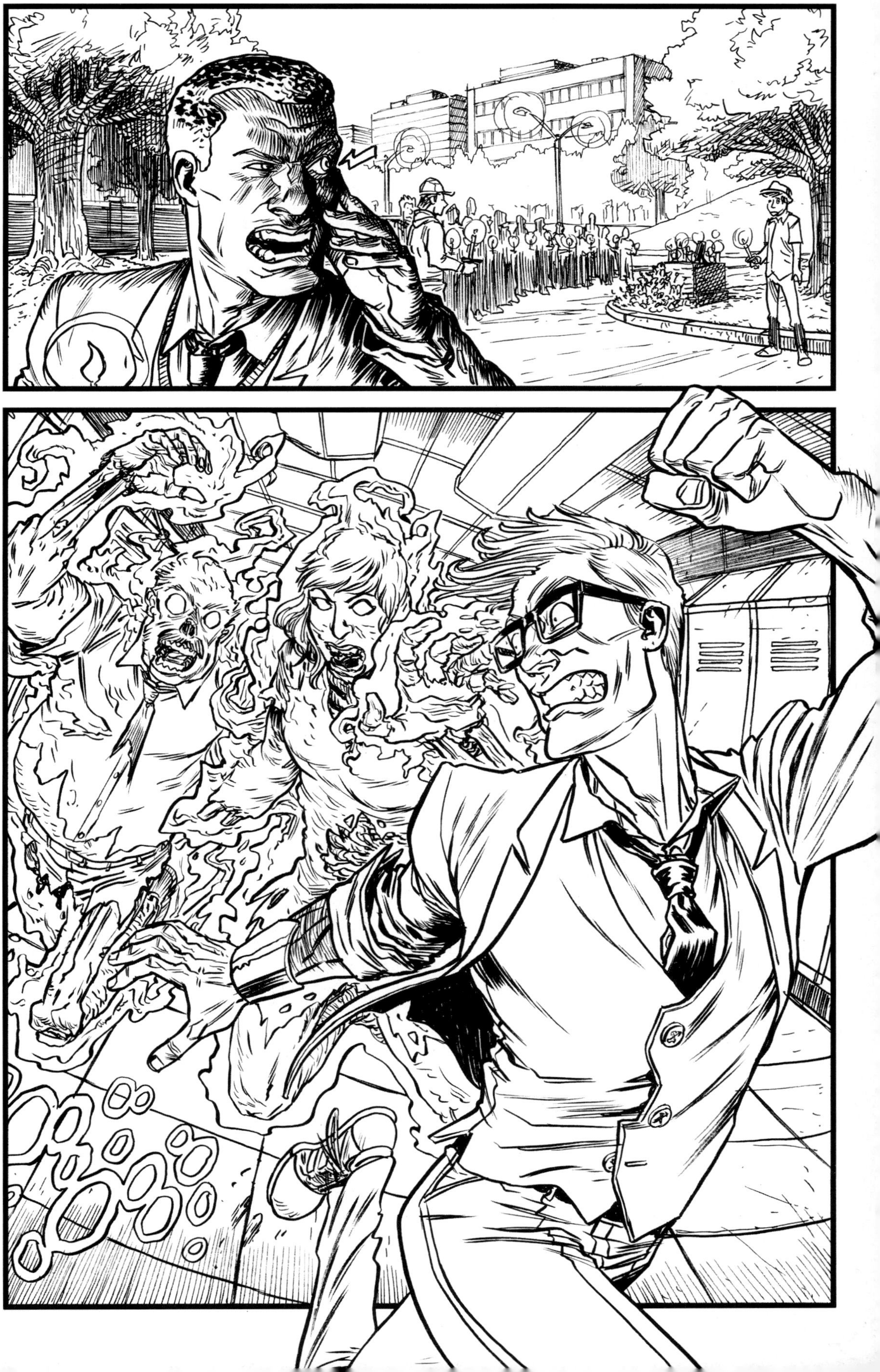

QUANTUM AND WOODY #4,
pages 18, 19, and (facing) 20
Art by RYAN BROWNE

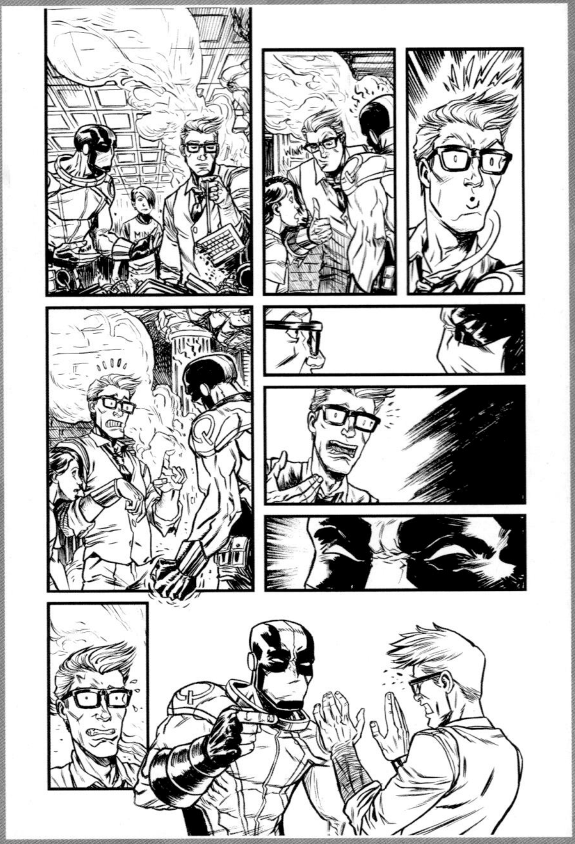

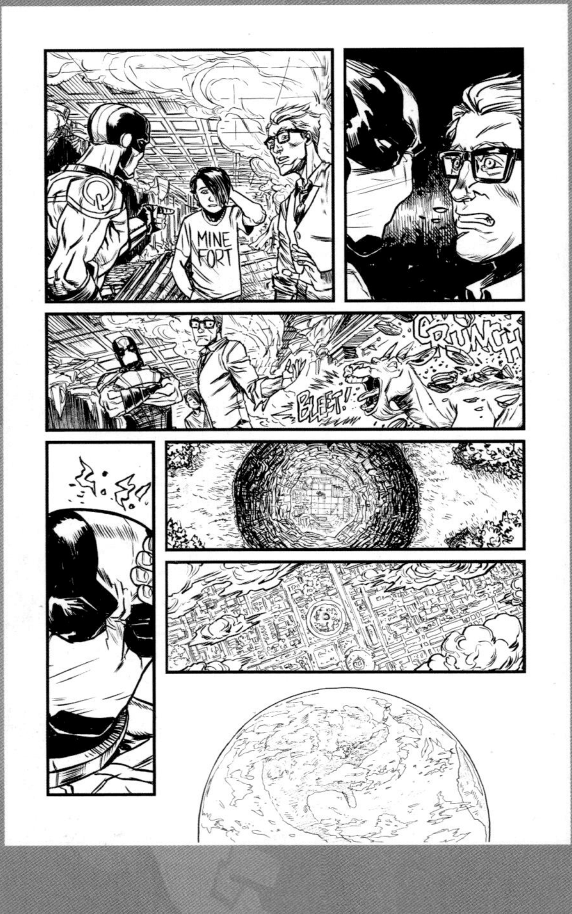
MINE
FORT
CRUNCH
BLEET!

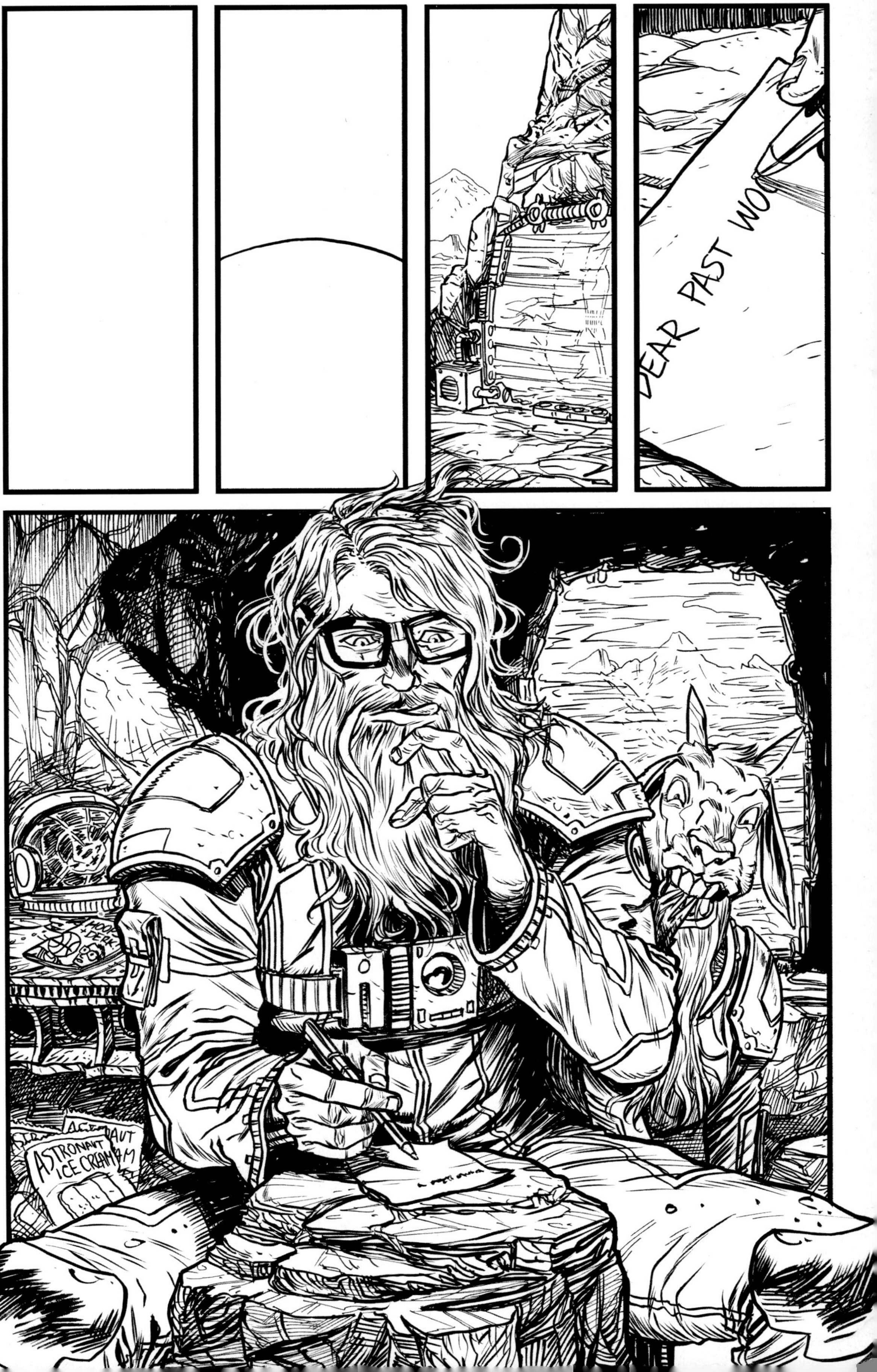
DEAR PAST WO
ASTRONAUT ICE CREAM

EXPLORE THE VALIANT U

ACTION & ADVENTURE

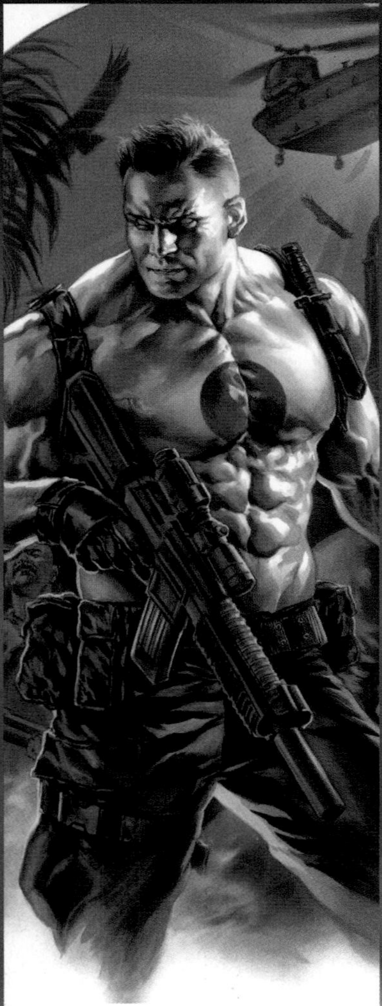

BLOODSHOT BOOK ONE
ISBN: 978-1-68215-255-3
NINJA-K VOL. 1: THE NINJA FILES
ISBN: 978-1-68215-259-1
SAVAGE
ISBN: 978-1-68215-189-1
WRATH OF THE ETERNAL WARRIOR VOL. 1: RISEN
ISBN: 978-1-68215-123-5
X-O MANOWAR (2017) VOL. 1: SOLDIER
ISBN: 978-1-68215-205-8

BLOCKBUSTER ADVENTURE

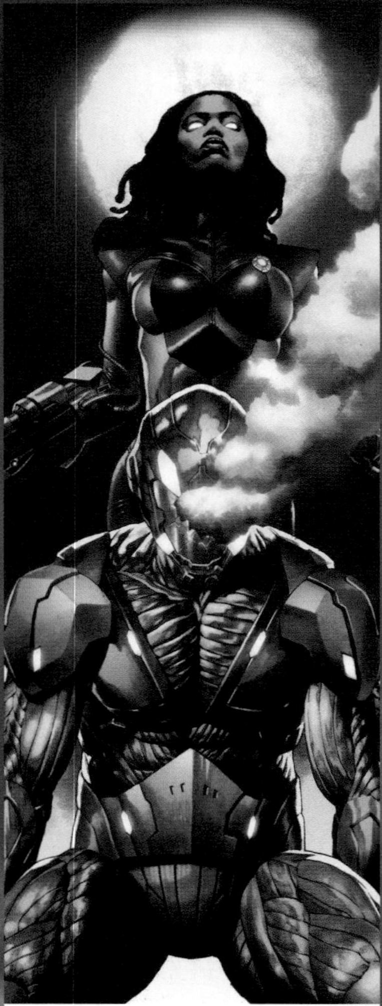

4001 A.D.
ISBN: 978-1-68215-143-3
ARMOR HUNTERS
ISBN: 978-1-939346-45-2
BOOK OF DEATH
ISBN: 978-1-939346-97-1
FALLEN WORLD
ISBN: 978-1-68215-331-4
HARBINGER WARS
ISBN: 978-1-939346-09-4
HARBINGER WARS 2
ISBN: 978-1-68215-289-8
INCURSION
ISBN: 978-1-68215-303-1
THE VALIANT
ISBN: 978-1-939346-60-5

COMEDY

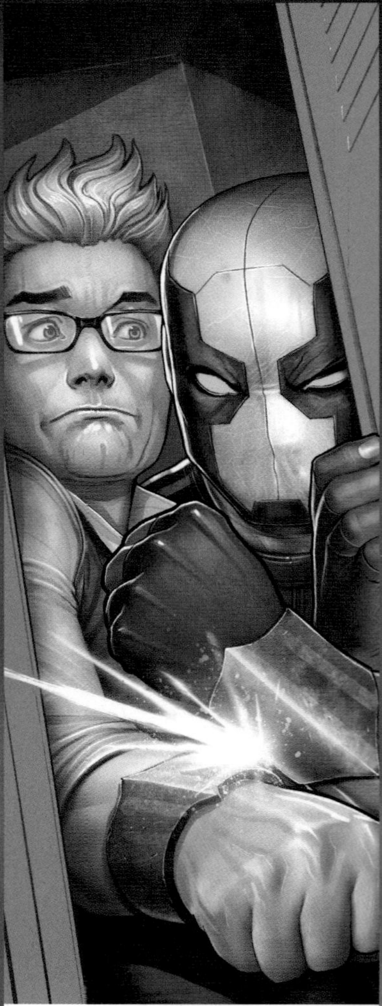

A&A: THE ADVENTURES OF ARCHER & ARMSTRONG VOL. 1: IN THE BAG
ISBN: 978-1-68215-149-5
THE DELINQUENTS
ISBN: 978-1-939346-51-3
QUANTUM AND WOODY! (2020): EARTH'S LAST CHOICE
ISBN: 978-1-68215-362-8

IVERSE STARTING AT $9.99

HORROR & MYSTERY

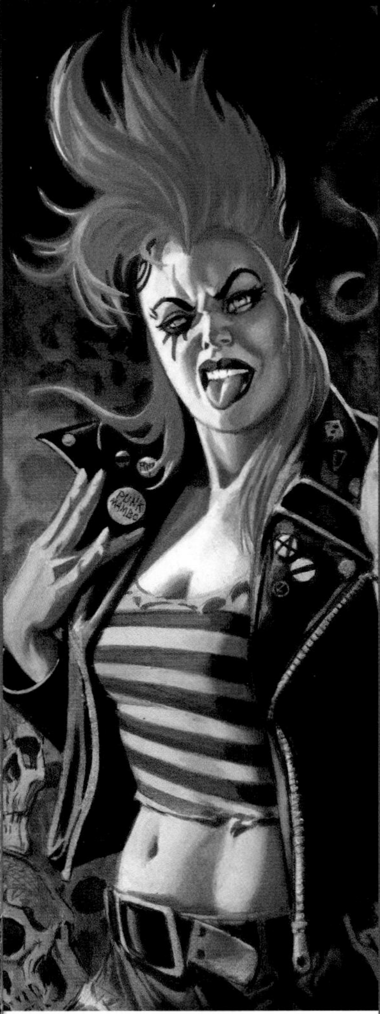

BRITANNIA
ISBN: 978-1-68215-185-3
DOCTOR MIRAGE
ISBN: 978-1-68215-346-8
PUNK MAMBO
ISBN: 978-1-68215-330-7
RAPTURE
ISBN: 978-1-68215-225-6
SHADOWMAN (2018) VOL. 1: FEAR OF THE DARK
ISBN: 978-1-68215-239-3

SCIENCE FICTION & FANTASY

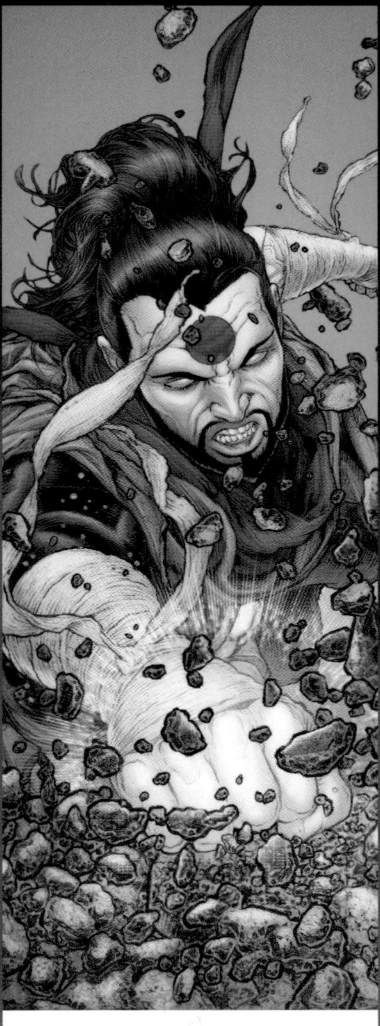

DIVINITY
ISBN: 978-1-939346-76-6
THE FORGOTTEN QUEEN
ISBN: 978-1-68215-324-6
IMPERIUM VOL. 1: COLLECTING MONSTERS
ISBN: 978-1-939346-75-9
IVAR, TIMEWALKER VOL. 1: MAKING HISTORY
ISBN: 978-1-939346-63-6
RAI BOOK ONE
ISBN: 978-1-682153-60-4
WAR MOTHER
ISBN: 978-1-68215-237-9

TEEN ADVENTURE

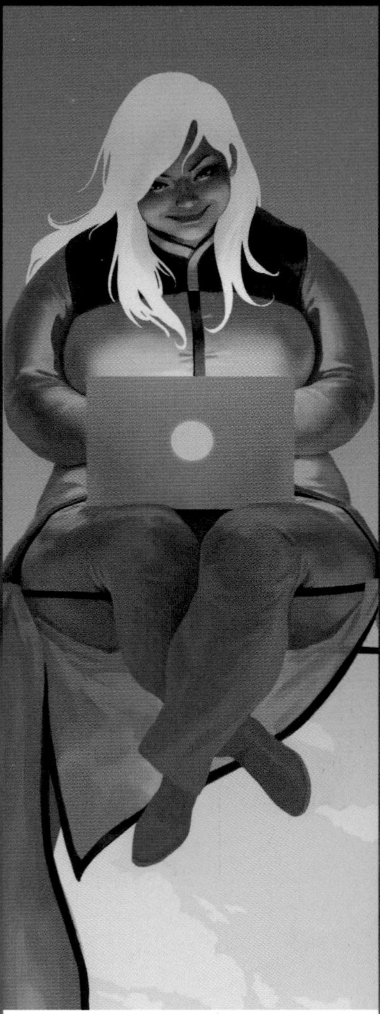

FAITH VOL. 1: HOLLYWOOD AND VINE
ISBN: 978-1-68215-121-1
GENERATION ZERO VOL. 1: WE ARE THE FUTURE
ISBN: 978-1-68215-175-4
HARBINGER RENEGADE VOL. 1: THE JUDGMENT OF SOLOMON
ISBN: 978-1-68215-169-3
LIVEWIRE VOL. 1: FUGITIVE
ISBN: 978-1-68215-301-7
SECRET WEAPONS
ISBN: 978-1-68215-229-4

Discover the entire Valiant Universe of titles at VALIANTENTERTAINMENT.COM/ALL-SERIES/

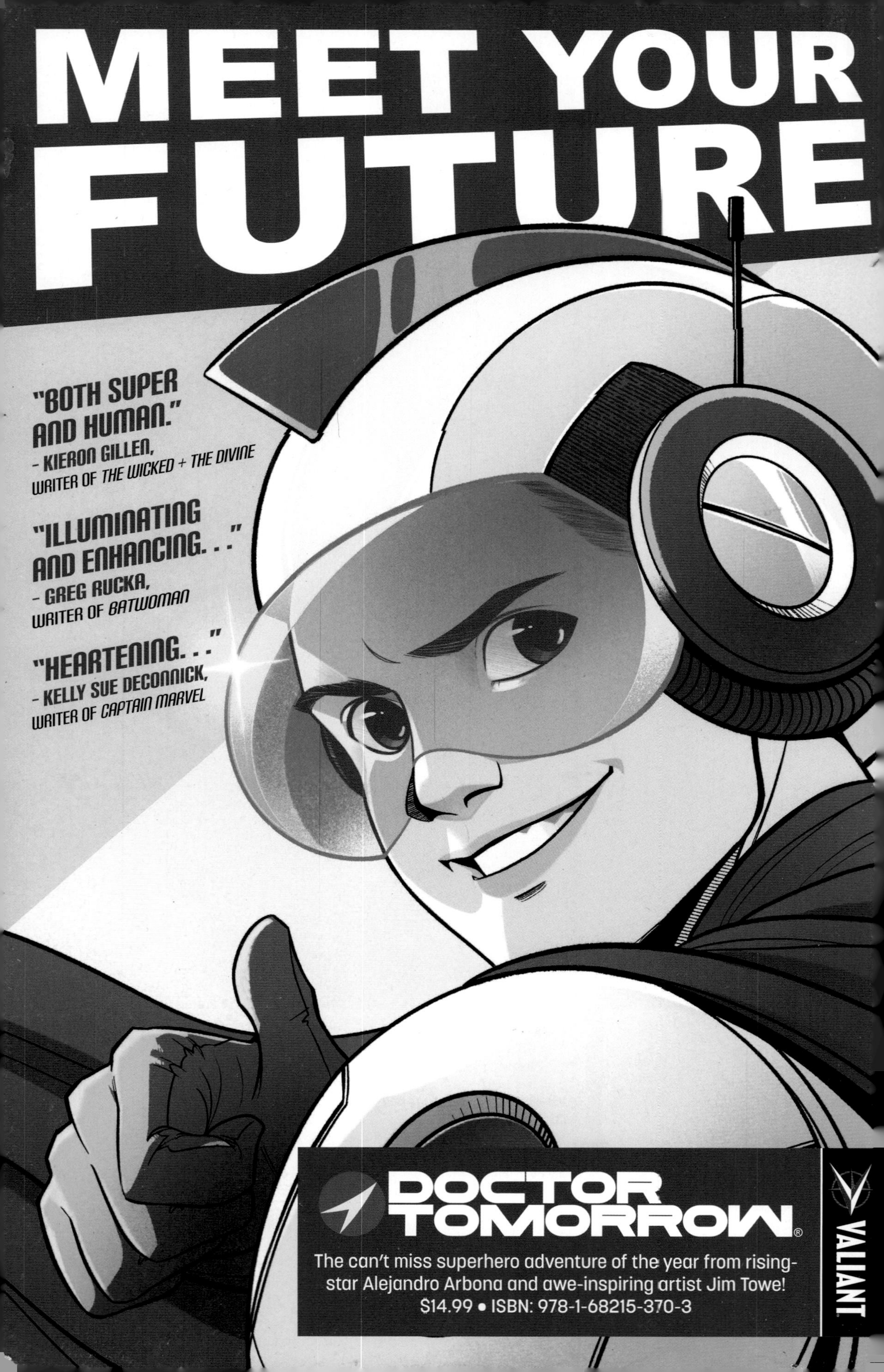
MEET YOUR FUTURE
"BOTH SUPER AND HUMAN."
- KIERON GILLEN, WRITER OF THE WICKED + THE DIVINE
"ILLUMINATING AND ENHANCING. . ."
- GREG RUCKA, WRITER OF BATWOMAN
"HEARTENING. . ."
- KELLY SUE DECONNICK, WRITER OF CAPTAIN MARVEL
DOCTOR TOMORROW®
The can't miss superhero adventure of the year from rising-star Alejandro Arbona and awe-inspiring artist Jim Towe!
$14.99 • ISBN: 978-1-68215-370-3
VALIANT